Her book is filled with personal anecdotes that reveal Mrs. Beadle's love for the academic life. With great insight and clarity she discusses the racial conflicts which arose in the university community over the surrounding ghetto area, and reports the amazing success of the resulting urban renewal projects under the direction of community residents and the University of Chicago. She also examines the complexity of managing a huge urban university today, citing the administrators' efforts to give dissenters a voice and secure relative order in a time of chaos. And on a lighter note, she tells what it was like to entertain such visiting dignitaries as Prince Philip and the Shah of Iran, and recalls her own problems of living in the creaky, sprawling Victorian university President's house. The result is at once a deeply personal and highly perceptive analysis of one of the most eventful decades in the history of American universities.

WHERE HAS ALL THE IVY GONE?

By Muriel Beadle
WHERE HAS ALL THE IVY GONE?
A CHILD'S MIND
THE LANGUAGE OF LIFE (with George W. Beadle)
THESE RUINS ARE INHABITED

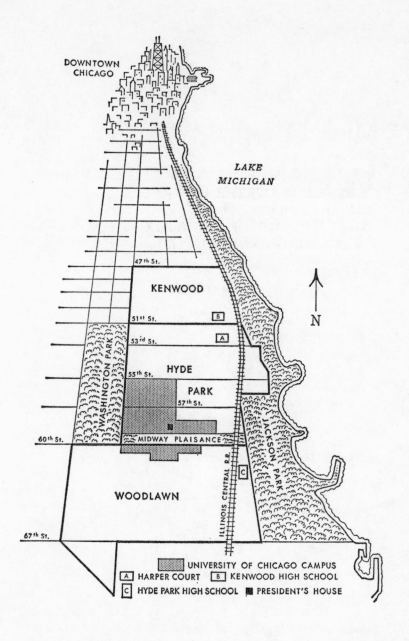

DOWNTOWN
CHICAGO

LAKE
MICHIGAN

N

47th St.

KENWOOD

51st St. B

53rd St. A

HYDE

55th St.

PARK

57th St.

60th St.

MIDWAY PLAISANCE

WOODLAWN

JACKSON PARK

WASHINGTON PARK

ILLINOIS CENTRAL R.R.

C

67th St.

UNIVERSITY OF CHICAGO CAMPUS
A HARPER COURT   B KENWOOD HIGH SCHOOL
C HYDE PARK HIGH SCHOOL   ■ PRESIDENT'S HOUSE

Muriel Beadle

WHERE HAS ALL THE IVY GONE?

A MEMOIR OF UNIVERSITY LIFE

FRONTISPIECE MAP BY E. JOHN PFIFFNER

Doubleday & Company, Inc., Garden City, New York, 1972

Library of Congress Catalog Card Number 78–186004
Copyright © 1972 by Muriel Beadle
All Rights Reserved
Printed in the United States of America
First Edition

To all the young scholars; and
in particular to Red and Suzie,
with love and admiration.

FOREWORD

About the title:

Some say "ivory tower," others say "ivied halls of learning." Either phrase conjures up a university which is remote from the everyday concerns of society. For the several hundred years of universities' history, they *were* remote; but during this century, and especially during the past decade, they have become actively involved in the social and political controversies of their time. In part, that's what this book is about.

The locale is the University of Chicago, which is an "ivied hall of learning." It also happens to be in the South Side Chicago community called Hyde Park-Kenwood, which has recently regenerated itself physically and has stabilized its population racially by using urban renewal as its tool. To chronicle that effort is another purpose of this book.

It also celebrates the academic life in general.

One of the annual rites on any campus is Alumni Day. In 1962, an alumna who hadn't been on campus for fifteen years strode up to me and asked, "Mrs. Beadle, where has all the ivy gone?"

As a newcomer to the University of which my husband had just become President, I had wondered that myself. You could see where the vines had been, but now the gray Gothic buildings were bereft of greenery.

I gave the lady the answer I'd been given.

"They thought it was beginning to split and crack the masonry," I said. "But so many people have disputed that belief that now they're going to replant at least some of it."

She did not look like an urban type, so I refrained from passing on the local rumor explaining the demise of the ivy. Besides, I'd only just heard it, and hadn't yet had a chance to check on its basis in fact, if any.

Whenever one demolishes slum buildings, swarms of rats are displaced into the environs, and the neighborhood gossip was that the ivy had been removed because rats were climbing up it in an effort to gain access through building windows.

The head of the University's grounds department later assured me that this was not true.

"We did have a rat problem in the steam tunnels," he recalled, "but we never had rats in our ivy."

Nevertheless, the alumna's query struck me as a good title for this book, for both metaphorical and parochial reasons.

About the place:

It is difficult if not downright foolhardy to write about a place that many others know better than you do. My husband and I have been here only ten years. The old-timers will undoubtedly find errors of fact or of evaluation. I'm sorry, friends: I've done the best I could.

As for what has been slighted, eliminated, or overemphasized? One couldn't possibly tell a complete story of what went on at the University of Chicago *or* in its community *or* in the city during the 1960's without writing a ten-volume work of surpassing dullness to people who don't know the places or people described. Anyway, it's an author's privilege to be selective.

In one respect only do I wish I could have indulged myself. I am especially fond of Hyde Park women, and some of the best of them do not appear in these pages: women I worked with on civic projects, like Nan Dunham, Edith Harris, Jean Block, Dorothy Gist, Barbara Fiske; women with whom I shared the fun and foolishness of the faculty wives' shows, like Mary

Schulman and Peggy Grant; women I love for themselves and for their wise counsel, such women as Florence Miller and Elisabeth Palmer and—well, you see the problem.

About the content:

This is *my* memoir, not my husband's. He read the manuscript, and declined to make changes except on matters of fact. The interpretation is mine. He says he believes in academic freedom, even for wives of university presidents.

Muriel Beadle

August 1971
Chicago

One

As the plane lifted off from O'Hare and headed west through the bleak December sky, I tilted my seat back and said to George, "Well, that's that."

He didn't respond. He didn't need to. Without words, we had agreed that the University of Chicago wasn't the right place for us.

In two days' time, we had lunched or dined with a representative sampling of the University's trustees who live in the North Shore suburbs, with another group who live in midtown Chicago, and with a final lot whose homes are on the South Side. We had met with members of the faculty committee who, with the trustees, had been seeking a new President of the University of Chicago for the past year.

They couldn't have been more pleasant. But there had been so many of them, and in the mass they were intimidating. Not because of anything they said or did; in fact, our mutual observance of the social civilities had been exemplary. The trouble was that observance of the social civilities hadn't masked the fact that this had not been a social occasion. Underlying all the inconsequential chit-chat had been the unspoken questions, "Are these the people we want?" or—on our part—"Is this the place we want to come to?"

The whole thing had begun, for us, two months before—in October of 1960.

George was then Dean of the Faculties and chairman of the Division of Biology at Caltech, in Pasadena. One afternoon he had received a call from the office of Caltech's president, Lee DuBridge. A Mr. Glen Lloyd had dropped in from Chicago and could Dr. Beadle see him for a few minutes?

George had been tied up for the next hour but had said that he'd see Mr. Lloyd at 5 P.M. Then he forgot the appointment. At five-thirty, he had found a dapper little man—obviously an "Easterner" because he carried a hat and was wearing a suit with a vest—patiently waiting in an outer office. Overcome with embarrassment, George had invited the unknown Mr. Lloyd to come home with him for dinner. I, most fortunately, was frying chicken (which stretches) instead of two lamb chops (which don't).

The conversation had been a bit strained at first, since George had no idea of why our visitor was there. Was he a possible Caltech donor? Or did he want something *from* Caltech? Was he selling something? Taking a poll? That noncommittal message from Lee DuBridge's secretary had given us no guidelines at all.

Soon, however, we had found that Mr. Lloyd was the chairman of the University of Chicago's Board of Trustees. The Board was hunting a new President, he had said, and one of their major requirements was that the man be an outstanding scholar. Did George have any suggestions as to candidates?*

George had produced a few names and the two men had casually discussed academic affairs in general until our unexpected visitor had taken himself off to the airport. We thought no more about that evening until, in late November, the first invitation to come to Chicago to meet the full committee had been issued.

This was not the only "first meeting" of its kind in which George had participated. But none of the others had gone further, it being one of the conventions of academic searches

---

* We learned later that this had been Glen's standard opening ploy upon first meeting the handful of prospects who had survived early screening and were on the list for personal interviews.

that the first meeting carries no obligation but subsequent ones commit both parties to serious consideration of each other.

George wasn't unhappy at Caltech. It is a fine institution, and he had invested fifteen years of his life there. We lived in the best house we will ever inhabit. We had a host of friends whose company we enjoyed. The mountains and the desert were easily accessible (George was then an active rock-climber), and our son Redmond was in his senior year of high school where he was happy and doing well. So why seek a change?

True, there had been a recent period of anguish for George, in his Dean of the Faculties role, when some of the Caltech trustees and administrators had responded in too harsh and repressive a fashion, in George's opinion, to some political activism on the part of younger faculty members. He also seemed to have run into a solid stone wall on a curricular reform that he had been trying for a couple of years to get the faculty to adopt. But in academic administration, one learns to define failure as incomplete progress. What loomed larger in his mind was the knowledge that most of the problems that now came his way were trivial ones. For a person who is happiest when grappling with unknowns—and George is almost the archetypal scientist in this regard—life at Caltech had become too predictable.

Therefore he had accepted the invitation for a first meeting with the University of Chicago's presidential search committee. The difference, this time, was that there had been a second and a third meeting.

George had been much impressed by the men on the University's governing board, a cross section of Chicago's most vigorous, sophisticated, and public-spirited business and professional men. They were varied in age, income, and background; and it was obvious that they were intimately familiar with the workings of the University.

I hadn't met any of them except their chairman, but they had endeared themselves to me in absentia by just one act. Having in mind the more usual kind of Board of Trustees, I had at one point said to George, "Listen, you've *got* to tell them that we're Democrats."

He had dutifully made this confession to Glen Lloyd, who had smiled broadly and replied, "If it had mattered, we would already have checked on that."

The members of the search committee said later that they had been impressed by George's "personal qualities of modesty, integrity, analytical ability, decisive and direct response in action, and the breadth of his scholarly understanding."

All parties, well aware of the brilliant history, high standards, and great prestige of the University of Chicago, realized that the choice of a new President—seventh in a distinguished line —was no casual matter. The what-would-you-do-if questions, George told me, had been detailed and probing. Enough mutual rapport had developed so that everyone involved knew, by the December weekend when I too went to Chicago, that a final decision was in the offing.

In addition to all the luncheon and dinner parties, we had been given a quick tour of the campus, an impressive pile of gray Gothic set on surprisingly spacious grounds. (It was not at all my idea of an urban university.) We had driven around the neighborhood, a dense forest of soot-begrimed brick and stone buildings bounded by sidewalks and streets littered with rubbish. (Which was exactly what I had expected of an inner-city neighborhood.) We had inspected the President's House, a Victorian mansion that had been standing empty for the past nine months and now had only oddments of furnishings in its vast and gloomy sixteen rooms. (I had hated it on sight.)

There had also been an unsettling cloak-and-dagger atmosphere about the whole visit. Another of the conventions for picking new university presidents requires that the parties should *sense* agreement before the formal question is asked. What should be avoided at all costs is for the trustees to make an offer which the candidate then refuses (an insult to the institution) or for the trustees to reject a candidate who has explicitly stated his willingness to take the job (an insult to the candidate).

No one therefore wants any publicity during the final period when the principals in this delicate confrontation are coming to their unspoken understanding. Consequently, George and I had been spirited in and out of University buildings separately, our guides keeping a cautious eye cocked for any casual passersby who might take undue interest in the presence together of the chairman of the Board of Trustees, the chairman of the faculty search committee, and two strangers on the doorstep of the President's House.

Taken together, it had been too much. Everything about the place was alien. Although small as major universities go (only eight thousand students, two thirds of them at the graduate level), the University of Chicago was nevertheless twice as big as Caltech. It had a thousand faculty members, four academic divisions including a medical school, an undergraduate college, seven graduate professional schools, an adult education extension, and a host of autonomous institutions loosely affiliated with it.

George, a geneticist, knew nothing about theology or law or musicology or linguistics—all of which were specialties of the University of Chicago. He would have to raise a lot of money. He would have to make public speeches about topics other than genetics. He would have to symbolize the University. He *is* a modest man: what the place needed, he was thinking as we flew back to California that December night in 1960, was another Kimpton, another Hutchins—big, handsome men with orators' voices, commanding public presences, academic backgrounds less specialized than his. Besides he'd reach retirement age in 1968. Would seven years in office be enough time for his presence to matter?

For my part, the idea of running that house was appalling. A thousand faculty wives to get to know. Eight thousand students. Goodness knows what other responsibilities. At Caltech, I had observed Doris DuBridge's activities with sympathy, and I doubted that I could be as consistently nice as she was to people I didn't like very much. Given my inability to dissemble, I'd surely lose the University some multimillion-dollar gift by insulting a potential donor. I am an activist; could I restrict myself to non-controversial kinds of activism? And I detest cocktail parties. What the University of Chicago needed, I was thinking as we flew back to California that night, was a First Lady who had more social savvy than I had.

George spent the following day figuring out polite phrases that would help Glen Lloyd break off the negotiations when the inevitable phone call came. What came instead was a request for one more meeting in Chicago. It seemed that the Dean of the Law School, Edward Levi, had been unable to attend the other meetings, and they all felt that he and George should have a chance to talk. So, on a Thursday, back George went.

I wish I had been present. Since then, however, I have watched Edward Levi in action. He has a soft voice, a mild—almost self-deprecating—manner, and an inconceivably shrewd mind. Not only did he like George, he understood him on first meeting. The others had mentioned the fact that the University of Chicago had problems, but Edward *stressed* them. The University was in desperate need of funds. It was still in danger of being blighted by surrounding slums. It had lost many first-class faculty members and had been unable to attract replacements. In short, it needed regeneration—and fast. Could George undertake a job that would be so difficult? The dare was implicit.

Thursday evening, when George returned from this final visit to Chicago, he almost ran into the house. I had only to look at his face for a second before I said, "Oh, Lord! When do we go?"

TWO

George went to Chicago almost at once; he could see no point in being a lame-duck dean at Caltech. He lived at Chicago's faculty club; ate breakfast at Billings Hospital cafeteria because it was the only place on campus where anybody was awake as early as he is; held endless conferences with other adminstrators; met with students; rode the campus police cars at night; and walked the streets of the neighborhood until he found the shopkeepers who were to be our special friends for all of the following years. When asked by newspaper reporters to announce his administrative goals, he would say, "I'm still doing my homework."

He had plenty of homework. Among the materials he had received from the Secretary of the Board of Trustees were the Articles, By-Laws, and Statutes of the University and the previous year's file of minutes of Board meetings and Board committees. He also got a huge pile of detailed reports from the Vice-president for Business Affairs. He was already familiar with the big figures—the $250,000,000 endowment, the $74,000,-000 operating budget (almost 70 per cent of it for instruction and research), the $5,000,000 earmarked for scholarships and other forms of student aid—but now he discovered how big the "little" figures were. For example:

Almost $700,000 went into steam to heat the buildings, and almost half a million dollars were spent on maintaining the campus police force. The postage bill was in excess of $200,000; it cost $220,000 to do the campus laundry; and dairy products added another $175,000. Almost a hundred thousand long-distance phone calls and two million local phone calls were made each year by University personnel: $480,000. There were 35,000 windows to wash, at one dollar per window, and they got washed once a year.

The University Press was housed in a Romanesque red brick building just across the street from the Administration Building, handy for a drop-in visit by a new President. Its mission was to print scholarly works, under the guidance of an editorial board of faculty members. In addition to some 150 books of this character published each year, the Press also published thirty-four professional journals. The Secretary of the Board of Trustees had sent George current copies of all thirty-four, and he tried to get through at least one issue of each. They included *Journal of Business, Classical Philology, Journal of Near Eastern Studies, Ethics, Library Quarterly, Elementary School Journal, Social Science Review, Journal of Religion,* and (at last! a familiar subject) the *Botanical Gazette.*

He learned that there were seventeen departmental and professional school libraries and reading rooms in addition to the main library, Harper Memorial. In one place or another, some two and a half million volumes were stored and thousands upon thousands of periodicals were coming in regularly to swell the total. About a million and a half dollars annually were spent on library facilities and collections.

The Medical Center alone would take a lot of learning about. There were eleven hospitals there—four square blocks of hospitals, each with a different specialty, and research labs and offices were intermingled with the areas for patient care. Something like 150,000 outpatients streamed through in a year; 30,000 of them came to the Emergency Room. Half a million dollars' worth of free medical services were dispensed annually to indigents. These were teaching hospitals, and the doctors who did the teaching were full-time professors. No private practice allowed. This policy made the medical school unique in the country.

There were museums on campus. None in the city was better than the one at the Oriental Institute.

There were art galleries and a nursery school and greenhouses and a bookstore and centers for student religious groups.

There were autonomous institutions which everyone counted among the University's assets: for example, International House, where foreign students found a pleasant introduction to the United States; and the Sonia Shankman Orthogenic School, where Bruno Bettelheim was doing pioneering work in the treatment of emotionally disturbed children.

The University was affiliated with such organizations as the American Council on Education, the Association of American Universities, the Institute for Defense Analyses, the Association of Universities for Research in Astronomy (Tucson) and the University Corporation for Atmospheric Research (Boulder). The last two were consortiums whose members used jointly maintained research facilities.

Chicago also managed the Argonne National Laboratory for the Atomic Energy Commission. That was a $75,000,000 operation.

George was expected to keep himself informed on the affairs of all these divers enterprises.

He was also expected to understand the subdivisions within the University's academic structure. These included Departments (such as German, sociology, biochemistry, anatomy, mathematics, and so on); Institutes (for computer research, study of metals); Laboratories (cancer research, astrophysics); and Committees. Getting the Committees straight was an especially formidable assignment—and perhaps this is as good a place as any to discuss them.

All colleges and universities have administrative committees, the kind that are set up to study a particular problem or advise on a recurring one. But Committees—with a capital C, and within the *academic* structure—have quite another function, and they flourish nowhere more vigorously than at the University of Chicago.

They are intended to promote interdisciplinary exchanges between departments, each bringing together specialists in a variety of fields bearing on a common interest. Hence: the Committee on Comparative Studies in Literature, the Committee on African Studies, the Committee on Human Development, the Committee on Mathematical Biology, the Committee on Social Thought. They were especially popular during the period when Robert M. Hutchins headed the University, then fell somewhat from favor, and are back full force today. "Interdisciplinary" is a campus catchword.

George didn't have to look far for a secretary. Doris Olson was a veteran of two previous administrations and consequently was an invaluable source of information for a neophyte President. He needed her guidance if only to decide which he should accept of the initial five hundred invitations to give speeches. (By year's end, the total was near two thousand.) Considering the prospect of being behind a podium far more often than he would like to be, George was tempted to accept the offer of one Mack McGinnis, who sold "humorous material to incorporate in talks and introductions" for five dollars a year—but finally decided to rely on his own store of jokes.

While all this painful self-education was going on, I remained in Pasadena. Redmond's stricken look at the possibility of being snatched out of high school only six months before his graduation dictated this course. Besides, what husband is ever reluctant to have his wife do the sorting and packing incident to a move?

During those six months in limbo, I made several trips to Chicago. One was to take part in the "Revels," an evening of original musical comedy annually presented by the faculty for the enjoyment of friends and relatives. Most academic people like to participate in amateur theatricals. I myself had been an enthusiastic member of the Caltech Stock Company, and it was fun to make my Chicago debut as Annie Oakley's mother in a rousing work called *Empty Saddles in the Bach Corral, or A Rolling Posse Gathers No Mosse*.

Another trip was for George's inauguration in May, a splendid academic festival.*

I also came to Chicago to consult with the University's architect and the decorator who were in charge of refurbishing the President's House; and to interview possible household staff. I still didn't like the house, but the prospect of living there was no longer so grim as it had been initially.

And finally, on the first of July, we shut the door of our beloved Pasadena house for the last time. Red was wrestling with a carrier holding two Siamese cats, who were screaming at the top of their lungs despite the fact that they hadn't gone anywhere yet. George and I were each clutching shopping bags full of his prize iris rhizomes, dug up that morning from our California garden and due to be planted by nightfall in Illinois soil. When we drove away, bound for the airport, we didn't dare look back.

Settling into a new place is never easy, and this one was a whopper of a place. It had been built, all four floors of it, for William Rainey Harper, the first President of the University. In the spring of 1895, the *University of Chicago Weekly* said of it:

> Those who have visited Dr. Harper's new house have united in pronouncing it a structure in which beauty of material and design are remarkably combined with commodiousness and comfort. Neither labor nor expense have been spared in its construction. The house and stable will possess every modern convenience. The architectural features of both buildings, without and within, are of a firm, even severe type, similar to that of the other University buildings. The woodwork is principally of oak.

* George was actually inaugurated as Chancellor, but within a few months had the title changed back to the one used by the first four heads of the University—so I have referred to him as "President" throughout this book.

The architect, Mr. Henry Ives Cobb, has skillfully met the purposes peculiarly characteristic of the house of a university president, especially in the library, and in the means of entertainment found in the reception and dining rooms. The first named is the prettiest room in the building. It is located on the west side of the first floor, and is entered through double doors, opposite which are the fireplace and mantel. The room is lighted by large, elevated windows. The west wall of the dining room is covered by an ample sideboard, and the room is abundantly lighted by windows facing the east.

The total cost of house and lot is $40,000.

In the intervening years, ten times its original cost had been spent on remodeling it for its various tenants. The "firm, even severe" exterior remained much as it had in 1895, except that the tan brick was sooty gray by now. A long porch extending across the front had been removed in the 1920's (an esthetic mistake); and several large plate glass windows, of a size and kind unknown to Mr. Henry Ives Cobb, bespoke some 1939 tinkering.

The characteristic that struck anyone accustomed to California's horizontal housing landscape was that this house was so high; perhaps fifty feet from ground to ridgepole. Its height was further accentuated by a steeply pitched roof, rising from the walls without the interruption of eaves to destroy the verticality of line. This roof was studded with assorted gables, all of which in turn had steeply pitched roofs. Ridge lines were edged with copper, which by now had become a luminous sage green.

The original entrance had been on Fifty-ninth Street. Around the corner on University Avenue was a family doorway which Harper's son was later to describe as "a friendly door full of red, green, and blue glass with many facets. It made a father coming home for supper seem to young eyes as though twenty fathers were approaching." This was the entrance—but not the door—that now admitted visitors to the house.

One came into a minuscule glassed entry, also a product of the 1939 remodeling, and then entered the gloom of a passageway so narrow that I always privately called it "the cattle chute." This led to some stairs and eventually into a large open foyer. On one side, the foyer opened into the dining room, long since bereft of its ample sideboard and now adorned with a monstrously showy crystal and silver chandelier. On another side, one of two doors allowed entrance into the living room, veneered with something blond that wasn't oak and ornamented here and there with bits of neoclassic carving. From the third side, a wide Victorian staircase rose majestically to the upper stories. It, and the dado around the foyer itself, were still of the original oak that Cobb had installed, but they were now painted beige.

The entire first floor and the staircase to the second and third floors were carpeted in a soft green wool, acres of it. Its color dictated the other colors in these rooms. I had blended my own furniture from Pasadena with things already in the house, painting and slipcovering as necessary to make a match between provincial maple and lacquered pieces from a Western ranch house and the Chicago assortment of Victorian, traditional English, and baroque French furniture. The Manse now vaguely suggested an English country house. It didn't really reach its arms out to enfold one, but the decorator and I had done the best we could with it and I did not brood further about its imperfections.

The library, which gave off the narrow passageway through which people entered the house, was still "the prettiest room" in the place—not that it was anything like Cobb's design. In the 1939 remodeling, the room had been gutted, beams removed, small Gothic-arched windows replaced with enormous rectangles of glass, and a sleek ivory marble mantel installed. What remained of the furnishings, when I had first seen the room, were some dirty white upholstered furniture and draperies and a huge rug of white rough wool, splashed with gargantuan flowers and foliage in hot orange, red, maroon, and several shades of green.

When this riot of tropical color had first burst upon my view, I was feeling virtuous because I had just saved the University a pot of money by deciding to keep some upstairs carpeting in a color that I disliked. So I said to the University architect, as we stood in the doorway of the library, "Good grief! That thing has got to go!"

"All right," he said. "But I think you ought to know that this rug was handmade in Morocco, cost five thousand dollars, and was given to the University by the alumni."

"By the *alumni?*"

"So I have been told."

I gulped. "Well, in that case," I said, "I simply love it."

Therefore the library had been redecorated to enhance the rug. The chairs were now dark green or black; new green-striped draperies had been hung; and a stormy green and gray landscape by Innes had been transferred from the dining room to hang over the mantel. Finished, it was a handsome room.

(And my pleasure in it was not diminished some months later when the myth of the Moroccan rug was exploded by that courtly gentleman Harold H. Swift. His memory was a kind of supplement to the University archives. He had been chairman of the Board of Trustees during the administration of Robert M. Hutchins, and when he overheard me telling someone about the history of the rug, he said, "I'm afraid that's not quite right. The rug was made in India, it cost seven hundred and fifty dollars, and it was purchased at Marshall Field's by Mrs. Hutchins.")

The library also had yards and yards of shelves, reaching to the full fifteen-foot height of the room. Upon these shelves rested some five thousand volumes of books. They had been removed and dusted in celebration of our coming to Chicago, but whoever had done the job had then replaced them *at random*. In short, the library shelves were a a mess.

My finger pointed straight at Red. In Pasadena, he had

worked after school as a page in the city library. "Get some order into that jumble, will you?" I asked him.

It took him over a month to sort and categorize the books, but quite early on he made his great discovery about them.

"Hey, Mom," he said one day, as he emerged from the library for lunch. "I've figured out the principle governing what's in there. Those books are the ones that all Pop's predecessors didn't want when they moved out, so they just left them behind."

He was right. The assortment ranged from *Through Routes for Chicago's Steam Railroads* to an aged collection of Stanford University yearbooks to *Identification and Analysis of Attribute Cluster Blocs* (a detailed account of the political behavior of members of the 1927 Minnesota State Senate).

After Red had Dewey-decimalized all the other occupants' leftovers, he incorporated our own books into the collection. As he did so, he put a red paper dot on the spines of our books, one with the kind of adhesive backing that makes it easy to remove.

"The dot is to identify your stuff," he said; and then, with a twinkle in his eyes, "But it will peel off easily. That's in case you decide to follow precedent when it's your turn to pack up and move out."

For an eighteen-year-old, he was remarkably prescient.

In one corner of the same room we had installed a huge philodendron in a blond oak planter transferred from elsewhere in the house and stained dark brown. There was a tale in connection with it, too.

Lawrence Kimpton, George's immediate predecessor—who had resigned in 1960 to take a job in industry—told us how touched he and his wife Marcia had been the year that a group of undergraduates had serenaded him on his birthday. (Even in the 1950's, the rapport between university presidents and university students had not been so close that one took for granted a birthday serenade.) In addition, the kids had given him the planter. The Kimptons were overcome with gratitude. The next

day they discovered that the students had stolen it from The
Tropical Hut, a neighborhood eatery.

"But," Larry assured me as he wound up the story, "when
we returned it, the people at The Hut said it was an honor to
have their stolen property in the President's House. So take good
care of it."*

The only major structural change that had been made in the
President's House, at our request, was the conversion of a room
between the library and the kitchen into a family dining room.
We did this because the "State" dining room was about as intimate as a hotel lobby, and the furniture was in scale. My
mind's eye had pictured George and me breakfasting at opposite
ends of the twelve-foot table in a modern parody of a Mary
Petty cartoon.

A large butler's pantry and enormous kitchen lay between
the two dining rooms. The equipment was old but counter
space was adequate, and the square footage invested in drawers
and cabinets was bountiful. We needed every inch of it, and
could have used more.

One of my welcome-to-Chicago presents had been a 150-page
inventory of everything that was supposed to be in the house. I
had been told to identify these items and, by signing the document, to accept responsibility for the household goods that I was
inheriting from six previous sets of occupants. Thus a great
treasure hunt was launched.

Page 67 of the inventory said that we had "403 miscellaneous
pieces of glassware," and page 102 listed "97 double-damask,

---

* And we too were to receive a gift of stolen property. Or perhaps I
should say "borrowed." One day we found on our doorstep—in a crate
rather than in the traditional foundling basket—the marble bust of Silas J.
Cobb (by Lorado Taft) that had disappeared from Cobb Lecture Hall
some years before. Cobb had arrived in Chicago from Vermont in 1833,
one of the flood of Yankees who were to strike it rich in the nation's
biggest boom town; and he had given the University its first building. I
can only guess as to where his bust had been when it was "away," but
suspicion most logically falls on one of the fraternities. Cobb is now back
on his pedestal in Cobb Hall—high above a door, where a ladder is
required for access.

hand-hemmed napkins." We found more than 403 pieces of glassware, and 96 napkins. Also the tablecloths that matched them. They were splendid monuments to the Irish weaving industry, the napkins a yard square, the tablecloths in lengths to twenty-two feet. I was so enchanted with this Victorian splendor that I used them for all our later entertaining, despite the fact that it cost fifteen dollars every time a tablecloth went to the hand laundry.

In time, we located the pair of three-foot-high gold-encrusted porcelain jardinieres (which we left right where we found them —in an attic closet); the forty-seven-star American flag; the two punch bowls and ten dozen cups to match; remains of two sets of Lenox china; and a footstool covered with a needlepoint version of the University of Chicago's coat of arms. We also found (unlisted) a desiccated wreath from William Rainey Harper's funeral, some moth-eaten livery for a chauffeur, and a tarnished brass pot with an unsigned note inside that said, "This was a gift from the Aga Khan."

What we did not find, then or ever, was "One prayer chair, walnut finished oak, late Victorian period, spiral turned legs, massive carved and pierced back with tobacco motifs and center cartouche, and top rail with prayer book compartment." Even in a house as big as this one, it seemed unlikely that one could overlook something as distinctive as *that*.

Upstairs, there were eight spacious rooms and a multitude of bathrooms and closets. Above that floor was the ballroom (which could, alas, no longer be used by large crowds for fear that the old plaster in the rooms below would crack or crumble). Here too were two maids' rooms and another bath.

There was no elevator. Its lack further limited use of the ballroom, because older people among our guests couldn't comfortably climb three flights of stairs. However, there *was* a dumb waiter which linked every floor in the house and saved us millions of steps. The basement eventually became our auxiliary storage space and warehouse, and it was a great saver of everyone's energy to transfer a case of soda water or the punch bowls and cups to the dumb waiter, then be able to remove them at the site of use.

The basement itself, which ran the full length of the house, was a labyrinth of pipes, ducts, corridors, closets, and shadowed cubbyholes. It was full of old kitchen appliances, garden furniture, and rolled-up linoleum. Smack in the center was a cold room, where some predecessor of ours had hung sides of beef (or venison?), but the machinery that cooled it no longer worked. I had Red twist wire over the door handles to prevent anyone's getting locked into and then suffocating within this anachronism.

In addition, the basement held a self-regenerating colony of cockroaches. These provided great sport for the cats and great anguish for me. (In all the years we spent in that house, we were never able wholly to eradicate these fellow occupants.) Only George, who is a biologist and therefore respects all living things, took a benign view of them.

"They're endured at least since Paleozoic times. Isn't that wonderful?" he'd say.

And who was to care for this establishment?

We were lucky. The queen of the kitchen, for the entire time we lived in that house, was Alta Rita Galloway. She was a short and buxom lady of middle years, fanatically tidy, and a passionate cook. She had recently been employed by a Rockford physician but, like us in Pasadena, had found life there just faintly too predictable. Like us, too, she didn't know what she was getting into when she came to the University of Chicago, which in all our cases was just as well.

The other member of our full-time staff was Jimmie Lee Carter, whose abilities as a housekeeper were unexcelled. She really liked to wash lamp shades and did it superlatively, along with everything else connected with keeping a house clean. She put in a forty-hour week doing nothing else.

Mrs. Galloway spent an equivalent amount of time on ordering, storing, and preparing food; polishing silver; and keeping glassware and dishes ready for service. In Chicago, it takes un-remitting effort to keep just one jump ahead of the soot.

A host of part-timers were to come and go, but Mrs. Gal-loway, Mrs. Carter, and I were the permanent triumvirate who kept the ship afloat. We worked like dogs all through that first Chicago summer. The time eventually came, however, when I had used up every last ounce of enthusiasm for getting settled. We then bundled up the leftover rolls of wallpaper, the un-examined contents of top shelves and bottom drawers, and the still-unpacked trivia from our Pasadena house; dumped them into a couple of closets; and firmly shut the doors. Enough is enough.

Three

Cats are an integral part of our lives. In Pasadena, we had seventeen. There, however, they inhabited porches, woodpiles, and trees spread over two acres, and came indoors only by invitation. Chicago would be different, so we had found new homes for most of them and brought with us only the dowager queen mother and one of her half-grown kittens.

M'zelle had come to us as a waif from a municipal pound, skittish and scrawny, with dirty tan fur that felt like straw. By the time we went to Chicago, her fur was like silk, her walk was a glide, and her self-assurance was total. She was, and is, what George calls a *good* cat: beautiful to look at, sociable, and (generally) sweet-tempered.

Mary K came to Chicago with us because she was too dim-witted to be foisted on any California foster family. Mary K was a great jumper when she was very young, and decided one day to try for a tabletop on the edge of which there was a toaster. She didn't quite make it; hooked her claws into the quilted cover on the toaster; and brought five pounds of metal crashing down on top of her small self. Ever since, viewing the world through blank blue eyes that never change expression, she has bounced gently around the house on her tiptoes—cheerful, meek, and moronic.

Inasmuch as Mary K accepts any situation as normal, she adapted easily to becoming a house cat. M'zelle, on the other hand, was furious. Because she had never experienced city streets teeming with traffic, they held no terrors for her. She equated "outdoors" with climbing trees, chasing butterflies, and eating grass, and she desperately wanted to do so. That longing encouraged her intimate exploration of the house, seeking a way out, and one evening she found it.

We didn't know that she had, despite Mary K's having sat by an open window in our bedroom and wailed through the night. Mary K's hearing was more acute than ours, for not until six in the morning, when the air was calm and the neighborhood was quiet, could we too hear distant meows that were recognizable as M'zelle's. It turned out that she had found an unscreened ballroom window that was open about four inches and had squeezed herself to freedom. Eventually she had marooned herself on the ridgepole of the house, fifty feet above the ground, and all through the night she had been proclaiming to an indifferent world that she couldn't get down.

We had had plenty of experience with treed cats, who always think they can't get down and always manage to, but this was a different situation. The roofing slates were so smooth that her claws wouldn't have much purchase if and when she decided to descend. It is very difficult for cats to go backward, anyway, and if she were to slip while she was attempting this maneuver— whoosh! There were no eaves to stop her fall. Cats do *not* necessarily land on their feet, unharmed, when they fall from heights.

George couldn't stand the thought of what might happen to his darling.

"I'm going up after her," he announced.

We were standing across the street, staring at the Mt. Everest where M'zelle, hunched into a small forlorn bundle, was perching.

"But we don't have a ladder that will reach that far," I reminded him. "You'd have to get Buildings and Grounds to send one over. And just *look* at the pitch of the roof . . ."

"Hell," he said, "I've climbed steeper pitches than that one.

See the gable on a line with the front door, how it makes a V where it meets the gable at the back of the house? I could climb out of the window there and use a friction hold* for at least ten feet. M'zelle is only a couple of feet from where it gets too wide for a spread-eagle, and I'll bet I could coax her to come down that far."

"You mean you want to *climb* the roof? As if it were a mountain? That's insane."

I had great confidence in George's ability, having gone on Sierra Club climbs with him, but this was a problem as unique in his experience as it was in M'zelle's. So I said that I positively wouldn't let him do it unless he went up on a rope with a proper belay, and cinched the argument by comparing him to a California climber whom he considered stupidly foolhardy.

He agreed to my terms then, but the problem immediately arose as to who his belayer would be. The Great Plains do not produce many mountaineers; Red was spending a few days in the country with a new friend; and I wasn't strong enough to control the rope if George did in fact fall off the roof. Which explains why a campus cop who had never been west of Council Bluffs suddenly found himself in the ballroom of the President's House at 7 A.M. that morning, being given a cram course on how to belay a climber.

He turned the color of putty as George wound up the lesson by saying, "Now, the main thing to remember is to keep the rope tight but not taut. If you feel me fall, slow the rope but *don't* try to stop me right away. If you suddenly yank on a nylon rope that's paying out fast, you'll cut me in two."

I stationed myself at the window, partly to keep an eye on the rope and partly to make soothing remarks to the luckless belayer. In case he fainted, which looked imminent, I figured I would be better as a backstop than no one. Mrs. Galloway and Mrs. Carter, in dumb terror, stationed themselves across the street—afraid to look but afraid to miss the spectacle. The rest of the

---

* Mountain climbers use this technique when ascending a fissure narrow enough so they can brace their bodies into it and hunch themselves along.

campus police force, a couple of city patrol cars, and a few early-to-work employees joined the cheering section.

It was a breeze. Barefooted for better traction, George went up that roof like a Sherpa. M'zelle was by now too dispirited to skitter away from him, came docilely into his grasp, and lay still while George backed cautiously down to the ballroom window. The two of them made a triumphant re-entry, to the accompaniment of huzzahs from below.

M'zelle raced down the stairs in search of breakfast, and an hour later was sitting in an open (but screened) window bemoaning the fate that kept her locked indoors on such a nice day.

George had an absolutely beatified look on his face for the rest of the day, and walked with a strut for a week.

Eventually, M'zelle accepted a compromise. I took her out for regular walks on a leash. She soon discovered that urban living has its own delights, especially a big parking lot just behind our house where there were dozens of fragrant hub caps to smell, but she remained edgy for a good many months.

Before she finally accepted the inevitable, she embroiled us in an incident with a less pleasant ending. The trustees and their wives were our dinner guests, and we were using the library for the cocktail period. M'zelle came slinking into the room from the kitchen, belly down, sniffing all the strange feet, just as Mrs. Glen Lloyd entered the room, her step springy and her head up. Thus it came about that neither was aware of the other until Marion stepped on M'zelle. The cat as quickly retaliated. Two screams rent the air: M'zelle's first, then Marion's.

There was stunned silence from the group, then Babel. The bite, deep into the instep, had drawn blood. I wanted to run and hide, as M'zelle had done. *Our cat has attacked the wife of the chairman of the Board. Oh, God.* We whisked our damaged guest over to Billings Emergency for a tetanus shot and a bandage, and the party proceeded.

Marion has never held M'zelle against us.

That was the first all-stops-out party that we had attempted, and it gave me confidence that I could entertain fify people for a sit-down dinner with some degree of ease. Such numbers were to be far from uncommon in the future.

The first University event that I attended in my official capacity was a late-July party for wives of the Medical School's new faculty, interns, and residents. University-based medical schools begin their year in July rather than in September, and I was asked to welcome the 1961 arrivals. Since I was as much a newcomer as they were, I profited as much as they did from conversation with the old hands.

As I moved from group to group, much of the talk was essentially what you hear on any campus on occasions such as this:

"Yes, Havill's. On Fifty-third Street. They'll install it in no time. They do radio repairs, too."

"You're an alto recorder? Great! I know of a couple of chamber groups you might enjoy. Give me your phone number and I'll have someone call you."

"At Mass General? Did you, by any chance, know the Winzlers? He's finishing up in Pediatrics there. He and my husband roomed together when they were pre-meds at Cornell."

"The National Tea is cheaper, but the Co-op is more fun. You can get bean sprouts and black radishes and gefilte fish there, along with all the usual supermarket stuff. It's got a coffee bar and a big bulletin board where everyone posts notices about lost pets and things for sale and rates for typing theses. People are always standing outside with petitions or having ad hoc committee meetings in the aisles. It's as much a community center as a grocery store."

But some of the talk had a distinctly local twist:

"You could try Delia's, on Fifty-fifth Street. So many shops have been urban-renewed out, there isn't much choice any more."

"The little wooden buildings on Fifty-seventh Street, the ones with the peaked façades Yes, they *are* quaint. They were souvenir stands for the 1893 World's Fair. We call them the Art Colony. Not that there are many artists there any more. . . . One of them is even a live bait shop now."

"And don't under any circumstances get a new bike for him. It'll be stolen the first day he has it. Don't get a wire basket, either. Get straw. For some reason nobody steals straw baskets. . . . A light? Why? Nobody rides bikes at night, not in *this* neighborhood."

"We got it cheap because we promised to reconvert it to single-family occupancy, but we must have been out of our minds. You should see the filth. Our next door neighbor says there were thirty people living in it at one time."

"Well, you can't have everything. We'd probably get better city services if we had a machine alderman. But it's a tradition in this ward to elect an Independent. He's usually the only one in the City Council. Leon Despres is the current one. Seems to be a nice fellow. Paul Douglas was our Fifth Ward alderman before he went to the Senate; in fact, they've all been a scrappy lot. . . ."

Going home that night, I had plenty to think about. And as soon as I could, I got acquainted with these new environs of mine.

Hyde Park-Kenwood covers less than two square miles, yet it then had 55,000 residents. I had never lived in a place with such high density of population, and was fascinated by the swift changes in neighborhood character that can therefore occur within only a few blocks.

For a starter, there was the strip along the lake front, east of the Illinois Central railroad tracks. Here were located massed ranks of high-rise apartments and hotels, many of them deluxe because of the views of Lake Michigan they commanded. These collectively were called either "the Indian Village" (so many of them having names like the Algonquin, the Saranac, and the Powhatan) or "the Jewish Alps" (because the population of this area was predominantly Jewish). There was a nice stretch of park land there—always alive with children at play, old people sitting on benches, or well-groomed widows walking their poodles. I noted that hardly any of the faces were black.

Set down in the middle of this section was Fifty Army Headquarters, housed in what had once been the most elegant hotel on the south shore of Lake Michigan. Its military personnel kept very much to themselves, riding or bussing miles north to quarters at Fort Sheridan, near Evanston.

Then there was Kenwood, the northernmost section of the community. At Forty-seventh Street, on the northwest side, there was an apartment house district whose occupants were almost entirely poor Negroes. But two blocks south and on the eastern side of the same section the residential pattern was one of large single-family homes on sizable lots—almost suburban in its character. These houses were mostly inhabited by a multi-racial mix of well-to-do professional class families who worked very hard at keeping their part of the community stabilized.

One of the first Kenwood residents I met asked me if any new Negro professors were coming to the University in the fall. Her block was "getting too white for comfort," she said, and the residents were hunting for a Negro with a large enough family and sufficient income to maintain one of the grand old turn-of-the-century houses.

Hyde Park Boulevard (Fifty-first Street) marked the boundary between Kenwood and Hyde Park. For some five blocks south of it, the land had been so overbuilt that one saw hardly a tree or a blade of grass. The most typical structure was a brick six-flat (two apartments on each of three floors), a kind of structure much favored in its day because it doesn't require an elevator. The rear staircases and porches of such buildings were stitched together by wooden railings, cross-bars and lattices, and were open to the weather. They struck me as of surpassing ugliness. (But, then, the façades of these same buildings would win no prizes either.) Tucked in among the ubiquitous six-flats were tall hotels and small town houses dating from the 1890–1910 period, most often of limestone with Palladian touches for ornament.

This mid-section of the community, I learned, was called "the village core" because the main shopping street—Fifty-third

Street—slashed through its center. Whenever land use is mixed commercial and residential, a population becomes very heterogeneous. Here it included fragile old ladies whose Social Security checks barely paid for tiny bed-sitters in run-down buildings; young employed singles who lived at the YMCA or shared rooms in one or another of the apartment hotels; non-students of the kind we then called beatniks, who liked being close to a university scene; bona fide students, married, who found that the cheapest apartments were located in this section; and the community's permanently floating population of winos and homosexuals.

The area around Fifty-fifth Street, I was told, had once been of this character, too. But its eastern end had recently been smashed to rubble by slum-clearance bulldozers, and a new shopping center, twin high-rise apartment buildings, and a double row of stark modern town houses now lined the street. At the *eastern* end. On the west, the winding roads of Washington Park now spewed traffic into a kind of no-man's-land: more six-flats, service stations, a few shabby shops and taverns, and a National Guard armory. This section was next in line for urban renewal, and already you could sense the shadow coming. Many of the shops were empty, with old newspapers and half-pint whiskey bottles lodged in their entryways; and foot traffic was scant.

South of Fifty-fifth Street and on to Fifty-ninth Street, the landscape changed again. This was the area dominated by the University campus—greener, quieter, and more spacious than any other part of Hyde Park. It was not wholly institutional, however. Many houses and apartments had been built there years ago, mostly to house faculty families (70 per cent of whom still lived within walking or cycling distance of their offices—most unusual at an urban university today). Property here, I noted, was better kept and the streets were fractionally less littered than in the village core.

There was a small shopping area on Fifty-seventh Street, in 1961 so run down that it took me a while to understand the affection residents felt for it. It included a drugstore in whose back booths several generations of faculty and students had spent long afternoons, over multiple cups of coffee, arguing the fine points of Kantian ethics. Here too, legend had it, Hugh Hefner had dreamed up his Playboy enterprises. In the same block was Woodworth's, primarily a bookstore, with a dead tree trunk outside to which people nailed notices.*

Across the street was The Tropical Hut, source of the planter in our library and purveyor of a garlic dressing so potent that it was still with you two days after you had eaten the salad it had seasoned. Next to The Hut was Mary Louise Womer's Little Gallery, one of a chain of very old and very small brick cottages which had been adapted for commercial use. Mrs. Womer had founded the Fifty-seventh Street Art Fair, the first of its kind in the city and then in its fourteenth year. This event was remarkable not only for the display and sale of work by local artists but also for the availability of balloons blown up (in the boiler room of a nearby school) by distinguished members of the University's faculty.

In a class by itself, toward the east end of Fifty-seventh Street, was the Green Door bookstore and Medici Coffee House (one establishment, with books and periodicals in front and the espresso machine in the rear). It was in a class by itself because it was the only place in the community that sold the Sunday New York *Times* on Sunday. Sometimes the supply ran out, so it was important to get in line early and hang on to one's place.

One Sunday, a new faculty friend told me, the line was already turning the corner down the block when a fire broke out in the coffee house section. Smoke curled up in wisps and then poured forth in billowing clouds. The proprietor called the fire department, and the firemen responded with alacrity. But the people lined up for the New York *Times* did not break ranks. The firemen went past them and around them and through them, and the queue remained.

---

* It blew down a few years later, and our alderman promptly got the city's Bureau of Forestry to find another one—which they anchored in cement.

When the blaze had been quelled, one of the firemen was heard to remark—to no one in particular, as he passed through the line of people for the last time—"It's like another world over here."

When I compared it to Pasadena, I thought so too.

Four

In the early 1800's, the part of Chicago that I have been talking about was a wilderness of marsh and bog laced with quicksand, reputedly one of the most dangerous sections of land west of New York. It had to be traversed on foot or on horseback because wagons couldn't get through. Nevertheless, and because a sure way to keep your bearings is to follow a lake shore, the Indians had established a trail through this country. It is believed that the Pottawatomie chief Winnemeg came along it in 1812 when he brought the message from General Hull in Detroit to Captain Heald in Chicago announcing the declaration of war with Great Britain and ordering the evacuation of Fort Dearborn.

White settlers later used the lake trail, and in 1836 a man named Nathan Watson had a cabin alongside it. Fifteen years later, he had about twenty neighbors. What started the local population explosion, however, was an 1853 purchase of three hundred lake front acres by Paul Cornell, a lawyer newly arrived from New York to make his fortune in "the West." When the Illinois Central Railroad decided to run a direct line between Centralia and Chicago, a route that crossed Cornell's property, he said that he'd sell a sixty-acre right of way if the IC would build a station on the property, call it Hyde Park, and provide daily passenger service to Chicago. The agreement was signed in 1856, and in the same year ground was broken for the first subdivision. By 1880, Hyde Park had fifteen thousand residents, a Mendelsohn Club and a Lyceum, and was thoroughly civilized.

The Illinois Central still carries Hyde Parkers to the city center, and a remnant of the Indian trail survives as "old" Lake Park Avenue—a short stretch of service road remaining after the street itself was moved east to abut the IC embankment. The site of Nathan Watson's cabin, at Fifty-third Street and "old" Lake Park Avenue, is now occupied by the Hyde Park Federal Savings and Loan Association.

Here and there through the neighborhood one finds farmhouses dating from the 1860's and 1870's. Left over from the 1880's are a number of mammoth frame houses rich with bays and turrets and stained glass and band saw ornament. One collection remains on what is now Harper Avenue: glorious white elephants, the residue of an 1884 subdivision called "Rosalie Villas," which was complete with such social amenities as a Club House and Masonic Hall.

I discovered immediately upon arrival in Chicago that I liked living in a community with a visible past.

At Thirty-fifth Street, as you ride downtown on the IC, you can see the granite shaft above the marble sarcophagus in which Stephen A. Douglas is interred. A tiny park, Douglas Square, now surrounds it. In the 1860's, however, there were two institutions of note on the land in this area. One of them was Camp Douglas, a Civil War prison camp where captured Confederates died by the hundreds. The other, on the west side of the tract, was the University of Chicago. Founded in 1856, its main objective was to educate young men for the Baptist ministry. (With the Presbyterians pouring money into Lake Forest College in the far north suburbs and the Methodists doing the same for Northwestern University in Evanston, could Baptists be idle?)

Douglas gave the land. The University of Chicago's trustees erected thereon an impressive towered stone building. It was so expensive, however, that they had to mortgage the land to pay for it—and that was their undoing. A series of financial panics and the Great Chicago Fire of 1871 made it impossible for people who had pledged support to honor their pledges. The holder of the mortgage therefore foreclosed; and twenty-eight years after its founding the first University of Chicago shut its doors.

(A piece of its building is set into a wall of Wieboldt Hall on the present campus. Hardly anyone now remembers that well into the 1900's the University on the Midway was called the "new" University of Chicago.)

The collapse of the original university was never accepted as final by a few of its most devoted friends, and all through the 1880's they continued to work for its re-establishment. They finally managed to do so, in 1890, with a new charter and a new Board of Trustees. The first building, Cobb Lecture Hall, went up on a piece of marshy land at Fifty-eighth Street and Ellis Avenue, in Hyde Park. It cost a staggering $222,000*—but Chicago was a boom town, and high prices were commonplace.

This was especially true of the Hyde Park area, because the gleaming white buildings of the World's Columbian Exposition were rising along the lake front at Fifty-seventh Street. The Midway Plaisance, that great double drive linking the Fair site in Jackson Park to Washington Park a mile west, was being turned into the Fair's amusement zone, and everything pointed to a very prosperous 1893. In anticipation, Hyde Park real estate developers erected many hotels, apartments, row houses, and cottages—thus opening the way for increased density of population after the Fair, and for the addition to the community of residents with lower incomes than those who could afford the splendors of the Rosalie Villas.

Chicago at the turn of the century was in many respects the cultural center of the United States. Its great burst of creativity in the arts, which spanned the years from the late 1880's to World War I, was reflected in Hyde Park. The first two directors of the

---

* In the 1960's, when the University sentimentally decided not to demolish this historic building but to gut its interior while saving its exterior, the bill was $2,225,000.

Chicago Symphony, and most of their musicians, lived in the community. Mary Garden had her first voice lessons there. The sculptor Lorado Taft established his studio in a coach house near Sixtieth Street and Ellis Avenue. Harriet Monroe founded *Poetry* magazine, and the "Prairie poets"—Edgar Lee Masters, Vachel Lindsay, and Carl Sandburg—joined the local art colony.

The presence of the University drew a cosmopolitan citizenry to Hyde Park. University faculty, of course, settled there. The student body was eclectic from the start. Thirty-three states and fifteen foreign countries were represented in the entering class, which included (astoundingly, for 1892) some women and some Negroes. Doctors, lawyers, and other professional men without a University of Chicago affiliation were attracted to the neighborhood, and the city's Russian and German Jews began to find that they were not unwelcome in Hyde Park.

In addition, the place was physically attractive. The streets were broad and tree-lined; there was plenty of open space; parks and beaches were near; and the wind off the lake made the hot Chicago summers more endurable than was the case a mile inland. Wealthy businessmen of conservative political leanings therefore continued to move in. One of the grandest houses extant is a mansion that was built in 1892 by Frank Lloyd Wright for a man named George Blossom. It is probably the only Wright house in existence with a porch whose roof is held up by Doric columns.

As I prowled about Hyde Park and Kenwood in my early days there, it was a delight to find such places, and to hear stories of "the old days."

In 1916, forty Hyde Park members of the Equal Suffrage League had been among those who had stormed the Republican National Convention at the Chicago Coliseum to demand the woman's vote. A surviving member of that group told me how carefully they had dressed for the confrontation. They wore broad-brimmed hats, divided skirts, and white shirtwaist blouses, and across their bosoms were ribbon sashes on which the slogan VOTES FOR WOMEN was lettered in red. While they were en route, alas, one of the worst rainstorms of the year came up, thoroughly soaking them and causing the red dye of the letters on their sashes to dribble down their once immaculate shirt fronts.

They stormed the hall anyway; and were in time rewarded for their wetting. When the Nineteenth Amendment was passed in 1920 and the Equal Suffrage League became the League of Women Voters, these same ladies helped to make the Illinois League the first in the country to be organized, and they established the Hyde Park League as its first local group. A few years later, one third of Chicago's total League membership lived in Hyde Park.

In 1888, the Hyde Park *Herald* had said, "That was a lively tussle the Democrats had at their primary last Friday. One would think by the fuss they were making that they had a chance to elect somebody. What reason a Democrat can find for going into a primary in Hyde Park is a mystery." Thirty years later, *Republicans* were a distinct minority; and twenty years after that, their candidates were the ones who didn't have a chance. Hyde Park was electing Democrats or Independents.

This political change reflected a shift in population. Many of the conservative, business-oriented, suburban-type families had departed. (The place was filling up; air pollution was becoming a problem; and, well, the farther-out suburbs were *nicer*.) They had been replaced by a younger, more transient group, the kind of people who a generation later would be called "swingers." They didn't necessarily live in Hyde Park because of the cultural benefits bestowed by the University— these being rather heavily directed toward uplift—but because the neighborhood was handy to the Loop and was developing a Greenwich Village sub-culture. During this same period, the community had also acquired a sizable population of people in semi-skilled or service jobs.

But the largest group, if not in numbers certainly in influence, were the professional class residents—cosmopolitan, live-and-let-live types, who were active in support of causes, liberal in outlook, politically sophisticated, and organization-minded. It was their character and behavior that gave the community its "tone." It was they who would determine its destiny.

During the Depression years of the 1930's, many of the families who lived in the grand old mansions couldn't afford to staff them. Lawns began to look ragged. Peeling paint on house exteriors was commonplace. Hotel owners and apartment house landlords also lacked funds to care properly for *their* buildings. The University's income shrank alarmingly; even with operating budgets pared to the bone, it was necessary to dip into capital.

After that dismal decade, World War II brought a new set of problems. There was money now, but many materials (especially metals) had gone to war. Basic maintenance of property still had to be deferred. At the same time, there was a tremendous shortage of housing for the thousands of people who were pouring into the city to take jobs in the war industries. It was patriotic to take in roomers. Or to cut up a big house into flatlets. Never mind if the original plumbing or wiring wasn't adequate for the four families who now lived in space originally intended for one family; with luck, the place would hold together another few years.

At the end of the war, therefore, Hyde Park and Kenwood found themselves with a badly deteriorated physical plant and a huge population straining their public facilities. The garbage collectors couldn't keep up with the refuse; the streets couldn't accommodate the cars; and the schools were shockingly overcrowded. What's more, an increasing number of those schoolchildren were poor, and black. Lower-class black.

Chicago's Negro ghetto, historically situated on the South Side of the city, was bursting out of its strait jacket. Some years before, the black tide had swept south along a line to the west of Washington Park. Now it was moving east toward the lake front—into the dilapidated mansions of Kenwood; into the Hyde Park row houses left over from the World's Fair of '93; into the aged apartments of Woodlawn, the community just south of Hyde Park.

The "holding operations" of the 1930's and early 1940's were clearly over. With the outlawing of restrictive covenants in 1948, there was no longer a barrier to black in-migration. And as the Negroes moved in, the whites moved out. Between 1950 and 1956, 20,000 white families (out of the 72,000 people then living in Hyde Park and Kenwood) picked up and left; and 24,000 black families moved in. At the beginning of the 1950 decade, Negroes had accounted for 6 per cent of the population; at the end of the decade—the year before we came to Chicago —the figure was 49 per cent.

During the late forties and early fifties, the amount of crime had steadily increased—until, by 1952, the police district of which Hyde Park and Kenwood were a part had the highest crime rate in the city. Over a six-year period, the University's undergraduate enrollment slid from 3,200 to 1,250, as parents became fearful for their children's welfare. It became easier for other universities to recruit members of the University of Chicago's faculty, and more difficult for the University to replace them. In fact, my own husband had snatched a couple of top Chicago men for Caltech, men whom he would now be trying to snatch back.

One of the favorite "if only" games that old-timers at the University of Chicago like to play swings around a memo that the sociologist Louis Wirth sent to Robert M. Hutchins in 1937. It said, in part:

> . . . My own conviction is that the University Real Estate Committee, in view of the allegations that the University has been obstructing the south side housing project in the Negro area [public housing, among the first in the country to be constructed with Federal funds], might well issue a statement indicating that it favors this project and disavowing any efforts on the part of members of its staff to obstruct this project . . .
>
> The University cannot, as an owner of real estate and as a member and financial supporter of the local property owners' association, escape responsibility for promoting segrega-

tion covenants. . . . They will increase racial friction and will
not bring about the ends which the proponents of these covenants seek to achieve through them, namely, the exclusion
of Negroes from areas now occupied by whites . . .

The business office of the University might well consider,
as a gesture of good will, as an incentive to others, and as a
sound investment, experiments with Negro housing in well
selected areas [in the University community]. . . ."

The story goes that President Hutchins responded to this
memo by saying, "Louis, you stick to your teaching and leave
the administration to me."

I cannot vouch for the truth of the story, but know that
Hutchins did take Wirth's recommendations to the Board of
Trustees. In due course, the following reply—with an aura of
having come straight from the Office of the Legal Counsel—
was sent him:

The University of Chicago never has been and is not now
engaged in any effort to obstruct the proposed federal housing project on South Parkway. Being an educational and research institution, the University does not have any opinions
or judgments on the matter, and if any member of its [staff]
has been either promoting or opposing this project, he has
done so as an individual and has not spoken for the University . . .

The University is interested in the efficient management
and conservation of its property values and incomes and
therefore . . . has participated in . . . neighborhood organizations and property owners' leagues. The fact that some
of these associations have promoted deed restriction covenants does not commit the University to [the same] policy.
Members of the staff have been free, and will continue to be
free, to oppose such covenants.

. . . Being located in an area adjacent to a large Negro
settlement, the University would of course like the living
conditions of its neighbors to be improved as much as possible but has no funds of its own available for such an undertaking. . . .

That was in 1937. Less than fifteen years later, the "neighbors" to whom the statement referred were no longer two miles west but had moved in next door, and it was beginning to look as if a $200,000,000 gray Gothic investment was going to end up in the middle of a slum. Of course, the community wasn't a slum yet, but the sociologists considered this outcome inevitable. The national experience had been that once an area became flooded with poor Negroes it inexorably became a slum. So the trustees studied in considerable detail the alternative of moving the institution to a Chicago suburb, but finally—to their credit—decided to stay in Hyde Park.

"We'd never have gotten our money out of it, anyway," one Board member later said. "What kind of market is there for a secondhand university?"

(With individual local variations, this is also the dilemma in which most American urban universities—from Columbia to the University of Southern California—have found themselves in the course of the past twenty or so years. Most were originally built "out in the country," and then were surrounded by the city and all of its modern problems.)

At Chicago, it was clear that something had to be done. But what?

The University's trustees and administrators couldn't bring themselves to work with the Hyde Park-Kenwood Community Conference, those "fuzzy-minded idealists" who were the most active and best organized of the several community groups then trying to prevent the decline of the neighborhood.

The Conference had been founded in 1949 by people from KAM Temple, the First Unitarian Church, and the Fifty-seventh Street Meeting of Friends. Many University faculty members were active in it. An inter-racial group, it was liberal to Leftish, social-action oriented, and aggressively pro-integration. In fact, its more articulate members had preached brotherhood with such a sanctimonious air of superiority that they had engendered enormous hostility among Hyde Parkers who were willing for Negroes to be equal so long as they kept their place.

The first executive director of the Conference, Julia Abrahamson, now believes that its militant stand on race relations was a mistake. In her book *A Neighborhood Finds Itself*, she says:

> We should not have made ideological demands on people and institutions, asking them to take part in the Conference program *for our reasons* . . . We should have concentrated on involving *all* community people in a common improvement program. The very process of involvement, the experience of working together, would have improved race relations more naturally than all the self-conscious programs we undertook in this area. An organization for community betterment needs more to achieve its purposes than the loyalty of churchmen, teachers, and social workers. The banker has a vital role to play, and the real estate man, and the shopkeeper, and the university trustee.

What finally brought all these types of people together was the ever rising crime rate. Between 1949 and 1952 it went up by 36 per cent. Purse snatching, slugging, burglary, rape: the police couldn't seem to cope with it. There were those who said that the police weren't even trying to cope with it; Chicago is not the only city where municipal services mysteriously deteriorate as soon as the word gets around that a neighborhood is "changing."

And so, in late winter of '52, the Hyde Park Community Council* had taken a significant step. Boy Scouts and Y Girls distributed Council-prepared fliers to every house asking,

ARE YOU NEXT? ARE YOU AFRAID?
Join more than 50 church, school, business, civic, veteran, fraternal, and other organizations of Hyde Park and Kenwood in a gigantic Citizens Mass Meeting at Mandel Hall on March 27.

* A co-ordinating agency to which most community groups sent delegates. It is no longer in existence.

Two thousand people came. The result was the appointment of a committee of five local leaders, including the new (as of the year before) President of the University, Lawrence A. Kimpton. They were instructed to report back to the community in May with a specific plan for getting better law enforcement.

On May 11, just before the report date, a burglar invaded the home of a University professor, kidnaped his wife, and subjected her to a night of horror. Repercussions of citizen outrage reached as far as the state capital.

"Would you consider using state troopers to control crime in Hyde Park?" the governor was asked on May 15.

"Yes, I would," Adlai Stevenson replied. "But so far I have received no request for such assistance."

It is no wonder, then, that the second community mass meeting on May 19 drew an overflow crowd, or that the citizens overwhelmingly endorsed the proposal of the Committee of Five.

What was proposed went far beyond crime control, for the committee recommended the establishment of a permanent organization that would also tackle a variety of other local problems. It would seek to achieve better enforcement of zoning and building-occupancy laws. It would try to obtain better municipal services of all kinds. It would attempt to redevelop slum pockets. The anti-Conference faction nodded in satisfaction when it was stressed that the approach would be "practical" rather than "idealistic." In short, what was being proposed was urban renewal.

The new organization was named the South East Chicago Commission. Since the University provided much of its operating budget, and Larry Kimpton became its president, the Commission became known as "the action arm of the University." This was not quite accurate, inasmuch as many people without a University connection also supported it financially and served on its governing board. Nevertheless it was and is the organization through which the University can channel such of its resources as can be applied to the solution of urban problems.

In 1952, then, Hyde Park and Kenwood were fast-deteriorating communities whose main assets were a big and powerful university and a well-organized, highly motivated group of citizens. All of them wanted to improve housing, obtain better municipal services, and reduce crime. One faction believed, however, that the community could—and should—assimilate large numbers of incoming Negroes at the same time. The other faction, the one supported by the University, had no sense of "mission" with regard to integration, and some members of that faction were even hostile to the idea.

To me, the most fascinating part of the story was that the two factions had managed to accommodate to each other as the years went along, so much did they prize the unique character of the community that all called home. The "conservatives" had to accept black people as neighbors. The "liberals" had to accept the imposition of economic controls which discriminated against poor people, most of whom also happened to be black.

The executive director of the South East Chicago Commission, throughout its history, has been Julian Levi—a big, tough, aggressive man; half lawyer, half politician. He responds to the prospect of a fight among competing power interests with a gleam in his eye worthy of Genghis Khan.

He has given the Commission its crime-busting aura. For example, when detectives hired by the Commission obtained evidence that a local hotel was the headquarters of a narcotics ring, a list of the hotel's multiple building-code violations was passed on to the firm that insured the property. The insurance company promptly canceled its coverage. Not wishing to have uninsured property, the mortgage holder demanded immediate repayment of his loan. Foreclosure followed, forcing out the operators of the hotel. The new managers took the hint, and thereafter screened their occupants with more care.

It was also Julian who took the fight to City Hall, and to

Springfield, and to Washington. New laws had to be passed on behalf of communities like Hyde Park and Kenwood, places that required rehabilitation rather than slum clearance. (Only about 25 per cent of structures in Hyde Park and Kenwood needed to come down.) The University's Law School did much of the research out of which grew the nation's urban renewal legislation of the late 1950's. An urban planning group at the University drew up the urban renewal plan which, much modified by the citizenry, eventually became the blueprint for the physical renewal of the community. The University's trustees used their personal connections with lawmakers, moneylenders, and real estate developers in order to help get the plan implemented.

But physical renewal was not and could not have been enough to "save" the community, nor could the University—gigantic presence though it was throughout—have done the job alone.

People had to want to live in Hyde Park-Kenwood. They had to care enough about it both to maintain what they had and to work for its improvement. Enabling them to do this was the triumphant accomplishment of the Hyde Park-Kenwood Community Conference.

Cracked sidewalks? Uncovered garbage cans? Abandoned cars pre-empting curbside parking? The Conference organized the residents of the community into block groups. By persuading small groups of neighbors to tackle problems that affected their own households directly, it taught them three important things: what their own responsibilities as citizens were, what municipal services they were entitled to, and that they themselves could supplement services which—even after the community had gotten its fair share—weren't adequate.

For example, the Conference created a citizenry that knew as much about building occupancy codes as the city inspectors, and was much more vigilant. Even today, people pop into the foyers of apartment houses which seem to be acquiring a suitcase population and check the number of names that are listed on the mailboxes. The constant feeding-in to Conference headquarters of such information from the grass roots level enabled its officers to keep hammering away at the municipal authorities for better policing, better street maintenance, more building inspections, more frequent garbage collection, and so on.

And, as things began to get fractionally better, the citizens discovered another important thing: that groups can exert political pressure more effectively than individuals can, so it's to your own advantage to work co-operatively with your neighbors—whether you like them or not. And often, as you get to know them within the context of this shared interest, you discover that they're not so bad after all. (As Julia Abrahamson said.)

In retrospect, most of the people who lived through the 1950's in Hyde Park and Kenwood agree that the urban renewal project could not have succeeded without the double-barreled approach that the accident of time and place provided: the human relations approach of the Conference, and the law-and-order approach of the Commission. They also agree that it was not a pleasant period. Exhilarating, maybe—but not pleasant.

"From 1952 on," one old-timer said to me, "it was a schizophrenic experience to live here. There was Jesus Christ walking down one side of the street, and Julius Caesar marching along on the other."

Finally, and this is the most poignant part of the story, no one knew whether all this effort was being expended in vain. To endure a cliff-hanger situation of that sort for year after year takes uncommon faith and fortitude. It was only as the calendar flipped to 1960 that people in Hyde Park and Kenwood began to realize that they *were* going to make it; and it was the emotional reaction engendered by that realization—a mixture of elation and disbelief, as when your long shot bet pays off—that welcomed George and me to Chicago.

By the end of our first summer there, I had pieced together the broad outlines of this story. That urban renewal had indeed become a fact was obvious on all sides. That crime was no longer a problem of overriding concern was also apparent. And it was far from an all-white community. The details would have to come later; for the moment it was enough to be aware of the magnitude of the effort that had been expended, and its duration.

I had just been through a heartbreaking period in Pasadena. An organization of which I was a member had unsuccessfully sought to distract that city's leadership group from its year-long preoccupation with management of the New Year's Day Tournament of Roses, in order to consider the needs of the public schools. So I could appreciate how much energy it must have taken and by how many people to have kept the Hyde Park-Kenwood urban renewal project moving forward for over twelve years. It was going to be wonderful to live among such people. And in the community that had inspired such devotion.

Five

I do not wish to paint a false picture. One *does* have to worry about crime in Chicago, and in Hyde Park; but one can learn to live with it. Our education began on the morning after George's inauguration as President of the University.

We had ordered a Rambler before we left Pasadena. My husband, who has never overcome his frugal upbringing in Wahoo, Nebraska, knew that we would save money if he were to accept delivery at the factory—which was only an hour and a half distant by train. The catch was that the train he wanted to take left downtown Chicago at 5 A.M. Early rising being no problem for George, he had simply left a call for a University driver to pick him up at 4:30 A.M.

The driver, however, was late. And George is punctual. So he simply set out on foot to a) flag a cruising cab on the Midway or b) walk, if necessary, to the Yellow Cab garage about six blocks from our house. When the University car did show up (ten minutes late), I confirmed that George was not in the house and guessed that he had done what in fact he actually *had* done.

"My God!" the driver exclaimed. "The Yellow Cab garage is only a block from where Professor Johanssen was mugged just two weeks ago!"

With visions of their newly inaugurated President lying unconscious in the weeds on the IC embankment, the campus cops immediately launched a manhunt. It was unsuccessful; George, of course, had found a cab and was already serenely on his way to Kenosha. When he came sailing home that afternoon in his brand new car, the head of the campus police force gave him a stern talking-to about taking care that left him sober and penitent.

The house was ringed with exterior floodlights which we were supposed to turn on at dusk. At first, I often forgot to do this. (After all, in the milieu from which we had just come, we had never even locked our doors.) One weekend a campus policeman came to the rear of the house when I was in the kitchen and asked, "Are you the new housekeeper here?" I said I was, and he gave *me* a stern talking-to because it was after dark and the exterior lights weren't on yet.

A faculty member who had come to the University the year before, from a state university out in the Missouri countryside, told me of the "culture shock" that he and his family had experienced:

We finally got tired of feeling that the mainstream of Western civilization was somewhere "out there," so we came to Chicago. I was excited at the prospect. Chicago's emphasis, from Dewey to Fermi, has always been on the use of intellect to solve man's problems. And that part of being here, the scholarly side, has been great.

But we weren't prepared for the feeling you get of having to be on twenty-four-hour alert. Old Hyde Parkers say, "It's ever so much better now," and I guess it is. But at the same time they don't want to feel responsible if you get robbed or raped. So they tell you not to go into the parks after dark, not to leave your car unlocked, not to admit a stranger to your apartment building. It creates a sense of menace.

One day we ran out of gas in a Negro district only a few blocks west, and coasted into a service station. There were four big tough-looking fellows lounging by the gas pumps, and my wife whispered, "They could rob you."

I said, "Don't be silly. It's broad daylight, there are police not far away, nothing like that could happen here—I think."

I too experienced the same sense of unease. One hot summer night, almost immediately after my arrival in Chicago, I was reading late in our upstairs bedroom. George was already asleep. The windows were open, and the night was quiet. When it occurred, therefore, the sound of breaking glass somewhere at the rear of the house carried clearly.

"George!" I yelled.

He came out of bed already standing up.

I told him what I'd heard and we hurried to the rear of the second floor and looked down. We expected to see broken glass on the sidewalk outside the kitchen window, or shadowy figures flitting through the bushes, but all appeared serene.

"I'm going down to see," George said.

"Well, for heaven's sake, take something to defend yourself with," I urged, looking around wildly for a weapon.

His mountaineer's ice ax, due to be hung on the wall of his study, was still standing in the corner of the room. While I was calling the campus security office, he grabbed the ice ax and padded noiselessly down the stairs.

I was unwilling not to stand by George's side as he defended home and family. So I grabbed up the handiest weapon *I* could find: a pressurized spray can of insecticide which I'd been using earlier to kill some insects that seemed to be hatching in the bedroom carpet.

By the time I got downstairs the campus policemen had arrived. It was the first personal contact that this pair had had with us. I suspect that it was as memorable for them to have met the new President—in pajamas and bare feet, armed with an ice ax on a hot July night—as it had been for their unfortunate colleague who had become an instant belayer. And behind the President, in nightgown and curlers, stood the new First Lady, with a fierce look on her face and her trigger finger on a can of RAID.

A search of the house revealed no occupants other than the soundly sleeping Mrs. Galloway on the third floor and Redmond on the second. There were no signs of attempted entry, and no windows had been broken. We did find fragments of glass in the gutter, and decided that someone driving past had probably tossed a beer bottle out of the car window.

I eventually learned to do what any other modern urban dweller learns to do if he is not to leap like a startled fawn every time he hears an automobile backfire. The trick is to observe the necessary safety precautions but to do so matter-of-factly and without emotion, and then stop worrying. This is the same attitude one brings to potentially dangerous environmental conditions everywhere. There is no more sense in getting uptight about the threat of crime in Chicago than in being afraid to live in Arizona because it has rattlesnakes.

Statistics help bring peace of mind, too. When we came to the University, there were over fifty thousand people living in its community, most of whom had never had their purses snatched, their houses robbed, or themselves assaulted, even when they weren't following the prescribed safety rules. On many a late summer night, from that same bedroom window in the President's House, I heard the solitary footsteps of nurses coming off hospital duty, or of laboratory assistants who had to check the progress of some experiment at midnight. Overall, people get home safely—even students, who are an especially foolhardy lot.

As time went on and I grew more urbanized, I found myself experiencing tangled emotions when the word came in that a girl student had just been raped. Nine times out of ten she lived in a first-floor apartment and had not only left her windows unlocked but open, and I was torn between wanting to offer sympathy and wanting to spank her.

As a newcomer to Chicago, there were more lessons to be learned than to turn on the floodlights at dusk. Some lessons were simple, like remembering to wash your neck because it needed it, not because that was the hygiene your mother had taught you. Some lessons required the unlearning of others. It took a while, for example, before I stopped observing the traffic laws. For months, I braked the car to allow pedestrians to cross the street on marked crosswalks. This California-bred courtesy invariably resulted in a jam of impatient drivers behind me and pedestrians stunned into immobility in front of me. (You should see me charge and scatter them now.)

There was also the problem of feeling my way into familiarity with the etiquette practiced in the diverse circles in which we now found ourselves moving. In which houses did I keep my hat on when I was a luncheon guest? If Red were invited to a debut dance (the trustees were very kind to all of us) and the invitation said 10 P.M., when was he really supposed to arrive? In which groups did one have to be alert for the hostess' rising after dinner as a signal that the ladies and the gentlemen would have their coffee separately?

One problem was very difficult indeed. What behavior was expected of the wife of the President of the University? There were no guidelines. The University of Chicago is tolerant of many life styles. If George wanted to get to the office at 7 A.M. and work in his shirt sleeves, that was all right. If I wanted to put a cat on a leash and walk her around a parking lot so that she could smell hub caps, that was all right, too. I am not saying that everyone approved of George's or my eccentricities. They didn't. But nobody interfered. I was never urged to carry on this tradition or engage in that activity or make friends among a certain group. The future was wide open to shape as I wished.

However, it would have taken a very dim-witted person indeed to believe that the University had spent all that money refurbishing the President's House for just the two of us. So my first project was to get as many University people as possible into it. I began with the faculty wives, nearly a thousand of them.

I may have entertained that many people at Caltech in the course of some previous five-year period, but now I was proposing to do it within a five-*day* period (so that nobody's nose would get out of joint because she had been invited at the end of a more extended series of parties). Therefore, the project required careful organization and planning, and presented me with an opportunity to become better acquainted with the wives of the deans of the Divisions and the Schools. (A lovely lot of women; our work on this activity forged bonds of affection that have never loosened.)

Each gave me a bundle of 3×5 cards listing faculty wives by their husbands' departments. Some cards were marked with red asterisks to indicate junior faculty, others were marked with blue asterisks to indicate widows, or wives of emeritus professors. It would have been cruelty to curious womanhood not to have allowed the ladies to tour the redecorated house, so we proposed to ask wives of junior faculty to act as tour guides and widows and emeritus wives to preside at the tea tables.

Next came the problem of dividing the total list into manageable numbers for each of the five days. Although I wanted each guest to find someone there whom she already knew, I did not want anyone to scan the name tags that all guests would be wearing and see only A–E's, F–J's, L–P's, and so on; this is a dead giveaway that guests have been drawn from an alphabetized list. So the deans' wives and I drew up each day's list by balancing big departments against small ones: twenty from Anatomy, eight from Music, twelve from Economics, eighteen from High-energy Physics, and so on until we hit approximately two hundred.

Then there was the job of getting the name tags prepared, the invitations written, and extra people hired to serve and wash dishes. All during this planning period, Mrs. Galloway was in seventh heaven. She baked and froze cookies by the hundreds. By the first of October, the motor on the mixer had burned out as the result of having put in too many eight-hour days.

The teas were a great success. This was a fashion era of high-heeled, pointed-toe shoes, and the cleverest thing I had done in preparation for the teas was to have found some low-heeled, round-toed shoes in which I could comfortably stand practically forever.

At each gathering, of course, the noise level gradually rose so that people eventually found themselves shrieking in order to be heard over the babble. As an English woman, wife of a visiting professor, was escaping the din, I heard her say to her companion, "Mercy! What would it have been like if there had been alcohol to set them off?"

With the dawning of each new tea day, I pulled out the dead flowers from yesterday's bouquets and added fresh ones; threw away the leftover name tags and laid out the ones for today's crowd; checked the tablecloth to see if yesterday's cream spot could be hidden by today's plate of cookies; and ran over the list of expected guests so that I wouldn't confuse a surgeon's wife with an archeologist's wife and ask if she had accompanied her husband on his latest dig.

At the same time that all this activity was centered at the house, we were going out nearly every night. Most of the Divisions and Schools had some kind of gathering to welcome their new faculty or graduate students, and we went to as many as we could. These were humbling occasions. One night we'd be with a group of linguists and would hear (although not participate in) conversations about tagmemes and double-base transformations. Another evening the geophysicists would talk past us as they discussed impulse waves of the Cauchy-Poisson type. The sociologists were hipped on value biases and implicit models, and the Orientalists on Ugaritic lexicography. George seemed to have a nodding acquaintance with the physicists' quarks and partons, but he didn't do any better than I did with the musicologists' Alberti bass figures and angular melodic leaps. As for the people in the Divinity School, their conversation was so esoteric that George came home one night and said, wearily, "Those guys may have a line to eternity, but it sure is a private one."

In the midst of all this, Red slipped away to Harvard.

I had made a dutiful attempt to get him ready for this new chapter in his life. "Shouldn't we go downtown and get you some Ivy League clothes?" I had said one day in early September.

He had snapped one word of refusal, and that was that. Now he was in Cambridge and, like the new undergraduates at the University of Chicago, was standing in endless registration lines; having physical examinations; going to pink-punch receptions; and in general trying to play it cool while he was churning inside.

American parents have in recent years done their bright children a great disservice. We have goaded them unmercifully, using admission to a good college as the carrot, and by the time they get there they are as high-strung as a wire across Niagara Falls. The University of Chicago makes their entry even more traumatic because of its "placing out" system.

In its pure form, as practiced in the heyday of the "Hutchins" College, this system involved the testing of incoming students in the fourteen general subject matter areas whose mastery was required for graduation. If you placed out, you needn't take the course. If you did well, you received what today would be called advance standing. Legend has it that one bright young thing placed out on all fourteen subjects and therefore qualified for a B.A. degree before actual college entrance.

Over the years, the organization of the College had been changed, the number of required courses reduced, provision made for upper-class specialization, and so on—but in 1961 there were still enough required General Education courses to continue the ritual. In the students' minds, the tests assumed fearful importance.

Inasmuch as it took a lot of time to administer and grade these tests, new students had to be on campus two weeks before classes began. This in turn required an elaborate extracurricular program—one in which we, as newcomers also, took part. We went to Orientation Camp, a dismal weekend in tents on the shores of a nearby Wisconsin lake. We went to the first service at Rockefeller Chapel, which is really a small cathedral, and were stirred by both the place and the preaching. We went to Activities Night, when every organization on campus puts up a booth and installs a pitchman to lure new members.

We ourselves were hosts at the President's Reception. It was hard work, for about seven hundred young people had to be herded through the receiving line in just over an hour and you must really concentrate on each person if you are to say something that recognizes him as an individual while at the same time you are transferring his hand like a hot potato to the hand of the person next in line. Afterwards, we went to a special outdoor performance by the University's Court Theater of *A Midsummer Night's Dream*. It was a memorable performance because we sat beside a boy from Big Timber, Montana, who had never seen live theater, let alone Shakespeare, and was transfixed.

"Such a bright, personable group!" I'd say after one of the evenings spent with students. Or: "Do you remember that red-headed kid from Memphis, the one who told you it was a honor, suh, to be here."

"No," George would say. "But I remember that cute little chick from Omaha. The one who blushed when I told her that the best people come from Nebraska."

For perhaps a month after these opening rites, the new undergraduates remained recognizably the people who had been admitted to the College. But by November they had dissolved into an amorphous mass. Proclaiming themselves to be nonconformists, the girls all stopped setting their hair and parted it in the middle, and the boys all grew beards. They looked as if they seldom bathed; their clothing grew stiff with dirt; and they never *never* smiled. Even the courting couples appeared to have indigestion.

I got a grease pencil, drew a beard on a snapshot of Redmond (ghastly!), and kept it tucked into the edge of my desk blotter. If I got used to the idea ahead of time, I thought, I might be better able to control my facial muscles—in case I needed to—when Red came home for the Christmas holidays.

Six

Although I had grown up in Chicago, the city of my childhood was not the one to which I returned. Part of the difference was, naturally, in me: the matron of the 1960's did not see things as the schoolgirl of the 1930's had. Part of the difference was a reflection of national changes during the same period. You don't send your young men off to a global war, invent jet airplanes, put a television set in every home, and at the same time remain a bastion of parochialism. But many of the differences were solely Chicago born and bred.

The great landmarks were, happily, still there. Chicago is the only American waterfront city that has dedicated its shores to parks rather than to commercial usage, and this glorious green belt still stretched for twenty-six miles along Lake Michigan. The fine museums still stood within those parks, from the Chicago Historical Society on the north to the Museum of Science and Industry on the south. The gray Gothic bulk of the Tribune Tower was still offset by the shining whiteness of the Wrigley Building, and the Old Water Tower—that utterly useless and universally beloved Victorian version of a castle in Graustark—remained inviolate on its small peninsula jutting into North Michigan Avenue.

As of yore, the Chicago River cut through the heart of the city and made a mess of traffic whenever the bridges were up. Yesterday's fondly remembered elephants and dinosaurs greeted me in the main hall of the Field Museum, and the bronze lions—their tails a bit shinier now as a result of millions more caresses by little hands—stood guard at the portals of the Art Institute. LaSalle Street was still the canyon along which bankers and brokers pursued the almighty dollar; State Street was still the place where one spent it; and the elevated trains still clanked and roared around the loop whose shape gave the downtown district its name.

But much was new. A fresh breeze had blown through the musty old Art Institute of memory, and it was now one of the liveliest places in town. The city, which in my earlier day had turned its back on the river, had rediscovered it and had sited several new buildings to face the water. Among them were the now rising twin columns of Marina City, which were soon to add an exciting new shape to the midtown skyline. High-rise public housing projects extended like a grim chain gang for block after block on State Street south of the Loop. The stock yards were gone (no longer could Chicago claim to be Hog Butcher to the World), and the mammoth railroad terminals that had once hummed with traffic slumbered uneasily.

Too much has been written of the Everleigh sisters, Bathhouse John Coughlin, and Hinky Dink Kenna. Al Capone, the 42 Gang, and the still surviving West Side Bloc have also had more than their share of attention. The important part of Chicago's history is not the vendettas of its vice lords but its geographic location and the acumen of its businessmen.

As the prairies of the Mississippi Valley were opened up to agricultural exploitation, Chicago became their great trading and processing area. All through the mid-nineteenth century, the nation's railroads came thundering in to Chicago terminals. The Chicago-centered network of inland waterways grew and expanded, until in time the system had no peer. Commodities traders, millers, meat packers, and merchants in coal, lumber, and steel came swarming in, too—most of them New England Yankees—and the fervid energy they expended on the production of agricultural and industrial wealth became the hallmark of the city. (And still is: a recent visitor said, "I like the Chicago style of work. Watch the Loop restaurants. They fill up and empty fast. Lunch is to eat so you can go back to work.")

In 1850, Chicago's population was 30,000. Twenty years later, it was 300,000. By 1890, it had passed the million mark. Within the same period its urban area had grown from less than 35 square miles to over 175 square miles. In short, early Chicago was a boom town of incredible vitality. But it was *not* peopled solely by hard-drinking, trigger-happy outlaws.

Carl Condit, the architectural historian, has said:

> The traditional view—still persisting among historians— that Chicago was a crude and illiterate frontier town is wholly false. To accept such a view makes it impossible to explain the phoenix that rose from the ashes of 1871. Even at the time of its incorporation in 1837 the city included a bookstore, a theater, a newspaper, and three debating socie- ties. By the time of the Great Chicago Fire, there were 68 bookstores in the city, or one for every 4396 inhabitants—a higher ratio than can be found in most cities today.
>
> This interest in literature was paralleled by equal enthu- siasm for music and the visual arts. Many of the wealthy families lived a cultivated and sophisticated life, with much travel abroad, and several had exceptionally fine private li- braries. This vigorous intellectual life made the citizens re- ceptive to new ideas and enthusiastic about their implications, a characteristic of the city that would be more widely ap- preciated if most of the evidence for it—letters, diaries, and books—had not been destroyed by the fire. . . .

And here is testimony from an observer of the city at a slightly later date. Writing to his friend Theodore Flournoy in 1896, William James said:

> I wish you were here with me to see Chicago and its in- stitutions. It is a stupendous affair—the "storm-centre" of our Continent, and already outstripping New York in civili-

zation, size, and importance . . . It is a place of vast ideas and titanic energy, and the largeness and ambitiousness of its beginnings must determine its character for all time. Money for public purposes is poured out like water, and although there is crime and corruption *ad nauseam* there is greatness of the greatest sort. . . .

The great esthetic achievement of the period was the invention of the skyscraper and its development by the Chicago School.

The great technological accomplishment was the reversal of the entire drainage pattern of the Chicago metropolitan region —a system of locks, canals, and dams that caused the waters to flow *away* from Lake Michigan.

The great civic achievement was the Burnham Plan. ("Make no little plans," said Daniel Burnham, "for they have no power to stir men's blood.") Between 1900 and 1920, it brought into being the great lake front parks and the Forest Preserve District. The latter still provides the city with green oases on the outskirts of town. The grand boulevards of the interior were completed, as was Wacker Drive—that two-level roadway along the river which must have seemed visionary in the extreme when automobiles were still a curiosity, but which now plays a key role in preventing the complete strangulation of Loop traffic.

The dynamism that had characterized Chicago in its beginnings never wholly perished, but it was pretty feeble by the 1920's. Beginning with the long reign of Big Bill Thompson— from 1915 to 1931, with a four-year break for a reform mayor whose record matched that of most reform mayors—a series of corrupt and apathetic city administrations nearly smothered public and private initiative. During the same period, Al Capone and his successors destroyed Chicagoans' pride in their city, and the Depression of the 1930's left it broke.

In 1955, when Richard J. Daley unseated an honest but ineffective mayor, the last thought that would have occurred to anybody was that a savior had arrived in City Hall. Daley, like Chicago itself, has been reported in the nation's press by recourse to stereotypes. Short, squat, and jowly, Daley looks exactly like what he is: grandson of an Irish immigrant, son of a sheet-metal worker, product of an impoverished upbringing in a stock yards neighborhood, high school dropout, lawyer via the night school route taken in young manhood, holder of city patronage jobs which he escalated into offices of greater power until he built himself a formidable political machine.

Given this background, one can understand the dismay of the Better Government Association and the delight of the Old Pols when Daley was elected mayor of Chicago. Paddy Bauler, a colorful character whose saloon served as his aldermanic office and whose history suggests that he could have defended honest graft as enthusiastically as George Washington Plunkitt, greeted Daley's victory with the jubilant prediction that "Chicago ain't ready for reform."

But then an astonishing thing happened. Richard J. Daley turned out to be more interested in the public welfare than in private gain. His political machine was harnessed to purposes of civic improvement, and Chicagoans began to be aware of the value of a political boss who is so strong that he doesn't have to yield to pressures from every interest group.

Programs that had been limping along under Daley's predecessor suddenly picked up speed, and almost before the city knew what was happening to it, a new expressway system had come into being; you could find a place to park downtown; O'Hare Airport had been built; hundreds of acres of slums had been cleared and new dwellings had been started. True, the mayor has always put more energy into projects using lots of steel and concrete than into those whose aim is to preserve historic buildings and park lands; but in the context of the late 1950's, this predilection seemed less important than it does today.

Finally, Daley brought to Chicago the country's top criminologist, Orlando Wilson; made him the superintendent of police; and gave him both adequate funds and a free hand. The people soon discovered with joy that police services were improving by leaps and bounds. As a result of all this, the Chicago *Tribune* found itself in the startling position of saying a good word for a Democratic machine politician, and so did the city's businessmen—most of whom are conservative Republicans.

Thus began a great civic renaissance in Chicago. By the time George and I arrived it was in full swing. The downtown area rang with the sound of pneumatic drills and jackhammers as new office buildings went up. The distinctive common denominator of most of the buildings that have been constructed in the Loop during the past fifteen years is that the men who commissioned them had taste and conscience. They bought good architecture in full awareness of its being a civic contribution.

Men of the same stripe—some of them bearing distinguished old Chicago names, some of them newly caught by the city's ambience in the late fifties and early sixties—also guide the great private foundations and organizations which devote themselves to civic betterment, culture, or education: the Metropolitan Housing and Planning Council, the Welfare Federation, the Urban League; the Art Institute, the Chicago Symphony, Lyric Opera; the museums, the hospitals, and the several universities in the area. Chicago has good reason to be grateful to them. I have come to take a jaundiced view of the younger generation's condemnation of Big Business as Bad, All Bad. Such amenities as we have in Chicago are largely due to enlightened businessmen.

There are, of course, other power groups in Chicago. In the early 1960's, men of substance in the Negro community were only beginning to test the fragile bridges that have since led to their greater involvement in the affairs of the entire city. The churches—which in Chicago tends to mean the Roman Church, almost half of the population being Catholic—concentrate on social welfare or localized parish matters. The "ethnic groups" (Germans, Irish, Poles, Swedes, and many more, most of them now American-born but in culture still closely linked to their homelands) are a very large segment of Chicago's population: 35 per cent in 1960, compared with 18 per cent in the nation as a whole. They characteristically channel their social energies into sodalities, and express their interest in civic affairs through the Daley machine.

Traditionally, these groups have not been greatly interested in the University of Chicago, whereas members of the "downtown business establishment" have had long-time links with it. So it is not surprising that this is the group among whom George and I found our new non-faculty friends. (Not that many of them *live* downtown. I wish I had kept cumulative records of the mileage we have traveled to and from the fashionable North Shore suburbs.)

From the beginning of our acquaintance, we were struck by the range of their attitudes toward the University, and by the intensity of their feeling. Some knew the institution well enough to be proud of it and to support it generously. Others thought it was a fine place but wouldn't send their children there (as undergraduates, anyway). Still others considered the institution to be so dominated by liberals and Left-wingers that it was a menace to society. The source of this latter attitude lay in the sometimes abrasive personality of Robert M. Hutchins, and in the Red witch-hunts of both the 1930's and the 1950's. I have never ceased to marvel at its persistence.

Only those who harbored such suspicions can say whether George and I, as symbols for the University, either reversed or modified their beliefs—but we tried. And in the course of the effort, we became extremely fond of some of the people in this category. One of them was General Robert E. Wood, builder of both the Panama Canal and Sears Roebuck, whose distrust of the University of Chicago was total. George never failed to come home in a state of high good humor after any contact with him.

The men of the downtown business establishment meet at noon in private clubs—the Chicago Club, the Standard Club, the Tavern Club, the Mid-America Club, the University Club. Their ladies cluster at the Fortnightly, the Woman's Athletic Club, the Casino, and the Arts Club. We were delighted to be welcomed to these gatherings, and took advantage of the opportunity—partly because we wanted to find out how the winds were blowing within an important segment of Chicago society and partly in order to keep the University of Chicago in the minds of people who seldom visit the campus.

In this last endeavor, George was not perhaps as tactful as he might have been, since he was not the only local college or university president to be included in these groups. He is the least arrogant man I know, yet he has always and quite unconsciously referred to the institution he headed as "the University." So he deserved the good-natured rebuke he got one day from Rocky Miller, the president of Northwestern.

"You know, George," he said. "There are *other* universities."

A third reason for mingling with such people was personal pleasure. Speaking for myself, I thoroughly enjoyed the company of the women. The majority are intelligent, attractive, and useful to society—and worth knowing for that reason alone. But I freely admit that I also loved to see the clothes they had just brought back from Paris.

A lot has been written about Chicago's "second city" complex. With poor old New York falling apart at the seams, Chicago certainly doesn't feel inferior today; but even a decade ago I didn't sense any particular competitiveness with Number One. Such defensiveness as I noted arose from a desire not to be categorized as a cow town.

For example, the late Mrs. Daggett Harvey once told me with both amusement and exasperation that a New York friend had just called her and said, "I'll be flying out to Chicago next weekend. Is there anything I can bring you?"

I would also be derelict in my civic duty if I did not retell the famous anecdote about the New York visitor who was shown the superb French Impressionists in the collections of the Art Institute of Chicago.

"Where on earth did you get *these?*" he asked. He was obviously astounded to find such treasures 'way out here in the trackless wilderness.

His hostess took great pleasure in replying, "We inherited them from our grandparents."

By December of 1961, then, the social pattern we were to follow throughout George's administration was set. We attempted to divide our attention among three groups: the University faculty and students; the people who lived in Hyde Park and Kenwood; and the downtown business establishment. As often as not, we did this separately. There were just too many invitations, especially when we were new in town and people were curious about us, to allow us both to attend everything. Sometimes, too, the events naturally sorted themselves into assignments for one or the other of us.

It became commonplace for me to lunch downtown with a citywide woman's group (sometimes making a speech) while George was elsewhere in the Loop, meeting with a subcommittee of the Board of Trustees. He'd hurry back to the campus for an afternoon session with the editor of the student newspaper, and maybe I'd see him briefly before he went back downtown for a Commercial Club dinner. While he was gone, I might be having a reception for one of the subsections of the University of Chicago Service League. He'd sneak in via the back staircase while the party was still roaring along, and be asleep by the time I had emptied the ashtrays and fed the cats any leftover bits of pound cake. We often had to communicate with each other by taping notes to the bathroom mirror.

Elected officials and their wives have the same problem, only in more acute form. They are together mostly in public, and also find themselves engaged in a multitude of separate activities which further fragment whatever may remain of a private life. This kind of existence can be borne with equanimity only if both are willing to give themselves wholly to the demands of the job.

A university presidency can similarly absorb all one's time and energies, and it is an advantage if both husband and wife are equally committed to it. George and I never agreed absolutely on the degree to which we should practice nose-to-the-grindstone versus self-indulgent activity, but our attitudes were similar enough, praise be, so that we never wasted our energies arguing about how much of our time the University should command. Any university president and his wife can almost count on celebrating their wedding anniversary by eating over-done beef at a Jaycees' Distinguished Citizens Awards Dinner instead of at a candlelit table for two in the city's best French restaurant, and their life will be much less stressful if they don't fight it.

Seven

From its first multipurpose building, Cobb Hall, the University grew rapidly. By the time it celebrated its first quarter-century, it had more than forty buildings, most of them Gothic. This mode was appropriate for the self-styled Oxford of the West; in fact, the University's Hutchinson Commons is a replica of Christ Church Hall, and the tower on an adjacent building is a squashed-down version of the one on Magdalen College.

Taken individually, these early University of Chicago buildings are nothing to get excited about, but as massed around the central Quadrangles of the campus they are stunning in effect. This austere "gray city" is set among broad lawns studded with massive oaks and elms and is that rarity on the urban scene: a place of cloistered serenity (visually, at least) that lies within a hundred yards of busy city streets.

In 1961, this effect was best appreciated at a distance. When one saw the buildings at close hand, it was apparent that they had had little maintenance in recent years. (And no wonder: the University had invested $29,000,000 in the urban renewal effort, money that had come out of both the instructional and the housekeeping budget.) George couldn't stand the shabbiness of the place, and he urged the business manager to spend *some* money on maintenance.

"An institution as great as this one ought to be able to keep its brass polished," he said.

There were so many other things that the University's scant funds could be spent on—things of more obvious utility—that the refurbishing program began tentatively and without fanfare. Surprisingly, there was no backlash. In fact, a professor here and there commented on how nice it was to see fresh varnish on the beautiful old oak doors or to lecture in a classroom whose cracked walls had been patched and repainted.

Thus encouraged, George attacked an eyesore that in his opinion was even worse than the state of the buildings. He is an enthusiastic gardener, and the condition of the grassy areas shocked him. The weedy lawns, scarred with brown spots or patches of raw dirt, had the weathered look of a city tomcat who is still alive only because he has become tough enough to beat the odds.

The beginning of the campaign was modest. All George attempted was to replant and nurture the grass on a circular island about fifty feet in diameter which had been created by the pattern of the driveway leading from University Avenue into the great central Quadrangle.

The replanting was easy. The nurturing was not. People habitually crossed the circle every which way, and when the first tender shoots of grass came up in late October, they got mashed down by scores of scurrying or scuffing feet. "Please Don't Walk on the Grass" signs were ignored. Visual barriers of clotheslines between low posts were deliberately breached.

"You'd think we were trying to interfere with their academic freedom," George snapped one night when he arrived home after passing the usual scene of devastation.

"Remember that they're mostly urban types here," I soothed. "Half of them have probably never even *seen* a lawn mower."

"You mean," he responded with a small flash of humor, "that they're horti-culturally deprived?"

We went out to dinner that night, a rare kind of dinner date because it had no purpose other than personal pleasure. Our host was Edward Maser, new chairman of the Art Department, who had come that year from the University of Kansas. The guests of honor were Dr. and Mrs. Franklin D. Murphy; he had been the chancellor at Kansas and was now newly appointed to the same position at UCLA. Inge Maser is a spectacularly good cook, and after dinner George was sufficiently relaxed (especially in the company of another university president) to vent his ire and to voice his perplexity about "the grass problem."

I don't remember which member of the company was the strategist and which was the tactician, but two brilliant minds—lubricated by brandy—came up with this pair of ideas:

"The main thing you have to do is to persuade people to walk *around* the circle instead of *across* it."

"And the way to do it is to post signs they'll want to read. Same principle as the Burma Shave signs."

"For example?" George asked.

"Well, certainly not 'Keep Off the Grass,'" Frank Murphy replied. "How do you like 'Don't Tread on Me'?"

And then the rest of us were off.

"How about 'That's Turf'?"

"Or 'Color Me Green'?"

"What's that line from Gertrude Stein? 'Pigeons in the grass, alas'? How about 'Where Is the Grass, Alas? You Are Not a Pigeon.'?"

"Or 'Be a Nonconformist—Stay Off the Grass.'"

"On the Grass, *Nyet!* Off the Grass, *Si!*"

"Ho! Let's form a Green International!"

"Good. 'The Green Front Against Oppression of Grass.'"

"That's not scholarly enough for the University of Chicago. It ought to be a Committee of some sort." That was Ed Maser speaking. He had been a Chicago undergraduate during the Hutchins-encouraged rise of interdisciplinary Committees, and was well aware of the University's passion for them.

So, naturally, we named our new organization the Committee on Grass, Interdisciplinary and International. That final word was added in order to make the title more impressive, but it turned out to be accurate. When the first signs began to appear on campus and even the New York *Times* took note of the new "front group" at the University of Chicago, slogans came in from all over the United States and from Canada, as well as from people in many scholarly disciplines at the University itself.

We charter members of the Committee on Grass decided at the organizational (and only) meeting that anyone who submitted a usable slogan would become a Lifetime Member, Entitled to All the Privileges Thereunto Appertaining. He would receive a membership card, printed in green ink, and a button for a suit lapel, reading GRASS ROOTS. These were subsequently dispensed by a lady who lived in the President's House but was identified only as The Secretary and was reachable only through a box number at Faculty Exchange (the University's campus mail service).

Another decision made by the charter members was that no sign, however exotic, would be explained.

"If they're at the University of Chicago, they're bright enough to figure it out," Ed Master declared.

Hence the contribution from a member of the Oriental Institute staff was most welcome; it said a little something about grass but was written in Assyrian cuneiform as of the eighth century B.C. A graduate student in the humanities provided *"Ou sont les tapis d'autrefois?"* The wife of a visiting professor of Swedish advised walkers to *"Gaa uternom, Peer Gynt!"* Seneca was heard from, via Classics, but in translation: "Shame may restrain what the law does not prohibit"; and someone in the Music Department set down the opening bars of Stravinsky's *Rite of Spring.*

Reporters for the student newspaper nearly went crazy trying to find out for sure who was behind all this calculated nonsense. But inasmuch as no student ever arose as early as 5:30 A.M., when the signs were posted by a gentleman who lived in the President's House, the anonymity of the Committee on Grass was preserved.

The campaign used up material as fast as a weekly comedy hour on TV, but it was worth the effort. People decided that they would indeed "Be Hip, Man—Orbit It!" (That was the contribution of the chairman of the Geophysics Department, who had teenage children.) The infant grass slumbered through the winter virtually inviolate.

Often enough in October to make one want to skip through piles of fallen leaves, the skies are clear blue and cloudless and the air is so invigorating that it blows all the cobwebs out of one's mind. Overall, however, autumn is not an especially attractive season in Chicago. One has to go miles out of the city for the showy splendors of flaming red or gold foliage. In town, the green simply drains out of the landscape, like a slow leak in a tire, and the only bright color is in the swarms of migrating monarch butterflies. On an occasional October morning, very early, one can sometimes hear the honking of geese, and see far above in the pearly sky the big wobbly V of a flock heading south.

In late October, the local soothsayers make their predictions for the months ahead. A restaurateur in Waukegan checks the distance from shore to which the Lake Michigan fish have retreated, and correlates the depth of water there with the expected harshness of the coming winter. A naturalist in Rockford counts acorns, a heavy crop of which means a long hard winter; and a bird watcher in Aurora also takes note of how high in the trees the wasps are building their nests—which indicates, he says, how deep the snows will be.

In November, chill rains fall from dismal gray skies. Sodden garments hung in hall closets give every house entryway a wet-wool smell, and leaf-clogged gutters allow miniature waterfalls to pour down the sides of houses and seep through cracks in masonry. In the fall of 1961, the dampness was so pervasive that many of our bedroom doors swelled and stuck shut, and I had to have the carpenters from Buildings and Grounds plane them down. (After which, of course, the winter overheating of the house dried and shrank them, and many thereafter refused to latch. This became a special problem *vis-à-vis* houseguests and cats. If a door can't be securely shut, what's to prevent a sociable feline from seeking out any available warm body to bunk with?)

Christmas festivities began early in December. These included a tree-lighting ceremony and wassail party for students at Ida Noyes Hall (the University's closest approximation to a Student Union building); a party for all the women employees of the University; women's club meetings featuring group singing of carols; eggnog parties and cocktail buffets at numbers of private homes beyond recall.

We had not yet made the great discovery of later years: that during a period when party giving is widespread, the people whose invitations you refuse assume that you are attending parties elsewhere. Therefore you don't have to go to *any*, and can sit cozily at home with your shoes off. That first year in Chicago, however, we rode the Yuletide circuit hard.

Red got home just before Christmas. He had not grown a beard, but perhaps he should have; it would have hidden the ghastly hollows in his cheeks. Sallow and gaunt, he looked exhausted. And no wonder: like many college freshmen, for the first time in their lives freed from schedules imposed by school or family, he had sampled too many of the available opportunities.

In addition to course work that in itself was demanding, he had become a gallery patron of the Boston Symphony; had attended Radcliffe-Harvard "mixers" and other social gatherings; had shopped around among the campus chapters of the Young Democrats, Young Republicans, John Birch Society, and CORE; *and* was working for ten hours a week as a member of a dorm-cleaning crew.

"It's not hard work, Mom," he said. "The rooms are so full of junk there isn't much open space to clean."

When I finally harassed him into admitting that his work schedule and his class schedule meshed so poorly that he didn't have time to eat lunch and that he got no more than six hours of sleep a night, I demanded that he quit the dorm crew. I also delivered an eloquent sermon on being intelligent about the expenditure of one's energy.

"Look who's talking," he murmured—but agreed to hunt for a full-time summer job as a replacement for a part-time school job.

Aside from taking the starch out of him physically, his first term at college didn't seem to have changed him. He wasn't saying "Baaston," nor did his manner suggest that the Ivy League had yet made a deep imprint. ("When a Yale man enters a room, he looks as if he owns it. When a Harvard man enters a room, he looks as if he doesn't care who owns it.")

His version of course abbreviations jarred on a University of Chicago-trained ear: Humanities I, we had learned, is "Hume" I, whereas Red pronounced it "Hum" I. Social Sciences I, similarly, came out as "Sock Sigh" I, whereas at Chicago it was "Sōsh" I.

The best thing he could say about the dormitory meals was that unlimited seconds were allowed (one up on Chicago). This damning of institutional cooking with faint praise, plus his weight loss, inspired Mrs. Galloway to new culinary heights, and every day was Sunday.

Just before Christmas, a great, soft, wet snow, the first major fall of the season, drifted silently down in the night. Its virginal beauty (in sooty Chicago, a matter of one day) enchanted us recent emigrants from California and provided us with a last-minute infusion of Old Tyme Cheer. We managed then to trim our Christmas Tree; put a sprig of holly on the door knocker; and dug out all our traditional music for the hi-fi.

Speaking of tradition: the most remarkable Christmas party we ever attended in Chicago was one given annually by Mrs. J. W. A. Young, and we attended it only in 1961. (Mrs. Young would live to give only one more such party before she had to enter a nursing home, where she remained until her death in 1964.)

Widow of a University professor and herself a graduate of a very early class, Louise Young was eighty-seven years old when we met. She had, of course, been invited to my teas for faculty wives, and on the day she was to be my guest she had sent a bouquet of roses. Included was a yellowed visiting card with her name engraved in the center and, in the lower left-hand corner, "Tuesdays." I puzzled over this word, then suddenly realized that in a more gracious era, Tuesday had been her "At Home" day.

Mrs. Young had played a key role in establishing what is now the Indiana Dunes State Park (a favorite summer recreation area for Chicagoans) and for fifty years had been its ardent defender. She was also an enthusiastic opera-goer, Wagner being her favorite, and wore her reddish hair in Brünnehilde braids. What more appropriate nickname could she have acquired than "Dune Hilda"? In short, Mrs. Young was a lady of strong will, Edwardian values, and firm convictions. I regret that we came to know her so late in her life that her fires were beginning to burn low.

When she telephoned to inform me that George and I were "expected to attend" her traditional Christmas party on the Saturday before Christmas, it didn't occur to me to refuse, only to ask if we might bring Redmond. We walked to her house, an old frame cottage on Blackstone Avenue, through glittery moon-washed snow.

Upon being admitted, we discovered immediately that we had committed a sartorial *faux pas*. Mrs. Young had not specified "black tie," presumably because anybody who was anybody would know that black tie should be worn to her annual Christmas party. There were even some white ties present.

But—wasn't there something odd about the assemblage? There were so many old people there, the men in dress suits with a faint greenish cast, the ladies in bias-cut gowns whose wrinkles hadn't quite hung out. Mrs. Young herself had a 1930-style bandeau around her head, and over what I am sure she would have described as an evening "frock" she was wearing an embroidered Spanish shawl (the kind that, in my youth, people draped on grand pianos). The scene, lit by candles, gave me a sense of being transported backward by some time machine whose lens was slightly out of focus.

My guess would be that Mrs. Young had for some years been living in very straitened circumstances. Such lighting fixtures as there were had forty-watt bulbs in them; the furniture was threadbare; and the "collation" bore the marks of friendly help from many hands. There may have been alcohol in the wassail bowl, but it tasted like Kool-Aid, and the finger sandwiches included a pile spread with pimiento cream cheese garnished with shredded coconut. George had forgotten about the existence of pimiento cream cheese, and Red had never seen any. Almost together, they whispered to me, "Do I have to eat one of those?"

Later, there was a procession through the lower rooms of the house, in which each of us marched—carrying a lighted candle—with a kind of desperate gaiety. A recital and group singing concluded the festivities. In its totality, the party was like the "social evenings" I had read about in the memoirs of the University's early faculty. We left a bit before the others, closing the door very gently on the Ghost of Christmas Past.

Eight

The sit-in of 1962 hurt like a kick in the stomach. There would be others, much more vicious in nature, but this one packed the biggest wallop because it was the first.

The issue was open occupancy in those apartment buildings owned by the University in which space was rented to people other than faculty, students, or staff. The local chapter of the Congress on Racial Equality (CORE), which initiated the sit-in, charged that University officials who set rental policies refused to rent vacant apartments in certain buildings to Negroes* but were willing to rent the same space to whites.

George, as spokesman for the University, replied with complete candor that the assertion was true. But he argued that this practice was a necessary interim step on the road to integration of those properties, given the temper of the times and prevailing conditions in the community. Here's why:

Nervous whites are the main barrier to residential integration. Some are reluctant to live in the same neighborhood with *any* black people, some simply don't want to be the only whites left in an otherwise black community. Experience (all over the country) had taught that whenever incoming blacks reach about 25 per cent of a neighborhood's population, there is no preventing its "tipping." Oakland, the community just north of

* "Black" did not replace "Negro" until late in the 1960's. I have used both words in this book, depending on context.

Kenwood, was a classic example: 22 per cent Negro in 1940, it had become 77 per cent Negro by 1950. Woodlawn, just south of Hyde Park, had "turned" within the five-year period 1950–56.

Unscrupulous realtors—of both races, since greed for a fast buck is not a racial characteristic but a human one—help the process along by barraging white homeowners with offers of good prices for their property *at this time*. Once these "block busters" acquire the property, they resell it at grossly inflated prices to blacks who are in such dire need of housing that they have no bargaining power.

Another way to profit from the economic helplessness of a ghettoized people is to become a "slumlord." Reduce services in an old building—a six-flat, say—until you have driven out the tenants, then rent the same space to twelve or eighteen families instead of the six families for whom the building was designed. The income thus realized will be enough to recompense the slumlord for the loss of the building, which (with that many people using its facilities) will be a ruin in a few years and can be abandoned.

Both practices had been widespread in Hyde Park-Kenwood in the 1950's, along with a variant aimed specifically at the University. Owners of old properties who didn't want to maintain them but couldn't quite bring themselves to become slumlords had instead blackmailed the University into buying their buildings by threatening to "turn" them. This was how the University had come to own the apartment houses that were the target of the 1962 sit-in. The business office's collective term for them was "threat properties."

To stop both block busting and the conversion of old buildings into slums was a major goal of the urban renewal effort. There were two approaches. One was simply to reduce the amount of dilapidated or deteriorating housing. When you did this, both whites and Negroes were displaced—but mostly Negroes. A group of white homeowners in southwest Hyde Park, watching their neighborhood population climb from 16 per cent Negro in 1950 to what would be almost 70 per cent in 1960, had formed themselves into a development corporation which bought and tore down the most blighted buildings. The slum-clearance projected at the eastern end of Fifty-fifth Street, initiated by the city, was using the same approach.

Another way to reach the goal was to prevent deterioration of housing, or upgrade it, and attempt to fill it with people whose incomes and standards matched those already predominant in the community. This was the course followed by a group of militant women, affectionately referred to locally as "the Kenwood Ladies." They had organized themselves to seek out responsible buyers (of any race) for houses or apartments that might otherwise be acquired by slumlords. Their effort had been highly successful.

The reverse was true of a similar undertaking by a group of Negro businessmen, alarmed as the Negro population in northwest Hyde Park began to skyrocket from its 6 per cent figure of 1950. They tried to attract more whites to that sector of the community, but by 1960 the Negro population there was almost 80 per cent and is higher today. It is much more difficult to integrate a black area than a white one.

A third example was the 1960 creation of the Hyde Park Federal Savings and Loan Association, a colossal community undertaking. Its purpose was to make money available to *any* responsible person who wished to buy or rehabilitate property in the area. Hyde Park Federal had to be created because established loan institutions in Chicago wouldn't touch Hyde Park-Kenwood with a ten-foot pole. Hard-headed businessmen "knew" that money invested in a changing neighborhood would be money thrown away.

In short, to make Hyde Park-Kenwood a racially stable community, it was necessary to do one of two things: tear down blighted housing, and thus displace the lower-class poor; or keep the property in such good condition that only the middle and upper classes could afford it. Either way, you discriminated against *some* blacks.

Community leaders had argued about this kind of interventionism at scores of neighborhood meetings—screaming matches, some of them had been—during the 1950's. Mike Nichols, who got his beginning as a comedian here, had memorialized the battle when he said, "This is Hyde Park, whites and blacks shoulder to shoulder against the lower classes."

But by 1962, when it had become obvious that the community *was* holding its whites (despite an overall Negro population far in excess of 25 per cent), the objections to "managed integration" had subsided—among the permanent residents. The University of Chicago chapter of CORE, however, would have no part of it.

George tried to illustrate the principle by discussing the case histories of thirty-three of the fifty-odd threat properties owned by the University and rented to non-University people.

"When we acquired them," he said, "twenty-six were all-white, five were all-Negro, and two had mixed occupancy. They were all old buildings, in great need of rehabilitation, and none was being maintained.

"Around here, knowledgeable tenants assume that when a landlord begins to let a building run down, he is about to 'turn' it. For a Negro tenant to come in at that point confirms their fears, and they move out. That's what had happened to the five buildings on this list that were wholly occupied by Negroes when we bought them, and what surely would have happened to the others.

"We have learned, over the years, that the best way to hold white tenants is to rehabilitate a building. But the cost is tremendous—hundreds of thousands of dollars per building—and we haven't been able to upgrade all the commercial property we own. We're doing it as fast as we can, and as each job is completed we introduce Negro tenants.

"The thirty-three buildings on this list I've given you all have mixed Negro and white occupancy—now. We did it gradually, and we'll follow the same practice with our other commercial properties that still have all-white tenancy.

"Believe me, it's the only way you can achieve residential integration—and it *is* integration you want, isn't it?"

Yes, the delegation said, but "segregation cannot be a means to integration, on either logical or moral grounds."

"Can you name for me," George asked, "any other successfully integrated neighborhood—by which I mean one that is stable, not one which is inter-racial only because all the whites haven't moved out yet?"

None of the students could.

"You've all seen Prairie Shores and Lake Meadows, the high-rise apartment complexes near Michael Reese Hospital and the Illinois Institute of Technology, haven't you? Around Thirtieth Street? They're integrated. But do you know how they're kept that way?

"The owners refuse to rent vacant apartments to Negroes when the white occupancy in a given building drops, and rent to Negroes preferentially in reverse circumstances. It's a good thing that the buildings are new and attractive and the location is convenient. If the space weren't in demand, the owners couldn't afford to hold some apartments off the market in order to get a good racial mix."

The students looked stubborn. He was not selling them.

One of the boys said, "Three of us did a survey. We talked to all the people—well, most of them—in the six buildings where our tests showed that the University won't rent to Negroes. And they all said they wouldn't mind having Negroes in the same building."

George sighed. "Yes, I know. People usually respond that way. But experience, here and everywhere else, shows that when Negroes do move in, those same whites suddenly discover that their apartments are too large, or too small, or that there's too much air pollution in the neighborhood, or that the children will get better schooling in the suburbs. They never move out because of racial prejudice, but it's funny how often those other reasons for leaving occur to them at the same time that the building gets its first Negro tenant."

A girl spoke up. "Mr. Beadle, it seems to me that the University has a responsibility to prevent that sort of thing."

"Well, that's what I've been trying to convince you that we . . ."

"No, not that way. You must educate them. Tell them to be *reasonable*."*

Such talks were fruitless. Eric Sevareid has said, "Youth has the equipment to measure in one direction only: ahead. It sees the great distance between today and the realization of our ideals. The older generation looks across and sees how much better we are than most other societies, and backward, and sees the great distance we have come in progress." Both viewpoints may be valid, as Sevareid asserts, but their validity doesn't necessarily prevent conflict. So, in late January, some thirty students moved into the small reception area outside of George's office, and settled down there.

This was CORE's first sit-in north of the Mason-Dixon line, and it therefore attracted wide publicity. The lunch-counter sit-ins had been tremendously effective in arousing the national conscience, and the University of Chicago's rental policy sounded just as indefensible as the refusal of a Deep South drugstore to serve a cup of coffee to a Negro. Worse, really: wouldn't you expect a big, powerful, and enlightened academic institution to behave better than a small Southern shop owner who didn't want to incur the wrath of the Ku Klux Klan?

Consequently, the press swarmed into the Administration Building, too, reporting to the world that "CORE condemns the University of Chicago's shameful policy of racial discrimination" and that its members would continue the sit-in "until the University states publicly that it will not discriminate in renting, leasing, administering, or selling any property it owns or controls."

---

* This was to become a grim joke in our household. When George came home beat to exhaustion by having tried to mediate a dispute between groups or individuals whose emotions were so strongly engaged that neither party could approach the problem rationally, I could usually bring a wan smile to his face by saying, "Why don't you just tell them to be *reasonable?*"

As I think back now, I realize how mild-mannered the protestors were—by comparison with what they were to become. But nobody then knew what lay ahead, and this first attack upon an educational institution was emotionally shattering. Universities are held together by bonds of mutual trust, not by laws and regulations. Yet here was a segment of the University behaving as if another segment of the University were its adversary, in the same sense that management is the adversary in a labor union dispute. The students were even using words like "capitulation" and "negotiation."

Not generally enough appreciated, I think, is the role that rhetoric played in the campus turmoil of the 1960's. Terms like "negotiation"—and, later, "non-negotiable demands"—struck the older generation as an especially gross violation of the spirit of the academy. To the kids, however, not having been through the labor union wars, these terms were not so emotionally "loaded." Because of the language they used, students also often found themselves publicly committed to positions or actions they did not really espouse. At the same time, university administrators and the general public responded to the words and not the intentions, and either yielded more readily or resisted more stubbornly than they should have. Words *do* have power, and their careless use *did* have consequences for individuals and institutions.

Well, what was this particular institution to do?

The officers and deans convened in special sessions, often in the library of our house—George having waded through a mass of hostile students in order to get there from his office— and decided right off not to call in the campus (or any other) police.

In the first place, the idea of using force was anathema. A university is traditionally a place where dissent is tolerated, and the administrators couldn't believe that reasoned discourse would not in the end prevail.

Secondly, given the current mood of sympathy and support for the idealistic young people in CORE, it was unlikely that many members of the academic community would focus on the real issue: that the method of protest was intended to coerce rather than persuade. After all, what were the students actually *doing?* Just sitting there, eating peanut butter sandwiches. A forceful ejection from the building would only win them more supporters.

Finally, they expected to be carried out of the building, to the accompaniment of flashbulbs and the whirring of TV cameras, and for that reason alone it made sense to do the unexpected. In a word: nothing. Therefore, the officers of the University adopted CORE's own tactic—to go limp.

So the students sat, mostly in relays, night and day. Others organized and ran protest rallies elsewhere on campus. The lack of "action" began to make them edgy, and several groups invaded the office of the realty management firm which acted as rental agent for the disputed buildings. There, the students could not claim that they were not trespassing upon private property, nor did the office manager feel about freedom to dissent as university people do, so he promptly called the city police and had the protestors carted off to jail. Predictably, this action caused a flurry of support for "the cause."

The University refused to change its stand on rental policy. Its spokesmen continued, however, to reiterate the reason for such discrimination as was being practiced and at the same time pointed out the institution's exemplary record of non-discrimination in hiring practices, admissions, and rentals to University-connected people. This may have been a net gain for the University's reputation nationwide; at least, it spread the word. George began to get a series of letters from a Mr. J. S. Johnston in Tallahassee (no return address given), with such comforting thoughts as these:

> George, you may have more degrees than a thermometer, but you cannot figure how to cope with this migration of negroes into Chicago. . . . There is no solution, if you want the honest truth. The experts predict that by 1970 you will

have 1,250,000 negroes and you will still have the same 207
sq. mi. you have in 1962 . . .

You thought when Abe Lincoln signed the Emancipation
that these negroes would stay in the South, but something
went wrong and they are pouring in on you. . . . We have
so many down here we could spare Chicago 3000 a month
for over 350 years . . . You Yankees are caught in a web
that your ancestors started spinning over 100 years ago, and
truthfully we couldn't care less. . . .

These were early days in the campus activist movement,
remember. If the CORE group had been politically more sophisticated, they would have pulled out at the end of a week.
To that point, public opinion was with them. At the end of
two weeks, however, the University's point of view had received wide publicity; faculty visitors to the President's Office
were getting tired of stepping over recumbent forms; and the
newspapers had begun to write nasty editorials. ("Throw the
bums out, beards and all! Then fire the timid administrators
who surrender so easily to a mob!")

Even the Hyde Park-Kenwood Community Conference—once
damned by the conservatives in the community as being "too
idealistic"—got a bit huffy. It issued a statement pointing out
that a "truly integrated community is very difficult to achieve
in a highly segregated city," and that the people living in the
university area "had committed themselves to the principle
of a stable integrated community long before any national
group began focusing its attention on Hyde Park-Kennwood."
It also suggested that CORE join with everyone else "in the day-
to-day implementation of the long range goals to which we can
all subscribe."

In short, everyone's patience wore thin, including that of
the protestors. When George finally announced that he wanted
the anteroom cleared, and the Dean of Students warned that
anyone who continued the sit-in might face disciplinary action,
they left.

Although I believe that the University's rental policy was justified and also that the use of coercive measures for resolving the dispute was not justified, I do not want to leave the impression that the CORE chapter lacked good reason for protest.

It is one thing to set a policy and another thing to enforce it, and no high University official had made it his business to see that "managed integration" was uniformly practiced; or even that newly hired people in the various offices dealing with rentals knew what the policy was.

From the time we came to the University, I had been struck by its "two cultures." People on the business side—from those in the Bursar's Office to the men of Buildings and Grounds—tended to have home addresses in the suburbs, whereas those on the academic side tended to live in the community. Even if the suburbanites didn't live where they did in order to escape Negro neighbors, their lack of familiarity with the Hyde Park-Kenwood community renewal effort would have made them insensitive to its goals. And these were the people who handled University housing.

CORE said that even University-connected Negroes were sometimes rebuffed, and I won't argue the point. I am sure that Negroes without a University connection were turned away, and not tactfully, by building managers who were civil to whites. The sit-in had the beneficial effect, therefore, of publicizing the official policy of the University, and of alerting its officers to the necessity of being better watchdogs.*

There was another valuable by-product. In the midst of all the essentially sterile disputation typical of this and other conflicts which pit idealism ("open occupancy is morally right") against pragmatism ("but managed occupancy achieves the goal"), a faculty member suggested that students who wanted to stand

---

* At about this same time, George discovered with horror that one of the University hospitals was segregating newborn babies into separate nurseries. For months, he had recurrent nightmares about the possibility of there being other as yet undiscovered discriminatory practices in one or another of the University's highly autonomous divisions.

up and be counted should undertake some sort of social service project.

Out of this suggestion was born the Student Committee for Community Cooperation, into which for several years thereafter many hundreds of students were to pour their energies. They would tutor culturally deprived youngsters in Woodlawn, take them on excursions, act as "big sisters" or "big brothers," and in general improve the drab texture of the children's lives. Only when the student activist movement turned radical and the tutoring projects became politicized would they lose the broad base of support they had in the early 1960's.

That first sit-in, then, left no deep scars on the University. The Dean of the College was able to say, in a speech the following June, "If I have to choose between students whose social conscience takes exasperating turns and students with no social conscience at all, I'm in no doubt where I stand."

And the student newspaper, in its year-end review, was similarly dispassionate (for a student newspaper). "The issue was not as obvious as some people had originally thought it would be," the editor said. "CORE's method of using sit-ins to call attention to the problem was both effective and valid, but nobody doubts that such demonstrations must be used infrequently."

So everyone went on to other things. Berkeley was still two years in the future.

Nine

I prefer not to chronicle our first Chicago winter. Part of the time I had the flu and the rest of the time I was cold. One day, when the headlines said "TEMPERATURE LEAPS TO ZERO," I went downtown. In addition to all the woolies underneath, I was wearing a fur hat with a head scarf over it, a quilted mask over my nose and mouth, and a muffler—a fine outfit for robbing a supermarket. As I was waiting for the train on the IC platform, a friend approached.

"Hello," I said.

She politely responded. "Hello," she said. And then bent closer. "Who are you?"

I felt a lot more like me in April.

Because Chicago winters are enervating, spring is an especially joyous time. The khaki-colored lawns green up, the first pale leaves come out on the trees, crocuses stain the remaining patches of dirty snow with color, and before you know it the golden hedges of forsythia are in bloom all over town. Out in the country, it is a delight to stalk the early wild flowers—spring beauties, buttercups, violets, anemones, and umbrella-like May apples. One glorious Sunday we spent a couple of hours tramping through the woods near the Glen Lloyds' place in Libertyville, trillium white at our feet and great drifts of hawthorne blossom overhead. The Chicago climate is particularly hospitable to flowering trees, and the massed crabapples, plums, redbud, and lilacs in Grant Park are a May extravaganza without peer.

The rebirth of life outdoors was paralleled by the coming of new life indoors. Mary K had been eight months old when we came to Chicago, and with tiresome frequency from then on had informed us that she was eager for love and motherhood. In due course we found her a mate—a handsome Siamese named Buster, owned by a professor in the Medical School—and in April she presented us with six kittens.

In this, as in everything else she did, Mary K was scatter-brained. She gave birth to kittens as easily as hens lay eggs, apparently without being aware that she had done so. Then she walked off and left them. My job, then and during her many subsequent accouchements, was to find and assemble her kittens. Once I had them all collected in one place and penned Mary K in with them, she became a good mother. We used a sun room at the back of the house as a cattery.

To come home to eight felines instead of the two who were permanently in residence delighted George and made his rare evenings at home more entertaining and relaxing.

There is never a time at the University when one is not being lectured at, but spring brings the visiting speakers in swarms. Gus Hall and Jimmy Hoffa were among them that year. So were Robert Lowell, Karl Shapiro, and Stanley Kunitz. (What a coup to collect all three for a super-poetry-reading at one time from the same platform!) Erich Leinsdorf, whose son Gregor was an undergraduate, enchanted me by his use of an analogy with baseball to describe the proper training of a young conductor. ("The European system of climbing through the minor leagues is far better than the American system, in which the choice is an assistantship with a major orchestra or becoming the conductor of a community orchestra. Both are dead ends professionally.") Billy Graham came to campus to preach conversion, and Santha Rama Rau came to advise that Kipling's Asia was gone beyond recall.

Of a somewhat different order was the visit of Karl Barth, whose son Markus was a professor in the Divinity School. This was, I believe, the first visit to the United States of the great Swiss Protestant theologian (then seventy-six years old). To see him in the flesh "was to ecclesiastics"—in the words of one of them—"what a personal appearance of Sir Winston Churchill would be to the House of Representatives." Both laymen and theologians converged on Chicago, many coming hundreds of miles, and each of his five lectures at Rockefeller Chapel had SRO crowds.

We had a cocktail party for him, and I lurked near the guest of honor in order to catch any words of wisdom. A small man with flyaway white hair, thick-lensed glasses which kept slipping down on his nose, and an impish smile, he talked about the Civil War battlefields he had seen en route to Chicago. What had turned him into a Civil War buff, I asked?

"I became interested," he replied in his heavily accented English, "after reading *Gone With the Wind.*"

One event in May brought me a special sense of satisfaction, as well as a lot of peripheral entertainment. This was connected with Hyde Park's Centennial Celebration, the planning for which had begun many months before.

The initial movers and doers were the businessmen of the community, who think like businessmen everywhere. If they could schedule some spectacular event, the kind that would pull crowds from the rest of the city, a lot of lovely extra dollars would flow into their cash registers. Nor would it hurt to show off a bit, now that the community looked better, thanks to urban renewal.

When I joined the Centennial Steering Committee, I was astonished to discover that there are enough American cities and towns which wish to celebrate centennials to support not one but several firms whose specialty is the planning and execution of such events. One of them had been hired to mastermind Hyde Park's celebration. And almost from the beginning its Field Representative had found himself mouse-trapped between Town and Gown.

Town had no objection to beard-growing contests, the election of a Queen, a plan to get the citizens into old-fashioned costumes during the final week of the celebration, and a Centennial Pageant complete with covered wagons, Indian war parties, slaves making good their escape from Ole Massa, and all the rest of it.

Gown was too knowledgeable to like the pageant as planned, and too sophisticated not to see the perils in some of the specific proposals.

"This sort of thing may be okay for Wichita," exclaimed an associate professor of history. "But for Hyde Park? My God! There was never a covered wagon or an Indian war party within miles of here!"

"You're going to have kangaroo courts that will 'try' people who don't grow beards, and fine them?" asked a horrified faculty wife. "All you have to do is haul in one visiting Russian scholar while he's taking his shirts to the laundry, and we'll have an international incident on our hands."

I also had reservations about the assignment that had been given to me. I was supposed to persuade the women of the community to buy and wear calico dresses and sunbonnets (on the sale of which the Centennial Committee would make a profit). I looked inquiringly at Marion Despres, the wife of our alderman. She shook her head. I had read the community right, then; its ladies would not take kindly to a proposal that they wear fancy dress to the supermarket.

"Well, okay, if you feel so strongly about it," the suffering Field Representative finally said. "But you'll have to figure out some other way to raise two thousand dollars. That's the amount budgeted for the Women's Division to earn."

So I teamed up with Eleanor Petersen, one of the community's most active and competent women and a militant of a type which is too little in evidence today. Eleanor did and does care very much about social reform. She was, for example, one of "the Kenwood Ladies" and had also played a key role in the creation of the Hyde Park Federal Savings and Loan Association. But she isn't *grim*. A little frivolity now and then? Why not? Let's go! We decided to have a show featuring fashions of the past century; called it *Hips, Hoops, Hooray!*; and scheduled it for May.

Between us, we put hundreds of women to work. One committee engaged in a treasure hunt for heirloom garments; another committee matched models to clothing; a third group sold tickets: in fact, the organizational dragnet missed hardly anyone who might have something to contribute. It was a glorious ethnic, racial, religious, and social mix. Many of the women who took part were active in community causes which were dead serious, or controversial, or both, and by their very nature attracted people of similar type. They enjoyed having an activity come along which cut across the usual spheres of interest, provided everyone with some new people to swap recipes with, and had no social significance whatsoever.

For me, it was the community equivalent of what the teas for faculty wives had been: it enormously broadened my acquaintance. I might otherwise never have known the tall and lissome Mrs. Thomas Lyman, who dressed herself and her five children in ivory lace and linen, c.1910, and created an Edwardian vignette of surpassing charm; or Mrs. Irving Harris, who belted out *The Birth of the Blues* in a way that made one's heart quiver; or Miss Avadner McGlory, who suffered having two buckets of water dumped on her just before she came on stage as "Miss Drip-Dry"—and smiled all the while.

The show escalated from a simple parade of fashions into one of those amateur theatricals that Hyde Parkers engage in with such zest. It had songs and dances and comedy turns, and was a great success. We netted $2,200. There were those on the Centennial Steering Committee who said that the energy put into *Hips, Hoops, Hooray!* was responsible for the failure of the pageant—but I don't really believe that the women of the community held the fate of the pageant in their hands.

What ailed the pageant was that you can't transplant Wichita to Hyde Park. It required masses of people surging across an outdoor arena, and surges of that sort aren't effective unless the masses of people have rehearsed them. The University-connected segment of the community was lost to the enterprise from the moment the date was set, for it fell during final exams. And the only others who came to the tryouts were members of the Senior Citizens Club and a bunch of teenagers—the two age groups, according to the Field Representative, that are most unreliable. The older people get sick at the last moment, and the kids hare off to the beach.

Several of the schemes intended to underwrite preliminary pageant expenses had met with moderate success at best, and when the Centennial Steering Committee in addition found itself trying to provide rest room facilities for a thousand people, parking spaces for hundreds of cars, and sufficient extra police for crowd control—not to mention the mammoth publicity effort that would be necessary to get the thousands there in the first place—they called it quits.

Of the less ambitious projects which took place as scheduled, I most enjoyed the Grand Centennial Parade. The local troops of Boy Scouts and Girl Scouts were on hand, moseying along or marching smartly according to how close they were positioned to the three bands. Organizations as disparate as Zonta International and the Women's International League for Peace and Freedom detailed local marchers. Jackson Park Bicycle Shop, Model Camera, and Drexel Chevrolet did their bit for the commercial interests, and the Fifth Ward Regular Democratic Organization saw to it that Chicago's political establishment was represented.

Interspersed among the marchers were those Chicago parade perennials that the municipal agencies always keep ready for St. Patrick's Day parades, civic welcomes for astronauts, Grand Openings at supermarkets, and neighborhood festivals like this one—floats urging co-operation with Mayor Daley's Clean-up

Committee or reminding citizens that THE FOREST PRE-SERVES BELONG TO ALL OF US.

Hyde Park does not have Pasadena's expertise in designing, building, or managing parade floats in motion, and the drivers of those that had been made by loving hands at home did not fully understand the relationship of weight to momentum—a fact that was most obvious in connection with the Centennial Queen's Float.

The Queen was to be the person in behalf of whose candidacy the most coupons for the now defunct pageant had been sold. Did she turn out to be some Junior Miss America for whom the parade would provide a day of adolescent bliss? Indeed not: it was the barmaid at Jimmy's Woodlawn Tap who shot into view as the Centennial Queen's Float barreled around a curve on Fifty-fifth Street.

The float was canted like a yacht in competition for the America's Cup. The Queen's hair was whipping across her face, her roses were bouncing on her lap, and she was clutching the armrests of her throne as if for dear life. She nevertheless managed a big smile, at once brave and beseeching, for the applauding VIP's in the reviewing stand, before she and her craft went sailing over the horizon and into the haven of the Co-op Parking Lot.

Among the money-raising schemes that didn't work was the minting of commemorative coins, the size of half-dollars, which were supposed to be sold and then used locally as currency. For as many coins as are in circulation, you deposit an equivalent amount of real money in a local bank. People may swap their commemorative coins for legal tender; only, the Field Representative had said, most people don't. They keep their coins as souvenirs. After a publicly announced cut-off date for redemption, the Centennial Committee would pocket the money remaining on deposit.

Unfortunately, "most people" in Hyde Park are unlike "most people" elsewhere—and our citizens, including many of the merchants who were allegedly sponsoring the Centennial, regarded the fake money as fake money, and wouldn't use it. So there were never enough coins in circulation to generate a substantial bank deposit.

I did my bit, though. I am still carrying, in a special section of my wallet (and in the company of my Kennedy half-dollar and my two-dollar bill) two Hyde Park Centennial commemorative coins.

Ten

That first spring, George and I went to everything we could: the student art exhibits, the film festival, the chamber concerts, the lectures, and the student theatricals (which ranged from a slighly raunchy musical comedy to a moving *Caine Mutiny Court Martial* staged in the Law School's courtroom).

As the mid-June crescendo approached, we added annual dinners: of the University of Chicago Press, of the Interfraternity Council, of the Women's Athletic Association, and more. We also gave parties at the house: for newly elected Phi Beta Kappas, for the Aides (students who act as marshals at University ceremonies), for visiting VIP's, for retiring faculty members, for prospective donors of new buildings, and for June graduates.

In June alone, we entertained almost six hundred guests for dinner, and Mrs. Galloway began to show signs of strain. So did we. I was reminded of a university president who was asked to comment on the intellectual stature of a man being considered for the presidency of another institution.

"Intellectual stature?" he snorted. "Hell, that's secondary. Find out whether he has good legs and a good stomach."

The University of Chicago is unusual in that it graduates students four times a year, at formal Convocations. This practice keeps the output small enough so that it is still possible for the President to present a diploma personally to each graduate as his name is read by the dean of his College, Division, or School.

Nevertheless, June is the "big" Convocation, with sufficient numbers taking their degrees so that in the 1960's the event was a doubleheader. Half the students were graduated on a Friday afternoon and half on a Saturday morning. This meant, in terms of presidential wear and tear, that George shook about fifteen hundred hands in the course of presenting the diplomas, and as many again at the receptions for graduates' parents.

At the first June Convocation over which George presided, the lead-off student among the College graduates, a girl, gave him a quick kiss on the cheek. Five years later, in similar circumstances, a student was to slip a notice of a peace rally into George's hand as he returned the handshake; and two years after *that*, a number of graduates would refuse to shake his hand. But in 1962 the mood was sweet. The only flaw was the omission of a scheduled song after the opening prayer, George having begun his Convocation Address too soon. This slip, however, had long-range benefits: at each subsequent Convocation, the soloist of the day launched into song only a split second after the Dean of the Chapel said "Amen," thus setting a nice brisk tempo for the rest of the proceedings.

What made the June Convocation weekend a nightmare, and turned us into walking wounded, were the concurrent festivities for alumni. We found ourselves attending breakfasts to welcome new graduates into the Alumni Association, brunches for alumnae, buffets for former and current members of the honor societies, faculty forums for keeping alumni abreast of new research, and luncheons for presenting awards to distinguished alumni. We ourselves gave a reception for alumni at the President's House.

In anticipation of that reception, I wanted to get the grandfather clock in working order. This required the services of someone who was not only able to clean and adjust the time-keeping mechanism but also (and this was much more difficult) someone who understood the operation of music boxes. Here's why:

The grandfather clock had been made for Harold Swift,

youngest son of the founder of the Swift meat-packing empire. His love affair with the University had started, he used to say, when he was eight years old. That's when he was taken to the World's Fair of 1893 and given a ride on the Ferris Wheel—a jumbo contraption, far bigger than any in existence today, that had been set up on the Midway. From the celestial eminence one attained at the top of the ride, young Harold could see far across the marshy flatlands to the west of the Fair site. He never forgot how beautiful Cobb Hall looked, far below, in otherwise barren environs.

Harold graduated from the College in 1907, became the first alumnus to be elected a member of the Board of Trustees, and served as that body's chairman for twenty-seven years (1922–49). A bachelor, he lavished on the University the devotion that another man might have given to a wife and children, and I doubt that the full extent of his services and his philanthropies will ever be known. Everything pertaining to the University was dear to him.

One of the treasures of the campus are the chimes of Mitchell Tower, which include a peal of ten bells cast by the same British foundry that created Big Ben. They were given in memory of the University's first Dean of Women, and when Coach Amos Alonzo Stagg made his contribution he had stipulated that every night at 10:05 the *Alma Mater* should be rung. Harold Swift had derived much pleasure from this end-of-day sequence: first, the chiming of the hour; then, the *Alma Mater*.

Years later, when he had commissioned the making of the grandfather clock, he had therefore specified that it should also contain a metal cylinder built on the principle of a music box or a player piano. The surface of this cylinder was studded with small projections which, as it revolved, caused concealed hammers to strike one of the eight chime tubes installed in the base of the clock case. The tune emitted was, of course, the *Alma Mater*. And the timer was set, of course, so that the *Alma Mater* would sound five minutes after the clock had struck the hour of ten.

The clock wasn't working when we had moved into the house. (It was Harold Swift, in fact, who had told me how it was supposed to work.) One repair man had had a shot at it in 1961, and it had functioned for a few months. When it had conked out again, I missed its sweet voice and its quaint 10:05 postscript—even though, truth to tell, the melodic tune that had issued forth didn't sound very much like the *Alma Mater*.

In 1962, then, I tried again. I found a new repair man, and he fixed the grandfather clock so that all parts worked. We were sitting there, listening to its one-selection musical repertory, when the thought suddenly struck me that perhaps the piece didn't sound like the *Alma Mater* because someone might have rehung the tubular chimes in an order different from the original one.

The clock repair man must have been as innocent as I was. In any case, he agreed to my proposal that we rehang the chimes in varying orders until we got a sequence that would give us a recognizable *Alma Mater*. We had just begun to remove the chimes when George—fortunately—walked in.

"What are you doing that for?" he asked.

I explained our great idea for solving the problem by the trial and error method.

"Good God!" He was horrified. "Don't you understand factorial eight? There are eight chimes, right? Which means"—he took a scrap of paper out of his pocket and did some quick computation—"that there are forty thousand three hundred and twenty different combinations you'd have to try!"

Therefore, I had found a mathematician who played in one of the local chamber music groups, and he had attacked the problem as if it were a cryptogram. He began with the pattern of pegs on the cylinder and in due course decided that they corresponded to the score of the *Alma Mater*. Then he directed some adjustments in the mechanism that activated the hammers (some of which were moving faster and hitting harder than the others, affecting the rhythm of the piece). The chime tubes

did not have to be rehung. At 10:05, one again heard an iden-
tifiable, if tinkly, *Alma Mater*.

I had undertaken all this, of course, in anticipation of Harold
Swift's being at the house on Alumni Day. I wanted him to
know that his clock was again proclaiming a proper "lights-out."
But as the day approached, we all realized that Harold had paid
his last visit to the University. He died on the day before Alumni
Day—aged seventy-seven, having given over half a century of
service to his alma mater.

The reception for alumni went on, anyway, and among the
guests was an uninvited one. Just before it was due to begin,
a pleasant-looking, well-mannered young woman arrived at the
door and announced that she was Ihr Kaiserliche Majestät Zaldemena M. W. von Hohenzollern, granddaughter of the late
Kaiser Wilhelm, and herself now head of the House of Hohenzollern. She extended her hand palm down; and I very nearly
kissed it, so assured and regal was her manner. Then she swept
over to the grand piano and gave an impromptu concert for the
alumni.

(I was to see Zaldemena Regina off and on for the next few
years. She popped in at various University events, and she wrote
me occasional letters. Sometimes she used English, sometimes
German. Once she read my fortune in Tarot cards and sent me
a précis of the forecast. This, she said in an appended note, was
a token of appreciation for my gracious hospitality on the occasion of her visits to my beautiful home. She happened to reside
incognito at the home of—and here she gave her sister's name,
which was also her own real name—where there was an Apollo
grand. "You are welcome to play it," she said, "when you return my visits according to protocol." I never did.)

Alumni Day at the University of Chicago is in most respects
like the same occasion at any other college or university. Re-
turning alums proudly present to each other the children who
have been dragged along, and then bore them to death by re-
calling their own youthful escapades. They fondly greet their
favorite professors—who have somehow grown older, whereas

the alumni themselves see each other as they used to be—and take nostalgic strolls around the campus. Yet in one respect our Alumni Days had a unique quality.

That first year sensitized George and me to the schism that had occurred in the 1930's, so different are the alumni from before and after that period. They asked the same two questions—"President Beadle what is your position regarding the re-establishment of intercollegiate football?" and "President Beadle, what is your opinion of the 'Hutchins' College?"—yet each group wanted different answers.

Neither the banker from the class of '12 (who had never forgiven Hutchins for taking the University out of big-time competitive football) or the attorney from the class of '37 (who had never forgiven the University for tinkering with the survey courses and the comprehensive exams that were the essence of the "Hutchins" College) would settle for less than partisanship, which George couldn't permit himself.

He tried to convince '12 that the existence on campus of over forty touch football teams "just for the fun of the game" was as good as producing the top team in the Big Ten, and much less expensive. He also tried to convince '37 that the "Hutchins" College had disadvantages even in its heyday; many graduate schools, for instance, and including some graduate divisions at the University of Chicago, had refused to accept its products. In any case, it would not now meet the needs of the majority of college students. The outcome in both cases was the same: no sale.

I'm going to talk about football at Chicago in a later chapter. This is a good place, however, to clarify a few misconceptions about the "Hutchins" College. First, it wasn't Hutchins' idea. Part of its program stemmed from William Rainey Harper, who had proposed in the 1890's that there be established on the south side of the Midway a junior college combining the last two years of high school with the first two years of college, and that its students be given the broadest kind of liberal education via general survey courses.

The University had been established primarily as a graduate institution, and after Harper's death the education of undergraduates received progressively less attention. Right after World War I, in fact, faculty and administrators gave serious thought to dropping the College altogether. What saved it was institutional inertia before 1923 and the appointment to the presidency in that year of Ernest DeWitt Burton, who was most interested in undergraduate education.

He and the Dean of the College drew up the first rough outline of what would become the "Hutchins" College, and raised ten million dollars to build quarters for it on the site where William Rainey Harper had envisioned it. Only one of the buildings intended for such use was ever erected—it now serves as a dormitory—but various people continued to refine the basic Harper/Burton idea. When Hutchins came to the presidency in 1929, he helped to complete the plan—which bears his name because it flowered during his regime.

Aside from willingness to accept bright high school juniors (not many of whom in fact ever enrolled), the salient features of the College were the requirement that all students take the same courses; a curriculum which skimmed over the body of factual information within any field of knowledge and concentrated instead on the great ideas which held it together; and a system of comprehensive examinations which students could take whenever they felt qualified to do so. Since graduation therefore did not depend on formal course work or class attendance, highly competent students could graduate in less than four years—an option that traditional educationists found highly unsettling.

"I think I'll run down to the U of C over the weekend and take a degree" became a standard wisecrack in such circles in the 1930's.

Controversial though the Chicago Plan was off campus, the intellectual atmosphere it generated on campus was exhilarating —for a great many people. College or university administrators who deal with alumni should never forget that any golden period in the institution's past was golden only for *some* of its students, and these are the ones who defend it. The "Hutchins" College was the right place, for example, for James D. Watson. This young genius entered at age fifteen, had earned two degrees upon his graduation at age nineteen, and at age twenty-five was the co-discoverer of the structure of DNA (for which he subsequently won the Nobel prize). In contrast, the same academic setting drove to distraction another, equally gifted young man named Saul Bellow, and he transferred to Northwestern.

If just one other major university had adopted the Chicago Plan, it might have spread to many institutions. George, who was on the faculty at Stanford in the 1930's and served on a general education policy committee, remembers that Ray Lyman Wilbur urged Stanford to adopt the Chicago Plan; but the proposal never got to the point of serious debate.

In the 1940's, and thereafter, the rapid growth of two-year municipal junior colleges (organized to follow a four-year course in high school) and the steadily increasing number of students who wanted to specialize in particular subject matter fields worked against any extension of Chicago-style undergraduate education. By the early 1960's, even the "Hutchins" College itself was but a pale shadow of what it had been in its prime.

It is ironic that college administrators, including those at Chicago, are still trying to solve the problem that so many Chicago alumni consider to have been brilliantly solved in the 1930's: how best to educate that portion of intelligent young people who are not yet committed to (and perhaps should not be channeled into) the professions.

George thinks that the timing of the Great Experiment was the reason for its limited impact. If the Chicago Plan for undergraduate education had been introduced during that exuberant period at the end of the nineteenth century when people seemed willing to give almost anything a try, it might have changed the course of higher education in America.

But in neither the 1930's or the 1960's was this the mood of the country; a by-then very large educational establishment was committed to a different kind of system; and no American university could successfully become a maverick. And so, although George could understand why that unhappy member of the class of '37 with whom he tangled in June of 1962 was grieving for the good old days, he could do nothing about restoring them.

The grand finale of Alumni Day is the Interfraternity Sing. At dusk, fraternity men past and present march (or in some cases stagger) into the cloistered Gothic setting of Hutchinson Court and belt out the old varsity songs. Their families and friends sit on the grassy banks and hum along with the massed voices on stage. At the end, the bells in Mitchell Tower play the *Alma Mater*, and for a moment in time everyone is young and beautiful and carefree again.

Given a balmy June night—and some Midwestern June nights are sheer heaven—the alumni depart the campus on a giant wave of nostalgia, full of peace and goodwill toward all. At my first and all subsequent Interfraternity Sings, I shared the emotion. I must in candor admit, however, that it stemmed in part from knowing that we could now at long last go home and wipe the smiles from our faces.

Eleven

During the spring of 1962, various changes in administrative organization and personnel had occurred, giving George a group of people with whom he got on well. The most important one from the standpoint of the University as a whole, and the happiest one for George personally, was Edward Levi's appointment as Provost.

This required that Edward resign the deanship of the Law School, which he had built into one of the nation's finest, obtaining for it into the bargain a building that was the architectural jewel of the campus. Like George, he is a scholar who enjoys teaching, and he realized that it would be only a matter of time before conferences and desk work would swallow him up. But when George reversed the technique by which Edward had hooked him, Edward was hooked too.

A provost is (usually) the administrative officer who ranks directly after the president, is his deputy, and is responsible for the academic side of the university. The specifics of the job are not clearly defined, however, and vary from university to university.

When Shannon McCune was provost at the University of Massachusetts, he wrote an article about the office in which he included some of the wisecracks that seek to explain it. One of them defines a provost as "the man who tries to develop at the university those programs which the president in his off-campus speeches says it already has." Another describes the president as "the shepherd of the university" and the provost as "the shepherd's crook." Then, in a more serious vein, McCune continues:

Not only the provost but the president by the delegation of duties helps to shape the position. The provost must, of necessity, disagree from time to time with the president; but such disagreements should take place only within the confines of the president's office. The provost must help to carry out the policies set by the president, the trustees, and the faculty. He should have a part in the formulation of these policies, but once they are established he has to live with them and make them operative.

As a consequence of all this, an intimate relationship must exist between the president and his provost. This must be based upon mutual regard and trust and preferably close personal friendship. The president by virtue of his position is essentially a lonely man; he needs someone with whom he can let down his hair—if he has any—and talk over problems.

This relationship did exist between George and Edward, and (as McCune suggests) it was often to be a safety valve for George. But in addition Edward possessed a knowledgeability about the University that George lacked. The Levi family was already deeply rooted in Hyde Park and the University of Chicago. Edward's grandfather had been a member of the University's first faculty, and he himself is a product of the educational chain that begins with kindergarten in the School of Education's laboratory school and winds up with the Ph.D. or its equivalent in one of the graduate professional Schools. Edward had been a professor in the Law School before becoming its dean, and was a personal friend of both Robert Hutchins and Lawrence Kimpton. Given this background of affection for, commitment to, and understanding of the history of the institution, he was bound to take seriously and eventually agree to George's appeal that he help to strengthen the whole University by becoming its Provost.

At many universities, the title for the same job is Dean of the Faculties.* Whatever else he may do, the holder of that position largely determines the quality and morale of the faculty. He works through a hierarchy of department chairmen (who are usually elected by their colleagues) and deans (whom he appoints—after consultation with department chairmen, if he's wise). Their requests for staff, equipment, and facilities channel through him to the budget committee of the university. He also nurses the institution through the periodic spasms of curricular reform that occur at all colleges and universities.

George and Edward both believed that a university's greatness lies in the stature and ability of its professors—first, because graduate students (and the University of Chicago, remember, is primarily a graduate institution) do not come to study *at* a place but *with* a person); and, second, because professors come to or remain at an institution which provides them with intellectually stimulating colleagues.

With Edward's appointment as Provost, a massive head-hunt got under way. The University's trustees had put together (from their own pockets) a three-million-dollar fund to be used for this purpose alone; and already in the late spring of 1962 the University had captured the country's foremost authority on Renaissance music, a noted economist, and a physical anthropologist of international renown. (This was just the beginning. In the course of the next few years, Chicago was successfully to raid every major American university and thus replace the top scholars and scientists who had been lured away from it during the bad times of the 1950's.)

* Which has the great advantage of using familiar language. One of the vexing problems associated with having, or being, a provost is that nobody knows how to pronounce the word. "Prah-vust"? Or "Pro-vohst"? Or maybe "Pro-vo"? Shannon McCune used to entertain himself at banquets where he was representing his university by betting with his head-table companions as to which pronunciation the person who introduced him would use.

You get a good faculty in a variety of ways. If a department chairman is alert and aggressive, he and his colleagues go head-hunting on their own and recommend to their dean that an offer be made to so-and-so. If a department or its chairman should be apathetic, the provost—working backwards through the dean —asks for, urges, and eventually demands nominations.

Redmond wrote us about witnessing a stage in this process. On a Cambridge visit, Alan Simpson, Dean of our College, invited Red to join him at dinner on the same evening that he was entertaining a young assistant professor of philosophy—I'll call him Cole—in whom the University of Chicago was interested. As Red told it:

> Mr. Simpson kept asking us—but especially Mr. Cole—questions about the administration and organization of Harvard. Somehow, the less attractive aspects were emphasized. When Mr. Cole mentioned the Confy Guide [*The Confidential Guide*, a student publication which rates the classroom performance of professors giving required or most widely elected courses] and said that most of the faculty didn't like it, Mr. Simpson led him into a discussion of the relatively greater weight given by most universities to research than to teaching, and the damping effect of this upon people who like to teach. But not at the University of Chicago, it appears; Mr. Simpson very neatly inserted a mention of the four $1000 prizes which you annually award for exceptionally good teaching. . . .

The next stage, if the candidate appears interested, is to pay his way (and perhaps that of his wife, if he's a full professor) to visit the campus. There, you expose him to a harder sell. Insofar as the family is concerned, what matters is not the University but the city, and Chicago's reputation can be a formidable barrier. It was ever so: on the eve of departure for his new home in the Midwest, the son of one of William Rainey Harper's first recruits ended his bedtime prayers by saying, "Goodbye, God. We're going to Chicago."

Whenever a wife accompanied a prospect, therefore, it was Kate Levi's job, or that of the appropriate dean's wife, or mine —or sometimes all three of us in concert—to convince the prospect's wife that making this change was the best thing that could possibly happen to her family.

We would take her on a sightseeing round of the campus and the community, hoping that the city litter baskets on the main streets would not have obvious garbage in them, and then show her some "typical" houses or apartments. These, it goes without saying, were typical only of the best the community has to offer—for example, places like the Julian Goldsmiths' modern town house.

Julian is not only head of the Geophysics Department but in addition is a great authority on Pre-Columbian art and has a notable collection. I doubt that any visitor has yet noticed that the *structure* of the Goldsmith house is typical of the newer Hyde Park town houses, so handsome are its furnishings and so meticulously is it kept. Ethel Goldsmith even said that she was grateful for being a way station on such tours; their frequency forced her to maintain standards of housekeeping appropriate for the visit of a mother-in-law.

For luncheon on these occasions, one gathers a selected group of faculty wives—e.g., those who are happy at Chicago. They should also be knowledgeable about schools both public and private; the availability of cleaning women and veterinarians; the latest crime statistics for the neighborhood; the cost of housing in the most accessible suburbs (in case the crime statistics have made the prospect jumpy); and the mean annual snowfall. About the mean annual *soot*fall there should be, of course, a conspiracy of silence.

In the evening, the prospect is fêted at a dinner given by a department chairman or a dean, at which his possible future colleagues and their wives are the other guests. There is a good deal of light talk about "when you come . . ." Either late that night or early the next morning, the visitors are put on a plane for their home city. Then the waiting begins.

The chances of our having captured the prospect were slim, I came to learn, if in the first possible post after the visit some one of the hosts received a carefully noncommittal note of thanks from the wife, one that was full of phrases like "delightful to have been with you," "most impressive to hear about the community," "always have had a warm regard for the University of Chicago and this visit further strengthened it."

That's how you recruit top faculty. For the younger ones, those with brand new Ph.D.'s, you rely on letters of recommendation from their major professors, or you scout the annual meetings of the professional societies. (Young aspirants to academic appointments refer to the latter as "slave markets.") What would seem to an outsider to be the most direct route—advertising and having prospects apply—is seldom resorted to, at least at Chicago. It and similar institutions prefer to "call" their new faculty.

But however you find them, once a tentative job offer is accepted, the dean then formally requests that the individual be appointed; the provost recommends that course to the president; and the president recommends it to the trustees. At the University of Chicago, the trustees have never refused to approve a faculty-initiated appointment. Other universities have not been so lucky.

It is also the provost's job (and sometimes the deans' and the president's, too) to prevent the recruitment of a university's most valuable faculty members by other institutions. What this requires is familiarity with the overall situation, professional and personal, of such individuals, and early application of balm to the purse or spirit of those who get restive. An increase in salary, more lab space, or even a parking space more convenient to his office will sometimes do the trick.

But sometimes the provost's hands are tied. If a man is an empire builder, and you don't want his kind of empire in your institution, it is better to let him go. Nor can the administrative officers do much to terminate the affair that a professor's wife may be having with one of his colleagues, or the asthma that his child suffers from in this setting but may not be troubled with somewhere else.

Also, there are always a few professors at every university who are brilliant but so obnoxious that administrators don't fight very hard to keep them if some other institution is foolish enough to make them an offer. When Barnaby Keeney was the president of Brown University, he complained to George about the problems they were having with a couple of distinguished but very "difficult" professors, and George made him a proposition.

"Tell you what," he said. "We'll swap five of ours for five of yours. Any five each of us chooses to send."

Barney didn't have to think it over. "Hell, no," he said. "You've got more to choose from."

Finally, it is the provost's job to challenge the reappointment to the faculty of people who are neither very productive as scholars nor very good as teachers, forcing departments to think carefully about the people who will be their long-time associates. Provosts are very useful to departments whose members, collectively, are chicken-hearted. They will sometimes recommend to their dean that a certain person be reappointed, or given tenure, even if they are lukewarm about him—because they don't want to hurt his feelings. They trust the provost to challenge the appointment and thus remove the responsibility from their shoulders. It is a dirty trick, but not uncommon.

A. Lawrence Lowell of Harvard once said that a university president is supposed to combine the qualities of a trained seal and a matinee idol with those of a foreign diplomat and an educational statesman. Henry Wriston of Brown said that a president should "speak continuously in words that charm and never offend, take bold positions with which no one will disagree, consult everyone and follow all proffered advice, and do everything through committees, but with great speed and without error." In short, he should be superhuman.

Richard W. Stephens, in a study of academic administrators, quotes a Yale trustee's account of just *how* superhuman the ideal president should be. In commenting on the election of Kingman Brewster's predecessor, the trustee said that the man they sought

> . . . had to be a leader, a magnificent speaker and great writer, a good public relations man and fund raiser, a man of iron health and stamina, married to a paragon—a combination of Queen Victoria, Florence Nightingale, and best dressed woman of the year—a man of the world but with great spiritual qualities, an experienced administrator who can delegate authority, a great scholar, and a Yale man. I don't doubt that you have concluded that there is only One who has most of these qualifications. But, we had to ask ourselves, is God a Yale man?

So they appointed Whitney Griswold, who did very well by them.

New university presidents know that they cannot be all things to all men, but only the most insensitive among them are free of the emotional pressures engendered by the ideal to which, in spite of themselves, they aspire. To reduce these unrealistic self-expectations is one of the virtues of the Presidents' Institute, an annual workshop now sponsored by the American Council on Education for new college and university presidents and their wives. In 1962, it was run by the Harvard Business School, and George and I attended it (despite certain mutterings on campus to the effect that anyone who was good enough to be chosen as President of the University of Chicago didn't have to go to Harvard to learn how to do his job). I won't speak for George, but *I* profited from it.

Merely running one's eye down the roster of institutions represented was educational. In the majority, as they are in the nation, were small private colleges such as Judson in Alabama (Baptist—400 students); Lincoln in Pennsylvania (non-sectarian —400 students); St. Francis in Maine (Roman Catholic—250 students); Maryville in Tennessee (Presbyterian—750); Cornell in Iowa (Methodist—800); Wells in New York (non-sectarian —475); and Miles in Alabama (Christian M. E.—800). Then there were a group of public institutions, ranging from Delaware State at Dover (500) and Virginia Polytechnic (5,300) to San Diego State (12,500) and Louisiana State (15,300). Among the private universities, the range was from Clark (1,150) and Chicago (8,000) to Houston (12,000).*

Given this much variety, how can there possibly be anything like a common standard among American institutions of higher education? Such diversity is both a strength and a weakness, for on the one hand it allows almost anybody to "go to college" but on the other hand it robs the bachelor's degree of any meaning until you know the standards of the institution that granted it.

The presidents and their wives at the 1962 session of the Presidents' Institute were just as diverse as their institutions. It did everybody good to realize that there just *isn't* a "presidential type," and to know that other people in the job had the same problems you did, and had flubbed some too.

Swapped shop-talk was constant, but there were "class sessions" as well, in which members of the group read case histories of situations which at one time or another had required action by a college or university president, and discussed whether his action had been correct. There was also a "faculty" of more experienced academic administrators, who gave formal lectures on various aspects of institutional governance.

One of the best of these was delivered by O. Meredith Wilson, then the president of the University of Minnesota. He said, in part, "It is a myth that if you don't get something done in the honeymoon year, you never will. This is to say that you push things through before you know anything about it. The fact is that a good president should be stronger in his fifth year than in his first. . . ."

He also urged the new presidents to remember that "most of

* All enrollment figures are as of 1962.

the things that need doing can best be done by the faculty, and that your job is to release their energies rather than to confer your own"—a theme that was repeated in an article by Eric Ashby which all of us were given to read. Ashby also suggested that "the secret of good administration lies not in the administrator's vast and exact knowledge but in his skill at navigating areas of ignorance."

In other words, a university president must develop the art of using other men's minds. He does not necessarily provide leadership, but should try to obtain and encourage leadership. He is a co-ordinator, consultant, and catalyst. He must feel his way into these roles; there are no "how to" books on their achievement. "In fact"—Ashby speaking, again—"books on how to administer are as unconvincing as books on how to make love."

This kind of talk was comforting because it helped the new presidents realize that they didn't have to know all the answers to the specific problems that were facing them on their home campuses, yet they also acquired a few general guidelines to apply locally as needed.

The same was true of the sessions for wives.

None of us was concerned, or expected to be, about the academic or business side of university administration; but all sought counsel on handling the social role into which our husbands' office had thrust us, and all were puzzled about how best to balance the public and private sectors of our lives.

One of the small-college wives said—in fact, she wailed— "I'm just automatically a member of every group in town and am expected to be active, and I have two little children. It's just killing me, and I can't get out."

One of the old hands replied, "That's why children are so useful. No one will sympathize, or even believe you, if you withdraw from something because you're being run ragged. But they *will* accept a withdrawal if you do it 'because the children need me at home more.' "

Another long-experienced president's wife added, "The best thing is not to join everything in the first place. A yardstick

I've found helpful is to accept only those civic jobs with a direct tie-in to my major interest."

A neophyte said, "We just don't have any time for *ourselves*. I've about decided to strike out every seventh day on the calendar and treat it like any other commitment."

"Sounds good, but it won't work," was the comeback. "Because *you* know that it isn't a genuine engagement. But I agree that you must find some island of isolation for the family. Ours is a shack in the country, and we go there as regularly as we take aspirin at home. Otherwise, we'd go crazy."

One of the case histories we were given to read had to do with a president's wife who scheduled dinner parties for a hundred students a week, her objective being "to present the President as a human being."

Someone in the group said, "She's nuts"; and a second woman said, "My husband is with people all day. The worst thing I could do to him is to force him to comb more people out of his hair when he gets home."

A third woman, after a bit of computation, said with horror, "Ye gods. At the rate of a hundred students a week, and if we stay at the university for fifteen years, that's seventy-eight thousand students."

A voice from the back row: "What makes you think you're going to stay fifteen years?"

Supplement from an old-timer: "If you do, you'll be three hundred years old."

The original speaker groaned. "I think I'm not cut out to be a university president's wife," she said.

Another case history described a president's wife who had obvious favorites among the faculty and invited them preferentially to her parties. Out of this discussion came a rule that I had unconsciously applied at Chicago, but hearing it articulated drove it into memory, and it thenceforth became the keystone of my social behavior as a hostess.

"To have a visible system at work is very desirable," the discussion leader said. "Invite those faculty members who have served on a college-wide committee, or department chairmen and their wives, or the members of a student honor society. When you need pourers at a tea, use the deans' wives, or the officers of the faculty wives club, or the first ten senior girls who sign up, or something of the sort. Then no one is disgruntled about favoritism shown."

"There's one danger to be avoided, though," an experienced wife warned. "Most faculty wives are flattered to be asked to help, but some will feel that they're being used as free domestic workers. I remember how upset I was once when I overheard a faculty wife saying to another, 'Well, have you done your dishwashing at the President's House today?'"

Thank goodness for Mrs. Galloway, I thought. She wouldn't let a stranger step across the threshold of her kitchen, even if she had to stay up until midnight getting the dishes done.

A highlight of the Institute was a speech by that great lady Mrs. Karl Compton, whose husband had been president of the Massachusetts Institute of Technology from 1930 to 1948. In years to come, her words of advice would flash into my head at the oddest (but always at the appropriate) times:

"You have yourself to give to the job; in fact, that *is* the job—the giving of yourself."

"One of the greatest arts you need to cultivate is to know when not to hear gossip—or to have a good forgettery."

"You can't permit yourself a clique of friends. Anyway, as one gets older, one doesn't need intimate friends in the girlhood sense. Your contacts may be brief, but they needn't be superficial. There can be depth in brevity if there is a spark of an idea between people."

"The greatest disservice you can do to yourself or your husband is to get so harassed that you show it. Part of your university function is to help establish the atmosphere that being there is a good life."

The upshot of all this was an easing of tension. At the final session of the Institute, one woman said, "I think I'll manage to muddle through this thing." I meant to keep in touch, to see how many of them *did* manage to muddle through, and for how long—but what university president's wife has time to write letters for pleasure?

Twelve

Because nobody had told us about the great summer exodus, its occurrence was the equivalent of a legacy from an unknown aunt. By the first of July each year, a sizable number of Chicagoans vacate their town houses or apartments and move for the summer to their country places in nearby Michigan, Indiana, or Wisconsin, with the result that the pace of life in the city slows down markedly.

Inasmuch as we had long avoided ownership of a second house or a trailer or a boat or any other kind of property that has to be looked after off-season, it never occurred to us to buy a little place at Fish Creek or Lakeside or Bariboo. But nobody in Chicago knew this, and the general expectation was that we would emulate our predecessors and many of the faculty and vanish from the city until mid-September.

Once we realized that this was the assumption, we took advantage of it and refrained from announcing that we intended to stay in town. We were therefore almost as carefree for three months as if we *had* taken ourselves off to some rural hideaway, and were much more comfortable.

Instead of being continuously on the go, I had a chance to sit back and reflect on the events of the previous year. I had learned something from my mistakes (those that I knew about)—specifically, that it is far better to ask for detailed guidance in meeting situations that one is experiencing for the first time than to extrapolate from some similar but not duplicate situation.

As I mentioned earlier, it was indeed pleasant to have had a totally free hand in shaping the style and tone that would be characteristic of the President's House and the activities stemming from it. However, there was a penalty. This freedom was due to the reluctance of anyone on campus to criticize the President of the University or his wife, whom faculty members (at any institution) want to be proud of because they symbolize the institution itself; and one form of criticism is to offer unsought advice. Because I didn't realize this at first, I had walked into some traps of my own making.

When it was announced that one of the University museums would display a collection of art objects of special interest to Jews, I had invited the wives of local rabbis and their heads of congregation to come to lunch and then view the exhibit. I had had enough sense to call a Jewish friend and ask what menu would be appropriate—since the group included members of Reform, Conservative, and Orthodox congregations—but I didn't have enough sense to realize that when she recommended fish she meant precisely that: the kind of fish that swims, not just anything aquatic.

After we were seated at the table, it had taken only a few moments to realize that half of my guests were not eating, and that all of them were embarrassed.

"What's wrong with it?" I had asked, having dipped into my ramekin and found the contents delicious.

"It *is* shellfish, isn't it?" one had replied.

"Yes, mixed crabmeat and shrimp."

That's how I learned that the Conservative and Orthodox ladies couldn't eat shellfish. Because we had no other protein in the house that wasn't frozen solid, their luncheon therefore had consisted of a not-very-filling green salad and a light fruit dessert.

The art exhibit was a further blow. The objects on display weren't as choice as they might have been; not that my guests said so, since by then they were in league to comfort me, but *I* knew.

I also found out shortly that, after they'd gone home, they couldn't resist telling just one friend about the luncheon *gaffe*—in strictest confidence, of course—with the result that the tale had spread through Chicago's entire Jewish community by nightfall. Ah, well: if to err is human, the shellfish disaster had made me more human.

The same friend who had advised me on the menu said, later, "Your basic mistake was to have invited them as a group. Each had to observe her particular dietary restrictions to the letter because she knew that the others would notice if she didn't, and none of them dared risk having that kind of report circulated. In a more mixed group, I expect most of them would have tucked right in."

A second mistake involved a speech I had made to the group of students who had been named that year to the Maroon Key Society, an organization whose members are appointed by the Dean of Students to serve as hosts for campus visitors.

Someone had told me that our undergraduates were not wildly enthusiastic about being appointed to anything, preferring to be elected by their peers—and I had unwisely attempted to convince them that much of the world's work would not be done half so well as it is if one had to depend on the electoral process to provide qualified workers. I had said that their being appointed to this honorary society was without doubt the first of many such appointments, predicting that within ten years they would be serving on the governing boards of community organizations whose directors *choose* their associates because of their ability to advance the objectives of the group.

All of this happens to be true, but the students didn't want to hear it. The romantic ideal of participatory democracy was already affecting their attitudes, and they were uneasy about the aura of elitism that clings to a selection process in which "everyone" does not have a say. My easy assumption that their choice as Maroon Key members confirmed their status as members of a meritocracy therefore made them feel worse rather than better about having accepted the appointment.

As time went on, I would learn—as those more experienced in dealing with our undergraduates could have told me from the beginning, had I asked—not to force the conclusions of my experience upon people who have not yet had the same experience. It is an exercise in futility, for example, to tell a highly intelligent college girl who sees her future as a choice between the "freedom" of a career and the "servitude" of marriage that these states are not necessarily exclusive, and that the descriptive nouns are sometimes reversible. Until such a girl holds her baby in her arms, she can't really comprehend that loving a husband and children can make marriage quite different from "servitude," so you might as well save your breath.

George had also run into difficulties of communication with students. At the dorm dinners we'd been to, he was typically asked if he didn't think it was wrong of Professor X to have put ten *hard-cover* books on the required reading list; why were the beginning biology courses so bad; and how would the rumored changes in the last two years of the College curriculum affect the General Education courses given in the first two years?

George refused to answer the loaded questions and didn't know the answers to most of the legitimate ones because they required detailed information about the organization of course offerings in specific departments. Being honest, he said so—with the result that the student newspaper began to lament his "intolerable ignorance" about the curriculum.

"Don't they realize," he said to me one night, "that I couldn't possibly know how every professor in this place has structured his course?"

"Nope," I replied. "The President is supposed to know everything. Think of all those affairs we don't get invited to because people assume we know that we are expected to attend. That Christmas tree lighting in Ida Noyes, for example—the one I was supposed to officiate at. They were miffed because I was late. But nobody ever told me that I was supposed to be there. I read about it in the Campus Calendar and just dropped in out of curiosity."

George tried to tell the students that his job was to find the people and create the conditions which would enable the various departments to improve course offerings, but this sounded too vague and generalized to young people who really *worried* about the dovetailing of Humanities I and Humanities II. It was the here-and-now of their courses that interested them, not the institutional processes which created, sustained, or modified the curriculum.

This was probably just as well, for there wasn't much that George could have told them about those of his activities that were relevant to the curriculum. Suppose, for example, that you had an undergraduate College whose faculty has long been separate from that of the graduate Divisions—the one having been chosen for teaching ability, the other for research ability—and you now realized that the teachers were getting stale because they had too little contact with the researchers, and that the researchers needed the stimulation that probing young minds can offer. But suppose at the same time that both groups were jealous of their autonomy and needed a lot of convincing that closer association might be mutually beneficial. In such an atmosphere, it would be foolish in the extreme to jeopardize the chances of bringing the two groups together by commenting publicly on the quality of the beginning biology (or any other) courses. Far better to be considered ignorant by the students than stupid by administrators who were trying to make a marriage between reluctant partners.

Red was home that summer, looking fit, and with a satisfying school year behind him. He had found a job in the library of one of the Chicago newspapers, on the evening shift, which meant that he slept late in the mornings and we met only at lunch. But on his days off, now that he was on vacation from his university and we had a respite from responsibility at ours, we could enjoy together a host of ordinary family pleasures.

There was open-air theater in the University's Hutchinson Court. Strolls on Wooded Island in Jackson Park. A series of lectures sponsored by the Art Department. (It gives one a great sense of freedom to sit on the grass and look at slides projected against the backdrop of a night sky.) Best of all were our al fresco dinner parties.

It was a joy to be able to eliminate temporarily the receptions, cocktail parties, and massive teas of the kind that had run up our first year's guest total to something in excess of twenty-five hundred, and instead invite eight or a dozen people to come for dinner in the garden, usually a barbecue with George as the cook. Nearly every Wednesday we had such a gathering, because the evening carillon concerts occurred on Wednesdays. It was pure bliss to sit outdoors in the dusk and give ourselves up to the bell-song that poured out from on high above us.

The carillon is in the tower of Rockefeller Chapel, which is adjacent to the President's House. John D. Rockefeller, Jr., gave the instrument to the University in 1932, and it is second in size only to the carillon in New York's Riverside Church. Its bells had been a joy and a comfort from the moment we had arrived on campus.

There are seventy-two of them, ranging from a small ten-pounder to the Great Bourdon, which weighs almost forty thousand pounds and is ten feet across. The heavier the bell, the deeper the tone, and it was the Great Bourdon that announced each hour with basso profundo sobriety. The quarter hours were sounded, too—originally with Wagner's *Parsifal Tune* (because Rockefeller had requested it) but now with the new *Chicago Tune.*

The reason for the change was that the long-time striking of clappers on the same spot had worn the bell walls smooth, threatening the purity of their tone. The usual practice is to give regularly used bells a quarter turn every quarter century or so; but to mount the machinery necessary to turn the monstrous weight of these bells would have been so costly that in 1961 the University had opted instead for a tune that would use different bells.

The composer Easley Blackwood, who is a professor of music at the University, therefore was asked to create a new four-bell melody (which the traditionalists on campus immediately attacked because it was "too mournful"; and now praise for its "subtlety"). In due course this new tune was programmed on a big drum called the chime barrel. It times the ringing and automatically plays one segment of the tune at each fifteen-minute interval, the full sixteen notes being chimed on the hour.

There was nothing at all automatic about the Wednesday night carillon concerts, however. I had not heard a manually operated carillon before we came to Chicago, and marveled at the difference between bell-sound made by man and by an electronic device. Aficionados can distinguish the individual touch at the keyboard quite as easily as if the musician were at a piano.

The University carilloneur was a young man named Daniel Robins. Since he had to climb 180 feet to the clavier room whenever he did a concert, his youth was an asset—although I must say that I sometimes resented his *running* up those stairs at the head of the puffing column of dinner guests whom we sometimes invited to watch him at work. They always appreciated the music more after seeing its source.

Dan had a passionate regard for the instrument; a missionary's zeal for educating those who came to watch him play; and a liking for pageantry. This last was reflected in his concert garb. He wore an Oxford jacket, striped trousers, and patent leather slippers, which looked very posh but certainly didn't help to dissipate the heat engendered by the physical labor of giving a performance in a hot room on a hot summer night.

A carillon keyboard is a cross between a power loom and a pipe organ. The carilloneur must do three things at once: he hits the spindles with the sides (not the flat) of his hands, using a crisp, chopping motion; he pedals with both feet; and he slides as necessary from one end of the bench to the other end. Playing a carillon therefore demands as great an expenditure of energy as a fast game of tennis, and at the end of a concert the carilloneur is ready for a hot shower and a drink of something cold.

A moment that has long remained in my memory is of Dan Robins turning from the keyboard to announce that his next number would be a Scarlatti sonata, and to watch him realize that he could not see his audience because of the steamy vapor that had fogged his horn-rims.

It must, I think, be frustrating to be a carilloneur. None ever hears the celestial concert that he produces. He is boxed in among his bells—some ranked above the clavier room, some below—and what one hears in the room itself is the strident noise of clanking metal or the dull reverberation of the big bells below. Nor can he rehearse on his concert instrument, unless he wants to risk broadcasting his mistakes for miles around. Carilloneurs therefore practice on a stand-in for the carillon that sounds something like a xylophone. Dan used to practice late at night, in a basement room at the Chapel, and the tinkling melodies that drifted across the lawns often served as our lullaby.

I never understood how he extrapolated from this instrument to the carillon; how a good carilloneur learns to anticipate the fractional lag between his activating the clapper of a bell and the moment of actual impact; or how he allows for the difference between a fixed bell (in which only the clapper moves) and a swinging bell. But whatever skills were required, Dan Robins had them. The music that poured forth from the Chapel tower made me so grateful for the location of our house that at times I almost felt fond of it.

The University of Chicago is one of the nation's great breeders of college and university presidents. In 1962, the heads of a hundred and eighteen American institutions of higher learning and thirteen in other countries had been educated at Chicago or had been on the faculty. That summer, we lost one more: Allen Wallis, Dean of the Business School, to the University of Rochester. I planned a farewell cocktail party for Allen and Ann, following the August Convocation. It was a nice party, but that's not why I remember the occasion.

The day was overcast, hot and humid, with rain threatening. I left instructions with the caterers not to set up for the party until four o'clock, thirty minutes before the Convocation would end. Then, if the skies looked no more threatening than they did at two-thirty, they were to use the garden. I hoped it would work out that way, for the house was stuffy. Because the campus cops had fits if I left the downstairs windows open at night, and we had no air conditioning, the end of a protracted hot spell found us at the mercy of fans that did little more than stir up stale old air.

As I sat in the Chapel and watched the by now familiar ceremony of graduation, I felt encouraged by the occasional shaft of sunlight that slanted through the windows. At four-twenty, when only the degrees of Doctor of Divinity remained to be conferred, I breathed a sigh of relief, and relaxed. Too soon. Just as the Dean of the Divinity School read off the name of his first candidate for the degree, there came a searing flash of lightning and a monstrous roll of thunder. The cloud-burst lasted exactly five minutes, and I was so bemused by the timing—was it a divine salute to the qualifications of those new Doctors of Divinity, or was it a warning that someone down here had goofed?—that I briefly forgot the chaos that must be reigning next door.

When I rushed home, glasses were feverishly being rewashed, fresh tablecloths were being laid, trays of hors d'oeuvres were being picked over for anything salvageable in the second layer, and emergency stores of canned peanuts and potato chips were being opened. But the air was now fresher, and we flung all doors and windows open to coax as much of it indoors as possible.

As George opened the front door, he saw two people standing just to one side of the entrance. The man was wearing a gown and carrying a mortarboard and diploma. The gray-haired woman with him was tall, erect, and well-turned-out. She was gesturing toward the upper part of the house.

"Can I help you?" George asked.

They were embarrassed. Finally, the man introduced himself and his companion—his mother. Their name was Kennedy, he said, and he had just received an M.A. after some years of part-time study at the University. He was the youngest of her children, all of whom had been educated at Chicago.

"Pretty good record for the children of an upstairs maid," Mrs. Kennedy said.

"An upstairs maid?" I repeated. "You?"

"In this very house," she responded, her voice still soft with the accents of Erin. "I came to Chicago from Sligo in nineteen twelve, and was hired by Mrs. Judson. I worked here for two years. But she never thought I was good enough"—a soft giggle—"to be allowed downstairs."

According to what I'd heard of her, Mrs. Harry Pratt Judson, wife of the University's second President, had run a very tight ship; and this testimony further confirmed the impression.

"Come in and have a look around," I said. "We can't take long, for guests are coming at any moment. But there's time for a five-minute run-through."

And I gestured the Kennedys inside.

"Oh, no!" she protested. "Not by the *front* door!" (After all those years!)

But George had them in hand, and we raced them through the place. Not surprisingly, in view of the various remodelings to which it had been subjected, the house looked unfamiliar to Mrs. Kennedy—until she got to the kitchen. There she recognized an ancient gas-fired bun warmer that I had never used but had preserved for sentimental reasons. She let out a great, hearty laugh when I showed her what we kept in it: aprons.

We showed our surprise guests out as the Wallises came in. All through the party I couldn't get the Kennedys out of my mind. The immigrant girl of 1912 . . . the well-dressed matron of today . . . all of her children now with college degrees, and undoubtedly people of substance in society . . . testimony to the validity of the American dream, and to the historic role of the American university as an avenue of advancement. It made me feel good to be associated with one, and to be saluting someone who would soon be guiding another.

Thirteen

The three men with whom I had lunched one day in May of 1962 had not been recognizable as Loreleis—but it certainly *seemed*, during the course of the next few years, that their siren sound had set me (and them, and a lot of other people) on a course leading to disaster.

Two of the men were members of the Hyde Park-Kenwood Community Conference's Community Planning Committee. One was Martin Lieberman, a big, hearty, foreman-of-the-jury type; as personnel director of the Toni Company, he was a labor relations specialist who knew just when to push and when to relax the pressure. The other was Bruce Sagan, younger and shaggier, publisher of the Hyde Park *Herald* (and a flock of other community newspapers), shrewd businessman, patron of the arts, dabbler in back-room politics: half con man, half knight in shining armor. The third was Irving Horwitz, executive director of the Conference; short, Puckish, genial—a man whose cheerful casualness made their preposterous proposal seem completely reasonable.

The problem was this:

When the community's urban renewal project began, the main emphasis had been on elimination of blighted buildings, upgrading of those that were merely beginning to deteriorate, addition of parks, improvement of street design, and other aspects of physical redevelopment.

Then the problems of displaced families had begun to loom large in the public consciousness. It was all very well for the planners to say that population density had to be reduced in order to make the community livable again (as indeed it did). But in human terms, did one just ignore the people whose lodging was to be demolished or renovated—leaving them literally or figuratively marooned on the sidewalk with their household goods heaped around them? The next big thrust, therefore, had been to provide new living quarters for those displacees who couldn't help themselves; a thrust that had as one of its features the acquisition of land for public housing units within Hyde Park and Kenwood. (What a storm of controversy *that* had aroused!)

The one group that nobody had given much thought to were the community's businessmen, and now the bitter fruits of this oversight were all around us.

It had made sense, from the physical planning standpoint, to consolidate into three major locations the commercial and shopping facilities which in the 1950's had been loosely strung along seven streets, most of them in property built before 1905 and much of it dilapidated. Because of the decline of the community itself, by 1954 large numbers of stores were vacant. Many others were being used for purposes incompatible with the maintenance of Hyde Park and Kenwood as residential communities.

Small factories and warehouses were coming in, along with cheap liquor stores, gypsy fortunetellers, and storefront churches; and the community as a whole had rightly been alarmed by the degeneration of its shopping streets. Those most heavily infested with taverns were veritable skid rows. And so, with hardly a protest from the citizenry, some 80 per cent of frontage formerly zoned for business had been rezoned for residential or institutional use.

(This, as it turned out, was overdoing things: most of the "good" taverns had been thrown out along with the "bad" ones. Residents mourned the passing of Hanley's, an old-time saloon; the Beehive, where one heard great jazz; and the Compass, which some say should have been preserved as a national cultural landmark because it had spawned Shelley Berman, Mike Nichols, Elaine May, and the whole Second City school of social satire. So grievous was the loss, in fact, that community leaders were to find themselves—in the late 1960's—using their influence *in behalf* of Jimmy's Woodlawn Tap, when its building was threatened by demolition.)

The experience of the Fifty-fifth Street merchants had been particularly traumatic. In the mid-fifties they had supported the urban renewal plan because they assumed that they would be relocated at or close to their established addresses. But what had happened instead? They had discovered, first, that no governmental agency concerned itself with the relocation problems of merchants; second, that their short-term leaseholds were valueless, and that they would not be financially compensated either for the cost of moving or for loss of goodwill should they move far enough away from their existing locations to lose customers.

This discovery had been just bearable; but there had been worse to come. The necessary demolition along the street was to have been staged so that the fine new shopping center at Fifty-fifth and Lake Park would be ready for occupancy before the merchants on the street were displaced. This would make possible their moving into it with minimum disruption to their businesses. Then the Chicago Land Clearance Commission had informed them that any private developer who got the land would be under no legal obligation to offer space to the Fifty-fifth Street displacees. The private developer who *did* get the land hadn't felt a moral obligation, either; and, in addition, he had scaled down the size of the shopping center so that there wouldn't have been room for all the displacees even if the developer had offered space to them.

Not that it had mattered in the long run, for the city authorities ran into so much trouble acquiring the land on which the shopping center was to be built that it hadn't even been started until three years after the first displacements of

Fifty-fifth Street merchants had occurred. During those three years, demolition of commercial properties along the street had proceeded piecemeal, giving shoppers progressively less reason for coming to the area, which in turn had played hob with business in those shops that were left. So it is no wonder that the Fifty-fifth Street merchants felt that they had been sold down the river.*

A few good things had come out of this mess, however. One of them was that the plight of the Fifty-fifth Street merchants had served to spur reforms in federal urban renewal legislation which later made things a bit easier for displaced merchants everywhere.

Another net gain was the creation of a second big shopping center a few blocks north and west of the one in which the Fifty-fifth Street merchants had expected to find refuge. This came about because a small group of displacees had decided in 1958—at the high point of their bitterness toward the developer of the Fifty-fifth and Lake Park shopping center—that their only hope of security was to get into the redevelopment business themselves.

* On this street alone, 194 businessmen were displaced between 1955 and 1958. Of these, 123 managed to survive in the neighborhood temporarily —most of them moving at least twice during the late 1950's in a grim kind of musical chairs that kept them just one jump ahead of the bulldozer— but when the final count would be made a decade later, only 31 would still be in business. As for the community as a whole, the final casualty list would stand at 641. Of these, 207 would have gone out of business altogether, 110 would have relocated in some other part of the city, and only 83 would remain in Hyde Park-Kenwood.

But before one damns urban renewal too harshly, it is instructive to read *The Impact of Urban Renewal on Small Business*, Brian J. L. Berry, Sandra J. Parsons, and Rutherford H. Platt. This case study of Hyde Park-Kenwood and three other Chicago city neighborhoods was published in 1968 by the University of Chicago's Center for Urban Studies. It makes, and documents, several important points: that the residents of Hyde Park-Kenwood *wanted* to get rid of certain kinds of businesses and designed the urban renewal plan to do just that; that in city neighborhoods without urban renewal to help the process along, approximately a third of small businesses fail within two years after they are started; and that in the renewed community of Hyde Park-Kenwood the currently established businesses are "about right" in kind and number for the present population.

Under the leadership of Everett Ramsey, who couldn't move elsewhere because his news service was franchised to distribute newspapers in Hyde Park and Kenwood only, fifteen of the neighorhood's most solvent small business men had incorporated for the purpose of developing the shopping center that was specified in the urban renewal plan for the corner of Fifty-third and Woodlawn. Their organization and financing problems were monstrous, but by 1960 they had managed to create a corporation that could build and operate a shopping center—if it got a chance to.

By 1961, when the land in question had been cleared and finally went to bid, community sentiment was so aroused that the American Oil Company and Jewel Tea didn't have a chance. Their bids were higher, but the Department of Urban Renewal had correctly guessed that it would have a riot on its hands if the valiant efforts of the community's displaced merchants were to go for naught.

After all, wasn't Ted Anderson among them—Ted Anderson, whose hardware store was such a community institution that when he had been displaced from his original location, sixty of his customers had transported his merchandise, in a shopping cart parade, to his new address? And what of Harold Jacobson of Kimbark Liquors? His shop had been on that very site, and for two years he'd worked at another job, marking time until he could get back into business for himself.

Mitzie Horky of Mitzie's Flowers . . . Gus and "Stevie" Breslauer, whose small department store had been a fixture in the neighborhood for twenty-five years . . . Gabe Stern's menswear store . . . the optometrist Dr. Kurt Rosenbaum, who had fitted two generations of Hyde Parkers with their glasses . . . these were all people the residents knew and liked and depended on, people who had stuck through the bad years. Were their hopes and their efforts to be denied now?

The Department of Urban Renewal had wisely accepted the bid of this group of merchants, and thus established a precedent that again had nationwide implications: that "community benefit" can outweigh purely financial considerations in disposing of urban renewal land.

That story had a happy ending; but it was the story of only fifteen merchants, and they were the ones who were economically most viable. In 1962, many *small* small business men were still on the edge of the precipice, and others like them had already pitched over.

What would happen to the Acasa Gift Shop, one of those remaining on Fifty-fifth Street? Miss Clarinda Buck had run it for umpteen years, and it was *the* place for children's books and stationery. But it was a tiny shop, a one-woman enterprise, and it couldn't be run profitably if Miss Buck had to pay the high rent that was being asked (necessarily, given the financing and construction costs of new buildings) in either of the shopping centers.

What about Peter Leibundguth, who repaired stringed instruments, and Rudolph Van Tellingen's used bookshop? These enterprises were as valued in Hyde Park as a drive-in eatery or a bowling alley might be in a different kind of community. They were housed in that quaint little chain of shacks left over from the World's Fair of 1893, which were in such disrepair they should have been torn down years before, and now were actually slated for demolition in 1963.

What about Mary Lou Womer's Little Gallery on Fifty-seventh Street and Staver's Book Shop in the English basement below it? The potter Dorothy Peterson and Eric the picture framer were already gone; and the Alpha Shade Works, the cabinetmakers of the Work Bench, Stahl's Glass Shop, and the upholsterer Jens Simonsgaard were going.

This was the problem that was troubling the Messrs. Lieberman, Sagan, and Horwitz on that day in May when we had lunched together.

"So what'll the community be like, five years from now?" Bruce had asked me, rhetorically. "It'll be a conglomeration of supermarkets and dry cleaners and chain stores. It'll be stripped clean of the little businesses that are allied to the arts and to the cultural interests of the community. *Sterile.*

"And there won't be any hole-in-the-wall space, where beginning businessmen, people like the Bordelons"—who had parlayed a tiny home furnishing shop begun in Hyde Park into a citywide success—"can make a start.

"Why? Because, as soon as the deteriorated old buildings go down, the artists and craftsmen will be priced out of the neighborhood. We surveyed those who are still here and found that they pay somewhere between a dollar-fifty and a dollar sixty-six a square foot, which is about half what it costs to rent space in new buildings. It's obvious that providing low rentals is the key to holding them here. And we know how to do it."

"How?" I asked. "Get the Department of Urban Renewal to leave more of the old buildings standing?"

"No. We're going to build a shopping center specifically for artists and craftsmen."

"A *new* shopping center? But you just said that the cost of construction makes it necessary to charge rents that these little people can't afford."

"If you develop in the conventional way. But if you get cheap land AND long-term financing AND restrict the return to investors to an absolute minimum, you *can* provide low rents in new construction!"

This statement, delivered in a ringing tone that was obviously intended to stir my blood, had not had the desired effect. I have always had trouble balancing my checkbook, and now in addition the University was requiring me to keep exceedingly careful records of household expenditures. As a result, financial topics made me feel like I do on the morning I have an appointment with the dentist.

"Really?" It was a polite comment, nothing more.

Marty Lieberman had recognized this as his signal to move in.

"The important thing," he had said, "is to get the project under way; to concentrate on the *human* side of it. We've done the feasibility studies. What's essential now is to organize the development effort, build community support, establish the sub-committees that will iron out the details."

"And that's what the Conference's Community Planning Committee is doing? You, and the others in the group?"

A moment of silence. A slight shifting forward in their seats. A corporate intake of breath. This was what they'd come for.

"No. That's what we thought *you* might do."

"Me? Why *me?* I don't know anything about . . ."

Bruce again, low key now: "Good organization was responsible for the success of *Hips, Hoops, Hooray!* A lot of us were very impressed by that."

Marty, with a touch of evangelical fervor: "This would be a similar job, only on a slightly bigger scale. It would be a great civic contribution, and I'm not referring just to bricks and mortar. It could bring different segments of the community under the same umbrella again. Have a good human relations effect."

Irv, as if the thought had just crossed his mind: "Relations between the community and the University aren't as good as they might be. . . ."

I knew that. The University, through the South East Chicago Commission, had played a dominant role in drawing up the urban renewal plan, in getting the enabling legislation passed, and in attracting the private real estate developers who were putting up new buildings, residential or commercial, all over the neighborhood. Therefore, the University was being blamed for a lot of the things that had gone wrong.

"But my being involved in a project like this wouldn't—*couldn't*—have any connection with the University," I said. "It would be highly improper of me to attempt to influence University actions. Besides, I happen to know that the University is selling its residential properties just as fast as it can get them renovated, and the Board of Trustees wouldn't want any part of commercial redevelopment."

Bruce, soothingly: "Irv just meant that if the wife of the

President were to support a project like this, it would imply an interest . . ."

Marty: "A completely *unofficial* interest, of course."

Bruce: ". . . in the welfare of the whole community . . ."

Irv: ". . . instead of in the academic segment alone."

Then Marty said, "Incidentally, nothing like this has been attempted, anywhere. In Hyde Park, the one appeal people are sure to respond to is that something is a 'pilot project' or a 'pioneering effort.' So I know you could count on lots of help."

His smile was the kind that people in the advertising business describe as "sincere."

"*Lots* of help," Irv murmured, looking as guileless as an angel.

I had told them I'd talk it over with George, although I knew perfectly well that he'd say what he did say: "If the idea appeals to you, honey, go ahead."

And it *was* tempting. Late May was the height of the University social season, and I seemed to be spending all my time in idle chit-chat with transient mobs of people. I was itching to do something with a beginning, a middle, and an end; something that involved me as *me*. The delegation from the Conference may have wanted me as a symbol of the University, or even as a port of entry to the University's pocketbook, but I could show them that I had some value in my own person, couldn't I? You bet I could! So I had said that I'd do my best to get the project under way; and that autumn, I did.

I was startled to discover that the "lots of help" which had been promised actually materialized. The finally assembled organizing committee included four men who had long been Conference stalwarts: Marty Lieberman and Bruce Sagan, of course*; Harry Gottlieb, vice-president of one of Chicago's real estate developers; and Calvin Sawyier, an attorney with a leading firm. We also persuaded George H. Watkins, vice-president of an

* Years later, when Irv Horwitz was no longer executive director of the Conference, we nabbed him too.

insurance company, and Edward Rosenheim, Jr., a professor of English at the University, to join us. On the distaff side, we had Eleanor Petersen, my erstwhile partner in *Hips, Hoops, Horray!*, and Connie (Mrs. Philip) Williams, who like Eleanor was one of the Kenwood Ladies. Each had a long history of involvement in civic causes of one sort or another. In a word, they were pros.

I had often before been struck by the widespread belief that interest in an organization's goals is adequate qualification for membership on its governing board, but during the 1960's I was to become even more aware of the fallacy in that belief. As citizens groups sprang up like toadstools, their objectives ranging from getting more neighborhood control of the public schools to expanding job opportunities for minority groups to reducing environmental pollution, it became apparent that many of them did not realize that having board members who are experienced in organizational procedures is as tangible an asset to an enterprise as money in the bank.

A governing board can carry one or two members who require in-service training, but if most members don't already know which matters should be brought to the whole group for discussion, and in what form, the meetings can exhaust the energies of the participants, waste their time, and delay or prevent progress altogether. In short: motivation is essential; but it must be allied with procedural expertise. (I would sometimes say this to student groups, and they didn't believe a word of it—especially toward the end of the sixties, when they were idealizing "the common man" and eschewing professionalism of any sort.)

For this particular enterprise, there was one additional requirement. The only reason that the nine of us dared undertake a project of such magnitude was that each of us was highly knowledgeable about particular aspects of it. Bruce and Harry were already familiar with the details of commercial real estate development; Cal knew (or could locate and interpret) the laws that might affect our proposals; George Watkins had been in public relations and was good at fund raising; and the rest of us were either capable community organizers or had influence among particular segments of the constituency whose support we were going to need if our "center for the useful arts" was ever to come into being.

(A silly phrase, that. The philosophers among us had a lot of fun trying to define the difference between the useful and the useless arts, but we let the slogan stand because we couldn't think up any better short version of "a center for artists, craftsmen, and specialty shops whose goods or services reflect the cultural character of the community.")

We met at two-week intervals all through the autumn—fortunately, all the opening-of-term events at the University went smoothly that year, and there were no visits of VIP's or crises involving students to distract me—and by January of 1963 we were ready to take the plunge. We incorporated ourselves as the not-for-profit Harper Court Foundation (a name suggested by Eleanor Petersen), whose purpose was "to study means to prevent or alleviate the effect of urban renewal projects in eliminating the low-rental diversified properties which are necessary for the continuation of small businesses of special cultural or community significance, including the development of a project to accomplish said purposes."

When Cal Sawyier delivered my copy of the charter, I plopped it down in front of my husband, and said, "I'll bet you never expected to be married to a corporation president."

He grinned. "Not bad for a gal who can't multiply eight times nine." And then he turned serious. "Do me a favor. If you talk about it to students, don't emphasize corporate structure. All corporations are bad corporations, and I've got enough problems without having the kids on my neck because my wife has sold out to Big Business."

"Big business? Holy cats, this whole enterprise is in behalf of *little* business, and we aren't going to make a penny of profit on it, besides. Incidentally, do you realize"—now I was serious, too—"that I may be getting us into a financial mess? Personally?

If this thing should fail halfway along, I suppose the incorporators would be liable for any debts."

"I know. It's all right. Just manage to fail, if you're going to, when the stock market is up."

In February and March, the organizing committee called a series of community meetings in order to explain the scheme and test the degree of support. We had some fine drawings to show—architects' renderings of three bi-level buildings to be clustered around a central courtyard on Harper Avenue between Fifty-second and Fifty-third streets—as well as a step-by-step explanation of how the center was to become a reality. It all sounded as good as done, until questions from the audience revealed how iffy the whole thing really was.

I presided, but Bruce and Marty were always on hand to field the sticky ones. For example:

A Hyde Park lady, one of those who had long served on a Conference committee checking building code violations and was therefore an expert on the laws and regulations affecting urban renewal sites, said, "The land you propose to build on is specified 'for institutional use.' It says so right here in my copy of the urban renewal plan. I don't see how a commercial shopping center qualifies."

Bruce: "It doesn't. The land was supposed to be used for the new fire station, for the police station, and for a church parking lot. But now neither the city nor the church want it. So we'll get it reclassified for commercial use."

She was relentless. "Which means that you have to get the Community Conservation Council to recommend reclassification to the Department of Urban Renewal, then the DUR has to ask the City Council to approve it."

Marty: "We've already discussed the possibility with the CCC and the DUR and also with Alderman Despres, and nobody seems to be against it."

"Yes, but"—the lady knew her urban renewal plan—"the parcels set aside for institutional use aren't contiguous. Your plot plan doesn't match the land you say you're going to build on."

"What we're going to do," Bruce replied, "is to swap a bit on the northeast for the footage at the south end. It's the City Parking Authority we'll be dealing with there."

Another questioner: "It's very pretty. Especially that big courtyard. But isn't that where Harper Avenue now is? You'd have to close it."

"Yes. The City Council will have to approve that, too."

"I'm not quite with you on the financing," said a big, solid, well-tailored man. "You say this whole thing will cost six hundred thousand dollars, which includes land cost. How can you know what the land will cost? It has to be reappraised for commercial use, and then go to bid, doesn't it?"

Bruce was running the show, now.

"That's right. But we've had it appraised, and we've based our figures on that appraisal. We assume, of course, that our bid will be accepted."

He slid over that last assertion very rapidly.

Same questioner, over whose eyes no wool had been pulled: "Hmm. And are you assuming also that the Small Business Administration will loan you the four hundred eighty thousand dollars you list here as your mortgage? That's—why that's *eighty* per cent of the project cost! What guarantee do you have that you'll get that much? Or any loan at all?"

"The project falls within the requirements of the agency, and the SBA is most encouraging. Of course"—very casual and offhand, now—"we can't actually file an application for the mortgage until the land has been acquired and specific tenants have signed their leases. But we foresee no problems there."

"Well, *I* do. Sounds risky as hell. And I can't say I like this idea of charging some tenants high rents in order to subsidize the businesses who need low rents. That's interfering with the free play of the market."

I didn't know the questioner, but he had to be a disciple of the University's very conservative professor of Economics, Milton Friedman.

Bruce was ready for him, though. "There's nothing unusual in a sliding rent scale in shopping centers. High rents are routinely charged the big-volume merchants like department stores, and lower rents are charged the smaller shops that are essentially convenience facilities. Shoe repairers, for instance. The rationale is that they expand the range of services offered the shopping center customer.

"Well, our equivalent of the department store is a restaurant or two of the type the community has already lost. Like the Continental Gourmet, say. And our equivalent of the shoe repair shop is a potter or an upholsterer or someone of that type."

"It still strikes me as a subsidy," his questioner insisted.

Bruce can be very patient, very winning, when he wants to persuade someone.

"Let me review it again, quickly. One way to lower rents in new construction is to obtain very long-term financing. Any commercial mortgage house, if they'd do it at all, would loan us maybe sixty-six per cent of total cost, for maybe fifteen years, whereas the SBA can loan us eighty per cent on a twenty-five year basis. Since the payback time is then so much longer, we can set lower rents than if the project were being conventionally financed. In fact, they can be something like twenty-two per cent lower.

"But we want to get rents even lower than that makes possible. Another step in that direction is to limit return to investors. We've set ourselves up as a not-for-profit corporation, and we propose to pay less interest on our debentures than is usual in real estate development. . . ."

"You said it. This equity money—a hundred twenty thousand, it says here—that you propose to raise by selling hundred-dollar debentures, how about that? These bonds won't mature for twenty-five years, and you're going to pay only six per cent. That's peanuts."

"Right. But it's not primarily the investor we're interested in; it's the artists and craftsmen. . . . And even with that low interest rate working to keep our costs down and therefore our rental rates low, the break-even point sticks at approximately two dollars a square foot. So that's the reason for the sliding scale on rents. If we're going to get some tenants at rents below the break-even point, some tenants are going to have to pay a rate above that amount."

Marty took over at this point, saying, "We don't expect people to buy these bonds as investments in the usual sense. When you buy yours, we hope you'll think of it as an investment in the future of the community. Remember that if there had been a place like Harper Court five years ago, maybe we wouldn't have lost the Continental Gourmet, and Webers—remember those German coffee cakes?—and Greenhuts."

"There's absolutely no place to get nice buttons any more," a woman said. Her comment was not a *non sequitur;* the Greenhuts' shop had sold yardage and findings, and local housewives still lamented its passage.

And so, little by little, we convinced the people—eighty of the community's leading citizens, anyway—that we had a fighting chance to build the center. By March we had formed them into The Committee for Harper Court, and had divided them into subcommittees: Finance, Construction, and Tenant Selection. All that remained to be done was to persuade twenty or more merchants to sign leases for non-existent shop space whose completion date we could only guess at; have the leases ready at precisely the same time that we acquired the land, said acquisition to involve four city agencies and one federal bureau; raise enough money, again within the same time span, to pay for land which we might not get and whose price we didn't know; and construct the buildings, using federal funds that might not be loaned to us.

H. L. Mencken defined faith as "an illogical belief in the occurrence of the improbable." If a plaque memorializing the efforts of the founding fathers were ever to be installed in Harper Court, it ought to read: THIS CENTER IS A TRIUMPH OF FAITH OVER REASON.

Fourteen

"But there's no reason for them to get into such a stew about it," I said. "It's just a *dance*. Do they seriously believe that the Wash Prom threatens their intellectual integrity?"

"A lot of them do," Jim Newman said.

He was an associate Dean of Students, especially close to the undergraduates. I had run into him at a cocktail party on the same day that I'd helped to pick the five finalists in that year's contest for the title of Miss University of Chicago. She would be crowned at the Washington Prom, the last surviving relic at Chicago of a frolic with Big Ten overtones, which occurred annually on the Saturday closest to Washington's Birthday.

Any campus group could name a candidate. It had been clear, that afternoon, that some groups had deliberately nominated girls who were unattractive, unpoised, or in personality and behavior were as unlike the popular image of a "campus queen" as it was possible to be. The intent was clear: to indicate scorn of the tradition, and of the dance itself.

These nominations had been cruel, I felt, because the girls in question were intelligent enough to sense the reason for their nomination, but at the same time were young enough to want to be "popular"—which was what, in essence, the title of Miss University of Chicago signified. And so, torn between coming and not coming to the interviews with the judges, the girls had come, as wary as deer who have scented tigers.

We had eliminated the ones who couldn't have walked down the grand staircase in Ida Noyes Hall without falling flat on their faces, or those who would have clowned while doing it, or those who might not have shown up at all, and had picked five girls whom the student body would now vote for. At midnight on February 23, George would crown the one who got the most votes and give her an avuncular kiss on the cheek, after which she would reign for the remaining hour of the dance. It didn't strike me as a fate worse than death, and this was what I was talking to Jim about.

"Our students never seem to have any fun," I said. "And it isn't just because they have to study so hard they don't have time for pleasure. According to Red, there's a certain amount of pure frivolity at Harvard, and academic standards there are the same as they are here. Caltech students are brighter than either those at Chicago or Harvard, yet they don't have the Chicago students' peculiar air of . . ."

I paused, searching for the right word.

"Deadly intensity?" Jim supplied.

"Absolutely. And what's even worse is that those of our kids who don't want to attend something as conventional as the Wash Prom try to prevent its being attended by *anyone*. They're real Puritans, aren't they?"

Instead of answering directly, Jim escorted me to a quiet corner where we could sit down; and then he said, "I've thought about it a good deal. You're right, of course, about their not having much fun. All of us involved in student activities get so tired of hearing them complain that there's 'nothing to do,' that there's 'no social life around here,' when at the same time there are so many social and cultural events programmed that there isn't enough physical space on campus to accommodate them. The majority of the undergraduates don't even date regularly, did you know that?

"So the real mystery is: why, with so much opportunity, don't more of them go to the concerts and the dorm dances and the athletic events? I think it's because—like this age group everywhere—they want to be part of something that *everyone* is involved in, and the only thing they have in common here is their commitment to intellectual endeavor. So the hostility toward events like the Wash Prom is probably based on the fear that anything which is not intellectual in nature will diminish the one activity that gives them a sense of community."

We were interrupted at this point, but in following time I often thought about that conversation, and came to agree with Jim's diagnosis. The College of the University of Chicago is not a distinct social entity; its students blend, in some classes and in all campus activities, with the graduate students (who outnumber the undergraduates three to one). The central interest of most graduate students is in scholarship, and this reinforces the younger students' respect for the intellectual life. In addition, our College curriculum has traditionally emphasized the development of a critical mind. The person who evolves from the Chicago experience is very intense, very independent, very questioning—all of which are qualities in such short supply in the nation today that one should cry an unqualified "Hurrah!"

But it is also true that the overall atmosphere at Chicago can be hard on all but the most mature of eighteen- and nineteen-year-olds. In the early 1960's, most colleges were dominated by an "in" group whose members set the standards for student behavior. The smaller Ivy League colleges, for one example, were WASP enclaves. For another example, the social life and mores at many state universities were dominated by fraternity and sorority groups. The predominant tone of campus life was set by these dominant groups, and there was social pressure for conformity to their values. A student who did not wish to conform (or who was excluded) knew exactly what he was rejecting (or why he was being excluded).

At Chicago, however, there has always been a highly diverse student body, one containing more members of racial or religious minorities and more children from working-class homes than at comparable institutions. There is also great tolerance for their varying cultural patterns. To have this freedom is good, overall; but it deprives newcomers of the sense of knowing what behavior is expected of them (which even adults, upon moving to a new job or a new neighborhood, like to have).

Deciding whether to conform to a dominant social pattern is easier on the psyche than to be given multiple choices, especially in the late teens. True, older adolescents are striving to establish themselves as individuals, but many of them still need the supportive feeling that comes with being part of "everyone"— the "everyone" who goes to football games or chapel services or college ceremonies or (latterly) participates in sit-ins and strikes.

If a young and immature person is confused and made anxious by having to accept too much responsibility for his own actions, the natural response is withdrawal. That's why many of our first- and second-year College students used to gather in small bunches in dormitory rooms and either gripe because there was "nothing to do" or talk exhaustively about the one thing they shared in common, their course work. Many of them simply didn't have enough emotional energy to overcome this group inertia and go out as individuals to participate in the multitude of extracurricular opportunities available to them.

(This pathological state of mind is not as common at Chicago now as it was in the early and mid-1960's, partly because students everywhere—like aristocrats of antiquity or trade unionists in the early years of this century—have come to think of themselves as members of a distinct social class. The youth culture itself has become the students' "everyone." But in addition, the University of Chicago has reorganized the College into five divisions, within which students have a greater sense of "belonging," and has strengthened its residential house system.)

It was the house system at Harvard that prevented Redmond's feeling as adrift during his undergraduate years as some of his counterparts at Chicago did. Harvard's environment is just as sink-or-swim as Chicago's, and it's bigger, besides; during Red's freshman year, for example, I had plenty of reason to wonder whether anyone would know or care or bother to notify us if he became ill or got into trouble. Fortunately, his inner resources were adequate to the demands imposed on them, but even Red needed a sense of place or status—and Lowell House, into which he moved as a sophomore, provided them. Its Master made a point of entertaining the residents in small groups in his quarters, and encouraged a full range of house-based social, cultural, and educational activities. The result was that the residents became, whatever else they may or may not have been, at least members of that cohesive social entity called Lowell House.

Don't misunderstand. To balance the lost and lonely students at Chicago or Harvard or any comparably open-ended environment, there are as many or more students for whom the freedom of such a setting is wonderfully nourishing. Jim Newman once said, in a formal report, "A high proportion of our graduates emerge as men and women with a genuine intellectual commitment, a well-established set of values which they themselves have determined, and a respect for and ability to live with people whose standards are different from their own. If there is a Chicago type, it is Riesman's 'Autonomous Man.'"

Chicago's administrators quite rightly don't want to tamper with an academic environment which produces that kind of person. Besides, as a practical matter, the development of a greater sense of community—for those who need it—is nothing you do by fiat. To *require* all students at Chicago to do anything together would create cohesiveness, all right: the brick-wall cohesiveness of faculty and students in solid opposition to the requirement.

What administrators can do, however, is to build on the spontaneous comings-together that occur from time to time in the life of any institution, and encourage their perpetuation. At the University of Chicago, each spring's Festival of the Arts and each fall's Folk Music Festival are such events. And almost any controversial issue affecting the intellectual or moral integrity of the University will also pull people together into a commonality of interest and activity. The visit to our campus of

George Lincoln Rockwell in February of 1963 was an event of that sort.

He had been invited to come for the wrong reason. A group of students at Northwestern had asked Rockwell to speak on their campus, and Northwestern's administrators had refused to allow use of the university's facilities for the purpose. Quick as a flash, therefore, and primarily to see whether the University of Chicago really meant it when it said that "any student organization may invite and hear speakers of their choice on subjects of their choice," the men of Vincent House fired off an invitation to Rockwell. *Then* they thought about it; and inasmuch as many of them were Jewish they were as appalled by Rockwell's acceptance of the invitation as were large segments of the student body, the faculty, and the general public.

This was not a simple matter of academic freedom (although it was that too). What made Rockwell's visit unique was the emotions it engendered. In the preceding year, speeches at the University by Gus Hall and Jimmy Hoffa had caused hardly a ripple, on campus or off, but Rockwell's prospective visit was of a different order altogether—as this letter from an alumnus made clear:

> I am a graduate of the University of Chicago, class of 1951. I am also a graduate of the Buchenwald concentration camp, class of 1945. My and my wife's families were among the five million Jews murdered by Nazis . . .
>
> There is no excuse for permitting a Nazi to speak on campus. What Mr. Rockwell and his Party represent, as you well know, is contrary to all concepts of humanity. What they represent is an insult to the memory of the millions of men, women, and children who died in concentration camps. It is an insult to the memory of millions of American, British, French, Canadian, Russian, and other GIs who died to preserve the freedom and dignity of mankind.
>
> I have been proud of the fact that I graduated from the University of Chicago. I am not proud any more. I am hurt and ashamed.

Many other alumni felt the same way, their comments ranging from personal attacks on George ("You are destroying the ideals the University always stood for before you came along as President") to the application of economic sanctions ("I am '09, my son is '34, my daughter '41. I regret that we shall henceforth not make any further contributions to our school.")

Then there were the communications (usually unsigned) from the citizenry at large:

> Northwestern University wouldn't allow that scoundrel to come there and poison the minds of those young students. Three rousing cheers for men who are true to God and this country—something you can't boast of.

> Why don't you let all the murderers out of all the prisons and let them lecture on *their* techniques? After all, these people are citizens, too—so, by your logic, they are entitled to be heard.

> My grandparents, cousins, uncles, and aunts fell victim to men carrying the swastika into the Ukraine in 1943. I can only wish that the same fate befall your loved ones. Then you will know how it feels!

This sort of mail had come in during the 1962 sit-in; and would again. The unique addition was a petition from eleven members of the *faculty*, asking George to "bar this despicable and dangerous man" from University premises. There was also a spate of protesting letters in the student newspaper, and an agonizing reappraisal on the part of Vincent House. The upshot of the latter was a decision (by a narrow majority) to let the invitation stand.

A year later, Harvard students were to be faced with a similiar dilemma, and Red's analysis of their reaction is so apropos at this point that I shall quote from a letter he wrote:

> The Young Democrats club has nearly been torn apart by an invitation to Governor Wallace of Alabama to speak

here under their auspices. In fact, the actual vote was 69–63 in favor.

Wallace is most aggressively on the wrong side of the civil rights issue, from a Harvard student's point of view. Most students feel that segregation and what accompanies it are great moral evils which must be rooted out quickly; there can be no compromise.

Yet this deep emotionalism runs into another emotion of great significance: student determination to make rational judgments. "Be reasonable" does not mean "be calm." It means "use your reason, your mind, your knowledge of logic."

The problem is the same as during the Rockwell thing at your place. Students, emotionally committed to being reasonable—which includes the exercise of academic freedom—are also emotionally committed to equal rights for Negroes (in our current case) or for Jews (in the Rockwell case). So, when a speaker is invited who is on the other side of the second issue, they have great difficulty reconciling the two sets of emotions.

One of the local synagogues even got into the act. Its rabbi publicly accused the young Jews among the Vincent House membership of "self-hate" and "morbid compulsions."

But no University administrator took any action, except 1) to reaffirm the right of the students to hear Rockwell speak, and 2) to batten down the hatches in order to preserve life and limb should the Jewish War Veterans' threat to prevent Rockwell's appearance take the form of anything more violent than picketing. (It didn't.)

The student newspaper showed that it could be a calming force in a storm by recommending that students refrain from demonstrations that would give Rockwell additional publicity. "This community can best show its objections by allowing his appearance to pass as uneventfully as possible," the editorial said. And, essentially, that's what happened.

Rockwell came; he spoke (in a moderate vein, as intelligent

demagogues usually do when they are with intelligent people); and the students enjoyed his speech. They were entertained rather than converted—which, again, is the usual effect of a demagogue upon college students. Why is it that so many adults are fearful that "our children" will be subverted by hearing someone speak whose ideas are generally unpopular? "Our children," if they are bright enough to be admitted to a selective college, are far more able to spot the fallacies in imperfectly reasoned arguments than most adults are.

As the tumult died down, the voice of a perceptive lady was heard. In response to the rabbinical pronouncement with its psychiatric overtones, Zoe Mikva (whose husband was to become a Congressman from Illinois) wrote, "When I was a student at the University in 1946, I traveled a considerable distance across town to hear Gerald L. K. Smith. This was my first contact with violent anti-Semitism. Believe me, it was enormously educational. I joined Hillel the following week—for the wrong reasons, to be sure, but you have to begin somewhere. In any case, I was motivated simply by curiosity when I made the pilgrimage to the racist, Fascist voice of *my* college days."

A student who had heard Rockwell unconsciously reinforced Mrs. Mikva's point when he said to me, "All my life my folks have talked about the Nazis. I couldn't wait to see one."

"And . . . ?"

"I saw one. Big deal."

The men of Vincent House ended up feeling rather proud of themselves for having proved once again that academic freedom is a fact of life at the University of Chicago.

"This whole thing had primarily a symbolic value," the house president said, "like our not having a football team."

Fifteen

The grass in the circle was well established by the spring of 1963. The tulips in the long beds leading from the circle to the Administration Building came up that year in even heights and looked just the way the seed catalogs promised they would. A few students found to their surprise that all this was nice to view, and George was encouraged to press the beautification program further.

A sprinkler system was installed throughout the grassy areas of the main Quadrangle, and hundreds of pounds of grass seed were sown. Until these new lawns got established, however, they had to be treated tenderly. Small signs wouldn't do; the area was too large. What, then?

One fine day in early May, a popular student named Joe Ford appeared on campus wearing a costume that was vaguely Elizabethan, and with a trumpeter in tow. The two of them took up a stand in the middle of the main Quadrangle. The trumpeter let loose a blast, Joe read a proclamation by the Committee on Grass, and then nailed it to the door of Cobb Hall.* The text, ghost-written for George by Jean Haskins of the Public Relations Office, said:

---

* Upon seeing a picture of Joe in the student newspaper, someone noticed that he had been standing on the grass when he read the proclamation. A counter organization therefore immediately sprang to life: The Committee to Keep the Committee on Grass *Off* the Grass. Lacking the hybrid vigor of the Committee on Grass, however, it perished young.

Let it be known by the students, faculties,
staff, alumni, and friends of the University of Chicago

Whereas: . . . Aprill with his shoures soote
The droghte of March hath perced to
the roote—*Chaucer*;

Whereas: 16 men from Joe Galatte & Sons Landscaping
Firm commenced planting 1,000 pounds of grass
seed on the main Quadrangle April 28—*Buildings
and Grounds*;

Whereas: . . . vegetable love should grow
Vaster than empires, and more slow—*Andrew
Marvell*;

Whereas: Kentucky bluegrass is a beautiful deep green color.
Extremely hearty. Withstands winter freeze and
summer drought if allowed healthy start—*Mont-
gomery Ward Catalog*;

Whereas: The flowers appear on the earth; the time of the
singing of birds is come, and the voice of the tur-
tle is heard in our land—*Song of Solomon*;

Whereas: The University Quadrangles constitute an intellectual greenhouse continuously producing fresh
ideas in the midst of an asphalt jungle—*Office of
Public Relations*;

Whereas: What shall we do in the heat of summer
But wait in barren orchard for another October
—*T. S. Eliot*;

Whereas: There are 172,500 square feet of concrete walks
on the main campus—*University Drafting Office*;

Whereas: Continued growth of this young grass is assured
only if it is not stepped on, at all, between now
and July 1st—*Department of Botany*;

Whereas: Brevity is the soul of wit—*Shakespeare.*

Now, therefore, be it resolved: That young grass, like ideas, be allowed to grow freely, and without oppression, on the campus of the University of Chicago.

> By virtue of the authority vested in
> me by the Committee on Grass of the
> University of Chicago
>
> George Wells Beadle
> *President*

The proclamation was widely circulated among other colleges and universities, and even found its way to a cabinet-level office in Washington. One day George received a telegram from Stewart Udall, Secretary of the Interior, who said, "YOUR INGENIOUS APPROACH TO SAVING THE BABY BLADES IS A TRIUMPH OF MIND OVER FEET AND SHOWS WHAT A HIGHER EDUCATION CAN DO."

The grass was respected, grew well, and became a great ornament to the Quadrangles. One pair of students, slightly intoxicated by young love and spring sunshine, even went so far as to write George a thank-you note.

Nor was that the only evidence that the sap was rising:

1) On the sidewalk leading into a dormitory, someone chalked a Valentine heart and within it wrote: ADAM LOVES EVE.

2) Mary K was pregnant again.

3) A number of rabbits inhabited the grounds stretching between Rockefeller Chapel and the President's House. (The Dean of the Chapel said they prayed at his place and preyed at ours.) One of them spent her nights digging holes in our lawn in anticipation of need, and every morning George filled them up. But one morning the hole had infant rabbits in it; and George was forced to put a small protective fence around it so that the power mower wouldn't decapitate the young. He was torn between delight as we watched the babies grow and annoyance because the uncut grass around the burrow made an unsightly hummock in the lawn.

4) The Alpha Delts undertook their spring housecleaning and retrieved a mountain of beer cans from their grounds. They also repaved their parking lot, then posted a sign that read: PRIVATE PARKING—UNAUTHORIZED CARS WILL BE DISMANTLED.

5) The April file from the Security Office included a report that had been written one morning at 4:10 A.M. It recorded a complaint from a citizen who lived uncomfortably close to the quarters where research animals were kept. The report, a model of succinctness, read: "A Mr. Hammet complained about the rooster crowing. Both cars went in. We chased him around, and he stopped crowing. He was the white one."

6) George and I were awakened one night by hearing what sounded like muffled screams from the vicinity of the Chapel. We called the campus police. This time the report was verbal. The officers had found a couple rolling around in the ivy under the hawthorne trees that flank the entrance to the building. All signs pointed to attempted rape. Both denied it, and the girl refused to press charges.

"Were they students?" I asked.

The policeman's face was impassive as he nodded. "In the Divinity School," he said. Then he grinned. "Maybe we'd better look around Botany Pond. Might find some biology majors in the bushes over there."

Crime was down. Figures just released by the police district in which the University was located showed that in the ten years since the urban renewal project had gotten under way "crimes against the person had dropped from 7.39 per cent of the city's total to 3.91 per cent, and within Hyde Park-Kenwood itself to 2.09 per cent."

The news caused a certain relaxation of vigilance. Responding to an alarm from one of the women's dorms, the campus cops left their car at the curb with the motor running. The prowler meanwhile exited by another door, hopped into the car, and made a clean getaway.

Our boys in blue redeemed themselves, however, when they

later spotted a youngster in the act of snatching a purse from a woman walking along Fifty-ninth Street. They gave chase, in a patrol car, and the boy tried to elude them by running down into the grassy stretch along the Midway that is depressed below street level. The police simply followed him.

It was pure Hitchcock: they gunned the car over the curbs and sidewalks and hurtled down the embankment in pursuit. The young thief was so unnerved by the sight and sound of a car where no car should be that he froze in fright. All the cops had to do was open the car door, and he meekly climbed in.

There was also raw material for farce in the visits that year of two VIP's.

One, alas, I cannot name. He was the Prime Minister and President-Designate of an African nation which was about to gain its independence from Great Britain. We made plans suitable for welcoming a Head of State, then had to backtrack when the slightly frosty voice of the British consul-general reminded us that Her Majesty Queen Elizabeth was still the head of that particular state. Further complications arose when His Excellency's advance men informed us that the party would include two ladies who were not to be named or listed or photographed; and what kind of award or medal or other honor did we propose to confer on the Prime Minister?

My Puritan back went up at the thought of entertaining a traveling harem in my house, but that part turned out fine. One of the ladies was about eighteen years old, sweet and shy; I quite understood why, once she had caught his eye, she couldn't have evaded a summons from His Excellency. The other lady was a police matron type whose job on tour was to protect the girl from improper advances or influences. They threw Mrs. Galloway into a tizzy by requesting orange pop instead of a cocktail.

The "award or medal or other honor" posed a problem. The University of Chicago is sticky about such things. Honorary degrees are given only to scholars, and the two medals which are sometimes awarded to non-scholars are restricted either to

alumni or to generally acclaimed public servants. Formally constituted committees act in each instance as guardians of the trust,
and they take their responsibilities seriously. Our distinguished
guest therefore had to settle for a flowery citation which was
hand-lettered on parchment.

Edward Levi, a great pragmatist, subsequently proposed that
the University have a medal struck which would be given just
to visiting Heads of State. The virtue of such a medal would
be that no one would have to determine whether the visitor in
question deserved recognition by the University.

"If it should turn out that he was unworthy of a medal,"
Edward said, "we could always say that it wasn't our fault but
that of his government."

I *can* name the second VIP. He was Premier Fanfani of Italy.
We were eager for him to come to campus because the University
was already looking ahead to the Twenty-fifth Anniversary of
the first controlled release of atomic energy, an event that had
been presided over by Enrico Fermi in 1942, and it was hoped
that Italy might contribute funds for a Fermi memorial.

Since Premier Fanfani's visit to this country was an official
one, he had come on from Washington with the full retinue
provided by the State Department and the national security
agencies. Consequently, after visiting the site where the Atomic
Age had begun, a cavalcade of sleek black limousines flying
Italian and American flags glided majestically up to our door
and delivered their passengers for a scheduled thirty-minute
cocktail party.

They must have been thirsty. Seemingly dozens of small dark
men in neat dark suits and neat dark ties came rushing into the
house. Five minutes of bedlam followed. Which was Fanfani?
Which was the State Department man? Which was Secret
Service? The man from the mayor's office? The correspondent
from *Newsweek?* The political assassin? Happily, there was no
assassin, and in due course I got most of our guests identified
and a receiving line of sorts put together in the living room.

We had invited all the Italian students we could round up, as well as an assortment of physicists, and everybody had a jolly time. None of the Italians spoke English; even the Premier bogged down after "Gin and soda, please."

The language barrier was surmountable at a party like ours—but that night, at the mayor's official civic banquet downtown, the head table was strangely silent. The city greeters had interspersed the visiting Italians with local bigwigs of appropriate rank, most of whom were Irish or Polish, and had neglected to provide interpreters.

Upon departure from the city, the Premier announced that he would recommend to his government that the finest sculptor in Italy be commissioned to do a sculpture as a Chicago memorial to Fermi. Joy reigned on campus. Unfortunately, the Italian Government fell, and Fanfani with it, before funds had been appropriated or the sculpture commissioned.

Other University visitors that year included two Britons—Sir Leslie Munro (who was charming) and George Brown (who was boorish); three Supreme Court justices; and a passel of writers and poets (among them Baldwin, Mailer, Spender, and Anaïs Nin, the latter enveloped still in the aura of Paris in the twenties). On the home front, William MacNeill's *The Rise of the West* turned into a national best-seller despite its being a work of impeccable historical scholarship.

Red came home for the summer and worked again at the newspaper library. When it was announced that Don Swanson had been appointed Dean of the University's Graduate Library School, Red's boss shook his head in amazement and said, "Where but at the University of Chicago would a *physicist* become the dean of a library school?"

The reason was simplicity itself. Don's specialty is the relationship between natural and computer languages and the use of computers in storing and retrieving information. The big problem that libraries face everywhere is how to store the weighty masses of volumes they already own, find room for the avalanche that keeps coming, yet make particular books or periodicals easily available to users whose needs are wholly individual. The answer lies in miniaturization and electronics, and the Graduate Library School was getting ready to point the way.

In '63, the Art Colony—those picturesque though decrepit shacks that had once been souvenir stands at the World's Fair of 1893—finally came down, an event that caused a small spurt in sales of Harper Court debentures.

We made further gains when we gave a cocktail party in the studio where Lorado Taft had once worked. Prospective investors were met at the door by a bigger-than-life-size plaster cast of a Greek goddess (nude) around whose neck was hung a sign saying, "I gave my shirt for Harper Court. What will you give?" A cast of an equally heroic male figure, with arms bound behind his back, was labeled, "I'm slaving for Harper Court. How about you?" Our third attraction was the artist Harry Bouras, whose golden tongue could convince anyone that found objects of metal, when welded together, are indispensable additions to the contemporary scene. He performed the same service for Harper Court.

By November 1, George Watkins' daily reports showed that we had raised $22,600. His big coup, however, was to have persuaded the Investments Committee of the University's Board of Trustees that they wanted to get in on a good thing, too. The upshot was a canny offer: the University would buy the *final* $35,000 worth of debentures. This reduced the amount we had to raise from $120,000 to $90,000, and at the same time acted as a spur.

"Great!" Eleanor Petersen said, when George broke the news at a Harper Court Board meeting. "Now we have only a little over sixty-seven thousand dollars to go."

We all groaned. This whole project was obviously impossible.

"Oh, come on," said George. "All we have to do is to find sixty-seven people with a thousand dollars each and an antique chair they can't get anyone to fix."

Put that way, it sounded possible after all.

At the same Board meeting, Bruce Sagan announced that the

Chicago Humane Society would give us one of its old dog-horse-and-people fountains, a cast-iron relic of a period in Chicago history when shoppers and strollers could pause for a sip from the top jet on the sidewalk side of the fountain, horses could be watered from a deep trough on the curb side, and dogs could drink from a small basin at street level. We accepted with enthusiasm; how nice to be able to provide amenities for all comers!

We had acquired a new Board member, Charles Reich, vice-president of one of the city's large grocery store chains, and put him in charge of Tenant Selection. He immediately informed us that he and his committee required guidelines. If they had to choose between a potter and a used bookstore, or between a Swedish bakery and a repairer of clocks, to which enterprise should they give priority?

Consequently, Ned Rosenheim found himself drafting a Standards of Selection and Occupancy Statement (which, if nothing else, was a change of pace for a professor whose specialty is the satire of Jonathan Swift). As soon as the document was completed and approved, Chuck Reich tested it by asking, "How do you people want to classify a dealer in tropical fish? Is he Category Two, 'a purveyor of esthetic materials'? Or is he Category Four, 'a retailer of unusual and superior commodities'?"

There was general laughter, culminating in some derogatory remarks about guppies and a spirited defense of swordtails.

"You won't think it's so funny when the time comes to actually choose the tenants," Chuck predicted. "Don't forget that Category Two takes precedence over Category Four."

So we sobered up and got back to work again. By golly, we *would* keep "the useful arts" in Hyde Park.

At home, there was a period when I had to soft-pedal any talk of the arts, or of building. The University's new conference center had opened, its cost having so far exceeded estimates and its losses in the first six months of operation having been so great that my husband got angry whenever he thought of it. In addition, the word "happening" was acquiring a new connotation in the national lexicon, and George's experience with that particular art form had been an unhappy one, too.

Instead of participating in a panel discussion on modern art (for which he had received a travel reimbursement and an honorarium), Bruce Conner had sat mute on the platform after having dumped a suitcase full of marbles on the stage. That had been his sole contribution to the "discussion."

At about the same time, Claes Oldenburg had come to campus and set up shop so close to our house that George could easily hear the motorcycle roaring around inside a building that had wooden floors. He was not amused to hear that a member of the College faculty had presided over the evening's festivities while wearing a steel helmet and swim fins; and when he found out that the "happening" had also included the throwing of mud at a freshly painted wall (to represent the passage of the sun from east to west) and the dropping of kapok-filled bags from the ceiling onto the heads of the spectators (to represent turds), he was outraged. The fact that the students had loved the shindy was immaterial. Didn't anybody have any sense around here?

Sixteen

A glance at a university's Table of Organization makes its governance appear pretty straightforward. It's a corporation. It has a charter. Like business corporations, it has a policy-making board, the trustees, who correspond to company directors. They hire a president to head the administrative bureaucracy that runs the institution. It's all there on the chart: vertical lines leading downward from the trustees past various groups to the students, and horizontal lines connecting the administrators at each level—the provost, deans, department chairmen, professors—to the particular segments of the whole which are their responsibility.

So why should universities be so difficult to govern?

The main reason is that orders do *not* pass down the line from the president to the provost to the deans and so on. True, the deans are there and so are the department chairmen, but even if born executives happen to fill these spots they have no authority to order the behavior of those who are below them on the chart. Their effectiveness depends on persuasion and example.

And the reason? No faculty member considers himself to be an *employee* of the university. Indeed, the shoe is on the other foot. He believes that the administrative apparatus of the institution exists to serve his needs as a virtually self-employed practitioner of scholarship. As indeed it does.

A new university president once made the mistake of referring to the people on the academic side of the university as "my faculty," and was immediately corrected.

A professor said to him, "You may be *our* president, sir, but we are not *your* faculty."

The only authority acceptable to the people on the academic side is that of their peers. It is difficult, for example, to live with your colleagues if you are the sole member of a department who refuses to teach a segment of a survey course for freshmen that the department has agreed to offer. It is equally difficult for a scholar to cling to a theory or research finding if other people in his field have shot either his assumptions or his data full of holes. But it is easy—in fact, obligatory—to resist anything resembling an order from any administrator who shows up on the Table of Organization as your "superior."

Shortly after he resigned as President of the University of Chicago, Larry Kimpton happened to meet a Chicago professor in another city. In the course of a brief conversation, he learned that the professor was there to act as a consultant for a business firm. Most universities try to curb activity of this sort, because (lucrative though it is for the consultant) it interrupts the research and teaching that the faculty member was hired to do.

So Larry said to his chance companion, "Well, I guess I'm in no position now to tell you how to spend your time."

"You never were," the professor shot back.

There is a good historical reason for this attitude. Universities began, in the Middle Ages, as a conglomeration of Masters around whom groups of students clustered. Only as increasing numbers of students wished to hear the great men lecture did it become necessary to have some kind of administrative apparatus. Someone had to rent a lecture hall; someone had to collect the fees that were necessary to pay for it; someone had to answer inquiries from aspiring students.

The Masters could have done this themselves, but very early on they discovered that if they hired someone to do the clerical work for them they would have more time for research and teaching. So they got themselves a registrar, or some similar functionary. However, *they* set policy for the university; the registrar and any other administrators were merely the hired help.

And that's pretty much how it stayed until the middle of the nineteenth century. The president of an American college—there weren't any universities in the United States before 1876 —was simply the senior professor and the presiding officer at faculty meetings. The institution's service staff could be counted on the fingers of one hand.

As colleges grew into universities, as universities took on a variety of jobs that universities had never done before (the community service role of the land-grant universities, for instance), and as the number of professors and students doubled and tripled and quadrupled, the modern university bureaucracy was born. The first vice-president was appointed in 1889; the first dean of the faculties in 1891; the first business manager in 1906.

When one knows this, an anecdote about the early days at the University of Chicago suddenly fits into context. In 1892, a visitor, entering Cobb Hall, asked a scrubwoman where to find William Rainey Harper.

"I dunno," she said, "I jes' scrub."

When the visitor repeated this remark to the President, Harper replied, "We are beginning to specialize, you see."

Colleges and universities have by now acquired a host of administrators whose jobs are directly related to instructional activities (student counselors, librarians, catalog editors, secretaries, and so on) and in addition employ a large number of people who serve the academics only in part or only indirectly. The bookstore, for instance, carries textbooks *and* office supplies. The personnel office keeps records on everyone in the place but hires only non-academic employees. The bursar and the campus cops serve the whole establishment.

Some of the people who are most intimately connected with the institution never set foot in a classroom or library, and might as well be working for a supermarket. Others, equally intimately engaged in the university's affairs, never have reason to visit the treasurer; don't know the name of the purchasing agent; and don't realize that one of the busiest offices in the place is that of the legal counsel.

What has evolved is two institutions in one: a businesslike organization that manages the university but does not set policy for the academic side; and the academic side, which determines its own destiny, thank you, but requires the services of the bureaucracy to handle the details. And that's why universities are hard to govern. You have on the one hand a group of people who are accustomed to the hierarchical relationships of business corporations and consider the administrators to be the holders of *line* jobs in the organization; and on the other hand you have a group of people who consider those self-same administrators to be the holders of *staff* jobs.

This, incidentally, is the reason that administrators dealing directly with the academic people are, in any well-run university, themselves the possessors of academic backgrounds. You can successfully hire a comptroller whose experience has been wholly in business, but a vice-president who has to deal with the faculty committees that plan new buildings is likely to have a nervous breakdown if he comes to the university setting from a business corporation.

That the general public doesn't comprehend this duality of university management, or appreciate why the faculty should control the academic program, is unfortunate but not necessarily disastrous. A college or university can get into real trouble, however, when its trustees don't understand its curious structure. Most trustees are businessmen, and much of their activity on behalf of the institution deals with such matters as the budget or the management of investments. So it is understandable that they often believe the place should be run on the chain-of-command basis which is characteristic of business firms. And many are never reconciled to the reality.

A recent survey of five thousand college and university trustees showed that the typical holder of that position is a business executive in his fifties, socially and politically conservative, who believes that the administrators' university should dominate the faculties' university (and also that the students should be seen but not heard). He is the kind of man who expects the deans to tell the professors what to do.

If he lives in the South, in the Rocky Mountain states, or in the Southwest, he is likely to be even more conservative than his counterparts in the nation's more populous and urbanized areas. If he is an elected trustee of a public institution (or a regent, a popular title for the same job), he is more conservative than his counterparts at private institutions. He is also more authoritarian, meaning that he balks at delegating responsibility to faculty or students.

Of all trustees, those who are appointed to the boards of private institutions are the most sophisticated about college or university governance. It is unusual to find a Reed or Swarthmore or Stanford trustee who seriously believes that he and his fellow board members should determine the curriculum or consider a faculty member's political views when deciding whether to give him tenure, whereas such beliefs are fairly common among the trustees of public junior colleges.

I do not suggest that trustees should rubber-stamp all proposals coming from the academic side of the fence. They are, after all, legally responsible for whatever goes on at the institution. But they should be more willing than many are to approve activity they don't understand or even like, taking a chance that what looks like heresy may instead be a step on the road to truth.

If a faculty or student body is free to follow any line of rational inquiry to its logical conclusion, there will inevitably be some people on campus who espouse unpopular points of view, or whose behavior deviates greatly from the accepted norms of middle-class society. Those trustees who can withstand the consequent viewing-with-alarm by fellow members of the Union League Club are the more likely to preside over a college or university of quality.

As a society, we would have been much more capable of intelligently handling the current "drug culture" if individuals and agencies external to the universities had not prevented research on LSD and marijuana during the 1950's and early 1960's.

The same danger lurks *within* the university family if any policy-making group can arbitrarily abridge academic freedom. If Big Brother types are in command, they can create a faculty and student body which spends a lot of time griping about restrictions, or actively opposing them, thus diverting energies that should be going into teaching or learning. Or they can create an intellectual wasteland by discouraging the presence on campus of the unconventional and controversial people who quite often make the big discoveries in scholarship and science, and who always leaven the dough.

George laughs every time he remembers a luncheon meeting arranged by one of Chicago's trustees for executives of business corporations who, it was hoped, might contribute funds to the University. As bait, our economist Milton Friedman was signed up as speaker of the day.

After his speech, the trustee who was the host—trying to make the transition from the marketplace to the ivory tower—said, "Don't you agree, Professor Friedman, that business corporations have a primary responsibility to support institutions of higher learning?"

"Certainly not," Milton snapped. "The primary responsibility of business corporations is to make money for their stockholders."

Happily, this testimony to the freedom of Chicago professors to speak their minds so amused and impressed several people at the luncheon that they did become donors (presumably of funds in excess of those to which their stockholders were entitled).

The university's president and other officers of the corporation are the middlemen. Their jobs are shaped by the attitude of the trustees toward governance of the institution and by the attitude of the faculty and students toward the policies set by the trustees. If there is distrust or hostility or even a serious misunderstanding of long duration between these two groups, the middlemen can spend all their time acting as buffers. This is joyless and exhausting, so men with good potential for leadership quit the job. Or else they choose sides, which is just as bad for them and the institution. What usually happens (in the words of the Harvard professor of government Stanley Hoffman) is that "they become unstuck, like hinges in a burning building, unsure of which piece of carpentry to fall with."

I don't suppose that any college or university has at all times in its history experienced harmonious relationships among trustees, officers, and academics. In fact, it was because of a dispute between two of this triumvirate at Chicago that an organizational structure was created which enables members of each group to keep easily and regularly in touch with each other, and for twenty years has prevented many an incipient crisis from developing.

For this happy circumstance one must thank Robert M. Hutchins, who so angered a segment of the faculty by his efforts to appoint professors that they asked the Board of Trustees to intervene. A wise chairman of the Board, Laird Bell, refused to establish a precedent for such intervention. Instead, he drafted a statute that clearly defines the responsibilities delegated by the Board to its officers and to the academic bodies, and in addition establishes a fifty-one-member elected Council of the faculty, which meets monthly and acts as a clearing house for all campus interest groups. It has an executive committee of seven, which meets at two-week intervals.

Student petitions to the faculty channel through the Council, or its executive committee. The College, Schools, and Divisions bring joint problems before it. Actions that the trustees are considering are reported to it. Because it is "the supreme academic body of the University," everyone knows where to go to get a hearing. Because it meets often, it can keep its finger on the pulse of University life, and can defuse potentially explosive situations before disputants' positions have hardened.

And what's so remarkable about that, you might ask? It's obviously a good idea. It is remarkable because it is such a rarity. When problems of concern to the entire faculty arise at most colleges and universities, the whole faculty senate must be convened. This is a large body even in small schools. It is so enormous in a big university, even if only tenured professors belong to it, that resolution of any but the simplest problems is impossible because the members of the group talk each other to death. Much of the turmoil on the nation's campuses in the late 1960's could have been prevented if administrators had been able *quickly* to sample faculty opinion, or obtain decisions from its members as a group. At Chicago, in contrast, the Committee of the Council (the seven-man group) routinely met with administrators.

The creation of that system of internal governance is an example of how valuable to a university a good chairman of a board of trustees can be.

When things go right, the chairman of the board has a relationship to the president of the institution that is comparable to that of the president to the provost. Although each has separate major concerns, each serves as informant and consultant to the other, and neither "speaks for" the university until he has discussed his proposed statement with the other.

During the 1962 sit-in at Chicago, George had to go to California to meet with alumni groups. While he was away, another University officer decided to "clear the bums out" of the Administration Building. But when he informed Glen Lloyd of his intention, Glen said, "I don't think I would, if I were you. It might compromise George's position with the faculty or students."

That's an example of how valuable to a university president a good chairman of a board of trustees can be.

At the new presidents' institute which George and I had attended in 1962, I had been struck by the combination of fear and hostility toward their trustees which some of the presidents' wives could not suppress. In contrast, George and I ranked ours high on our list of blessings.

Chicago has had only eight chairmen of its Board, and we have known six of them. Their personalities and backgrounds have been very different, and the University has required different kinds of services from them, but in their attitudes toward the institution and its governance they have been astoundingly alike. They have taken the job seriously, worked hard at it, and maintained a scrupulous correctness in their relationship to both administrators and faculty.

Nothing changed for George, therefore, when Glen Lloyd retired in June of 1963, and Fairfax Cone became the new chairman of the Board. Happily—as with the Lloyds—we could also call the Cones our personal friends.

A good chairman can establish a climate within the Board itself which provides on-the-job training for those of its members who don't at heart believe in academic freedom. At Chicago, faculty members are often invited to attend trustees' meetings and report on their work. In addition, all trustees are assigned to visiting committees. Many institutions use this device as a bridge between the campus and the man on the street outside. They appoint a lay group of "visitors" who periodically meet with faculty and students in one of the academic disciplines. The usual result is the development of more trust in the educational process on the part of the laymen.

This outcome is especially desirable in the case of trustees, because their major role outside of approving policy for the institution is to act as its ambassadors to the public. One of the saddest effects of the student rebellions of the 1960's was that many boards of trustees became punitive toward the institutions they were supposed to defend from public attack. When this happens, the effect upon the institution can be as tragic as when one member of a family stabs another.

Without trustees there would also be far less money in the college's or university's bank account.

Any institution that appoints a trustee primarily because he or she is rich is likely to rue the day, but nothing is nicer than to find someone who will be a good trustee and is rich *too*. Without soliciting outside their own ranks, the University of Chicago's trustees put together a three-million-dollar purse to help George lure eminent professors to our faculty, and the benefactions of individual trustees over the years (frequently anonymously given) have added up to ten times as much.

In addition, trustees can help a university obtain funds or assistance from outside sources. The little old lady who is unknown to anyone at the institution but bequeaths it ten million dollars hidden in her mattress is more myth than reality. The little old ladies who *do* give money to colleges and universities are usually friends of the trustees, and give the money at a trustee's urging. Often, too, officers of fund-granting foundations—money-management men, most of them—are more comfortable discussing possible grants with men whose background is similar to their own.

It is doubtful whether urban renewal in Hyde Park-Kenwood could have succeeded without the University of Chicago's Board of Trustees. Real estate developers reluctant to invest in what was clearly a "changing neighborhood"? Mortgage money hard to come by? Legislation bogged down in some congressional subcommittee? Police services slacking off again? Usually, someone on the Board had a friend who knew someone who was close to . . .

Show me a good university and it will have a good Board of Trustees.

Seventeen

Ralph McGill is respectfully remembered as the publisher of the Atlanta *Constitution* and, as such, the major voice of moderation in a South torn by civil rights protest in the 1950's and 1960's. But Ralph McGill was once a scrawny kid from Chattanooga who was a freshman at Vanderbilt University in 1917, and who got a spot on the varsity football team because older and bigger men were off at war. In his autobiography, *The South and the Southerner*, he told of a memorable experience:

Alonzo Stagg's Chicago team was on our schedule and as that game approached, excitement mounted. Freshmen made up a good half of the squad. Few had ever been in a Pullman sleeper and not one of us had ever been to Chicago. We arrived on a Friday morning, and some of us rode the elevated in from the Midway hotel where we were housed, and walked along by Lake Michigan, thrilled by its beauty, awed by its size . . .

The two coaches were friends. They arranged for the teams to have dinner together on Friday evening. We from Tennessee were somewhat self-conscious and when, dinner done, the Chicago squad began to sing some of their university songs and one or two made popular by vaudeville, we were tremendously impressed. When they were done their captain said that perhaps we would like to sing some Vanderbilt songs.

Sing? We were struck dumb with an agony of fear. Sing? We had never sung. At Vanderbilt, singing was done by the glee club. We had never thought of singing together. So we sat there, dry of lips, tongues cloven to the roofs of our mouths. Then our coach, God bless him, stood. Surely he would rescue us. But no. Though neither he nor we could carry a tune, he would not have us fail to respond. We would, he said, have a try at our Alma Mater.

And so, with our tuneless coach leading us we lifted up our voices and sang, thinly and awkwardly, the one song whose words we knew. Its tune and its words, like so many, many Alma Maters of secondary schools and colleges over the land, revealed a liberal borrowing from Cornell. The urbane Chicago squad sat without smiling. They even gave us a nice round of applause, though I'm sure they all howled when we were gone.

The next afternoon they ran us into the ground, 42 to 0.

I quoted that passage in a speech I gave annually to new women students (one whose purpose was to give them a taste of University history), and they were always amused by the anecdote. But they never connected the Chicago of 1917 with the one at which they were enrolled. To a college generation which in general had demoted the star quarterback from his once high place in the hierarchy of campus heroes, and at Chicago in particular had also added a deep distrust of competitive sports, the period of collegiate athletic history dominated by Amos Alonzo Stagg and his contemporaries was impossible to understand.

I told them, and other people told them, that when William Rainey Harper appointed Stagg to the University's first faculty, people really did believe that physical fitness was akin to godliness, and that organized sports such as football were important vehicles for building character in young men. It was also a fact that Stagg's character was so exemplary and his personality so winning that students played football as much for the honor of being associated with him as for the excitement of the game itself.

Stagg had invented the tackling dummy when he was a student at Yale. His later innovations included the numbering of players' uniforms, conceiving the end-around play, the fake place-kick, the man in motion, and the T formation. He also pioneered the use of the forward pass. With these, plus painstaking coaching, he built great teams, the best in the country. In 1905, for instance, the Chicago Maroons won every game, with a total of 245 points to 5 for their opponents.

They were still great in the 1920's, but in the 1930's they began to slide—not because Stagg had lost his touch but because he refused to go professional. Other universities in what was by then called the Big Ten Conference not only had many more students to choose from than the University of Chicago but in addition had begun to recruit men just to play football. Chicago still required its football players to carry the same academic load that other students did, and couldn't field enough brainy young men who were at the same time brawny enough to withstand the manhandling that the college football teams of the thirties gave and got from each other.

After Stagg retired (in 1933, at the age of seventy), it was downhill all the way. In 1939, Illinois beat Chicago 46–0; Virginia, 47–0; Harvard, 61–0; Ohio State, 61–0; and Michigan, 85–0. So Robert M. Hutchins pulled the University of Chicago out of big-time football and announced that *this* university, for one, was going to concentrate on private education instead of public entertainment. "The Monsters of the Midway" were no more.

It was a situation made to order for satire, and the wits of the Second City troupe—most of them University of Chicago alumni, who then played from a stage in the heart of Hyde Park—took full advantage of it. In one of their most fondly remembered routines, the University proposes to return to Big Ten competition, and the coach is interviewing possible players.

Throckmorton, a Divinity student, is among them; and the dialogue goes this way:

> Coach: So you want to play football, Throckmorton?
> Throckmorton: Indeed, I trust I may, sir, yes.
> Coach: I think you can. You look to me like you'd be . . . oh, about a hundred and ninety-five.
> Throckmorton (obviously pleased): Do your really, sir?
> Coach: You weigh about a hundred and ninety-five?
> Throckmorton (disappointed): Oh I thought you meant my IQ.

Another segment involved a mathematics major named Morgenstern.

> Morgenstern: Mr. Throckmorton, he's our center?
> Coach: Right, he's the center.
> Morgenstern: But you can't begin in the middle.
> Coach: We do . . .
> Morgenstern: Oh no, you have to have a beginning to get through the middle to get to the end.
> Coach: Who says so?
> Morgenstern: Aristotle.
> Coach: And who did he play for?
> Morgenstern: Oh, Alexander the Great, Philip of Macedon, that whole crowd.
> Throckmorton: St. Thomas Aquinas said the same thing, sir.
> Coach: Oh, a Notre Dame boy. All right, fine.

The latter exchange was a play within a play. It was the kind of general gibe at anti-intellectualism that any sophisticated audience would appreciate, but at the same time it was a parochial poke at the "Hutchins" College, where heavy emphasis was given to philosophy and logic, and the "Great Books" were required reading.

To the extent that University of Chicago students of the

1960's knew anything about the institution's football history, their knowledge was colored by emotionalism. They strongly disapproved of the double standard of contemporary admissions policies which at many universities differentiated between "athletes" and "students," and were proud of the fact that at Chicago one engaged in sports only for fun. In addition, they were passionately devoted to the ideals of the "Hutchins" College. In fact, twenty-five years after its peak, and ten years after the University had begun to change it, it was so romanticized by many College students that one could only describe them as members of a cult. As the president of Vincent House had said after the visit of George Lincoln Rockwell, Chicago's *not* having a football team had great symbolic value.

In 1904, when the University had dedicated its new Bartlett Gymnasium, William Rainey Harper had turned it over to Stagg with a light and fanciful remark: "May you live a hundred years to enjoy it." And Stagg *did;* in fact, he lived to be 101. After his retirement from Chicago, he had gone to the University of the Pacific in Stockton and coached for another twenty years. He had hit 100 in August of 1962, and although by then he was too frail to travel to Chicago, the University had had a centennial celebration for him in absentia.

Dan Robins had been asked to play a special carillon concert at noon on Stagg's birthday, and readily agreed. But when he learned that the Stagg Centennial Committee had in mind such tunes as *Wave the Flag for Old Chicago,* his back went up.

"I do not play folk music on my carillon," he had said; and that was that. The committee members were distraught but helpless, and Dan had saluted Stagg with a fine all-Bach concert.

However, at that night's reunion banquet of Stagg's "boys," they had managed to be both more frivolous and more nostalgic, and in the course of the event had announced that efforts to raise money for scholarships in Stagg's name had been so successful that two full-tuition awards could be made in the following year.

When the student newspaper had subsequently reported that two "scholar-athletes" would be coming to the campus in 1963, one could sense a small stirring of unease among the undergraduates. Then they had discovered that thirty men were already enrolled in what the athletic department called a "football class," and had played two games—officially called "scrimmages" because no scores were kept—with another college. In 1963, over forty men signed up for the football class; three "scrimmages" were scheduled; and the fat was in the fire.

A spokesman for the anti-football faction wrote in the student newspaper that

> . . . the common distractions from the academic aspect of most universities are sports, fraternity-sorority life, and pressure to conform to some social pattern. At the University of Chicago, all three are of minor significance. Our atmosphere is one of intellectual intensity, non-conformity, and involvement in the social and political problems of our society . . .
>
> Until this year, the absence of intercollegiate football was an important symbol of this unique character and spirit. With destruction of the symbol may come the destruction of that which it symbolized. The return of intercollegiate football will encourage the application and subsequent admission of non-academically oriented students, which in turn will change the spirit of the University by changing the character of its student body.

In rebuttal, another student wrote that *he* didn't credit the intellectual aura of the University of Chicago to the absence of a football team but to the presence of a capable and dynamic faculty and student body.

"If the people on this campus cannot remember that they are serious students, merely because there are forty-some men playing football in Stagg Field," he wound up, "then the disintegration of the College is not beginning, it is complete."

The University's administrators, of course, agreed with this

second view. George and I, for one example, had gone that fall
to a football game at Northwestern, as guests of the Roscoe
Millers. It had been a marvelous change, one of those it's-a-
great-place-to-visit-but-I-wouldn't-want-to-live-there afternoons,
and on our way home George had talked a little about the
effect on a university of big-time football.

The costs of maintaining a stadium, personnel to service the
players, team travel expenses, and so on are so great a drain on
funds, he said, that the institution *has* to fill that stadium with
paying customers. The customers won't come unless they get a
good show for their money. Hence the pressure to recruit good
players, and the temptation to find (or create) special courses of
study for the not-so-bright ones.

Knowing all this, neither he nor any other officer of the
University of Chicago could foresee a time when the University
would return to the Big Ten. The foolishness of such a move
was so self-evident, they thought, that they failed to gauge
correctly the mood of those students who saw the "football
class" as a portent of worse evils to come. They didn't, for
example, formally respond to a Student Government resolution
which approved the return of intercollegiate football *on condition that:*

1) The budget of the athletic department be made a public
document;

2) No admission charges be levied for football games;

3) The expenses of any projected football team not exceed
those of the basketball or track team;

4) The Stagg Scholarships be awarded primarily on the basis
of academic achievement and only to students in financial need;

5) No formal recognition be given for excellence on the football field;

6) A committee of faculty members be appointed to review,
at two-year intervals, the status of football at the University of
Chicago, and that the University disband the program if the
faculty committee so recommended.

Either these conditions were already in effect or, in the opinion of the administrators, could be so taken for granted that it was unnecessary to formalize them. And one was downright discriminatory. ("So it's all right to get a letter for basketball but not for football?" George snorted.) Nevertheless, it would have been wise of him to have cooled things down by officially responding to the Student Government resolution.

Instead, things heated up—with television providing the flame. There were plenty of old-timers in Chicago who remembered Jay Berwanger, the University's "one-man team" of the mid-thirties, and it suddenly struck CBS that a little footage of a University of Chicago scrimmage with the junior varsity of North Central College might be an entertaining feature on the evening news. When the camera crew turned up at the game site, word spread across the campus like wildfire. A couple of self-appointed leaders of the anti-football forces hastily gathered some troops; and, a hundred and fifty strong, laughing and chanting, they advanced on Stagg Field.

The students who organized the march didn't think beyond "going over there to protest," and once they got there they didn't know what to do with their followers. Nor, because the demonstration had erupted so suddenly, was there anyone at the game site who knew anything about crowd control. After milling about for a bit, then, a few of the students marched onto the field and sat down on the fifty-yard line. With whoops and hollers, the others followed suit. CBS loved it: a football sit-in was going to be far more entertaining than a football game.

Taking a firm position in a dispute forecloses options for compromise, and the longer the kids stayed seated the harder it was for them to stand up and leave. The protest had started out at least partly as a lark, but now the mood became sullen. The campus cops commanded them to leave, which only made them pugnacious. Assorted deans tried persuasion—"Come on now, you've had your fun; let other people have theirs"—but it was too late for that approach, too. The protest had ceased to be "fun" and was now a righteous crusade.

Both the Chicago and North Central players climbed into the

stands to get a better view of the sit-in. Other students, drawn to the site by the fast-spreading news on the campus grapevine, stood on the sidelines and either encouraged or denounced the sit-inners. Finally, in twos and threes, they left; and when only a stubborn trio remained, the campus cops carried them off. The sit-in had lasted for ninety minutes.

The game was played (with shortened quarters), and North Central won. Not that it mattered. The news story was the sit-in, not the score; and it got a big play in the press. The students' impulsive action had accomplished exactly what they had wanted to prevent: nationwide publicity about the "return of intercollegiate football" to the University of Chicago. Even worse, the news coverage made them look silly.

By the next day, most of them realized that it *was* a trivial cause and they *had* been juvenile in their behavior. But even supposedly mature adults get defensive when they have been revealed as fools, so it wasn't surprising that these young people couldn't find a graceful way to admit error.

Their sense of shame was intensified by the attitude of many fellow students. Some were angry because the sit-in, at that point in history still identified with the high moral purposes of the early civil rights movement, had been "cheapened." Others felt that the sit-in had suggested—to a nationwide audience!— that University of Chicago students were a bunch of "un-thinking, obstructionist reactionaries" instead of the cool-headed intellectuals that our students then prided themselves upon being. Oh, how the recriminations flew!

Even the University's administrators were swept along by the passions of the moment, George among them. Under pressure from the press, he issued a statement in which he said

> . . . A demonstration that transcends reason, as did that of last Friday on Stagg Field, must not recur. Any student who feels so seriously compelled to deny his fellow students the freedom to engage in a particular sport that he resorts to

such methods of protest, might more appropriately express his disapproval by withdrawing from the University.

The rhetoric was too strong for the occasion. The proposed solution was too drastic for the provocation. Neither he nor anybody else thought to mention that it was the students' concern for the unique character of the College which had motivated the protest. Nobody realized that the University's stern *in loco parentis* stance would leave a residue of resentment among immature young people who were desperately determined not to be regarded as immature. So the football sit-in, ludicrous though it was, left scars.

Berkeley was now less than a year away.

Eighteen

The date was November 22, 1963. The time was about 1 P.M.
I had just left off a piece of china for repair, and was descending
from the top floor of the loft building in a rickety elevator run
by a grizzled old man. I was the only passenger.

As we pulled level with the first floor, the operator said,
"Passenger I just took up told me that President Kennedy has
been shot. In Texas. It was a news flash on the radio."

"Shot?" I replied. "Or shot *at?*"

"That's all I know. Just what the other lady said."

He spoke matter-of-factly, without emotion. So did I.
Stretched between us was an instinctive realization that such
news must be approached cautiously, non-committally, because
if the President *had* been shot . . .

There are few newsstands in that part of town. When I
found one, the headlines of the papers on display had to do with
a local scandal. The newsstand was unmanned. Was the news
flash true? Did anyone know? I wanted to ask someone. But
which of the people hurrying by, apparently intent on their own
business, should I ask?

I dropped in at a restaurant on Jackson Boulevard. Aside
from the usual hum of conversation and the clatter of crockery
one hears at such places, all was quiet. I ordered a hamburger.
Should I ask? When it came, I said to the waitress, keeping my

voice low and the query casual, "I just heard that the President has been shot."

"Yes," she replied. "We heard it on the radio out back. The governor of Texas was shot, too. Killed, they say. But the President wasn't."

She was as matter-of-fact as the elevator operator had been. The presence of a radio "out back"—but tuned so low that the people in the restaurant couldn't hear it—also testified to subconscious recognition of possible calamity in the offing, and reluctance to spread the word.

A few minutes later, the waitress came back to me.

"They say now that he's dead. The President. Not the governor; *he's* alive."

The man on the stool next to me said, "May I have another cup of coffee, please?"

This marked the onset of a curious pattern of behavior that I noticed in myself, and in others, and that extended throughout the afternoon. People mechanically continued their normal activity but at the same time disassociated themselves from others on the personal level. I did not speak to the man on the stool next to me, nor he to me. On the streets, no one looked directly at anyone else, and if eyes happened to meet, each person glanced quickly away.

On Friday afternoons there is a matinee performance by the Chicago Symphony. I had a regular seat. It didn't occur to me not to go; that's what I had come downtown for. All the other ticket-holders were there, too.

The normal time for the concert to start came and went. There was no unusual buzz of conversation as the audience waited. When the manager came onstage and announced that John Kennedy had been assassinated, there was no outcry—just hundreds of indrawn breaths that gave the effect of a small wind sighing through the hall.

The concert was played. There was no applause, little movement. During the intermission, most of us just sat, invisibly walled off from our neighbors, and when the concert was over we silently filed out.

Dusk had come early that day, and there was gusty wind and rain. People were walking heads down, briskly, as if they had definite objectives. They grabbed up newspapers, glanced at the headlines, then folded the papers—quickly, as if by shutting out the headlines they could shut out the news—and hurried on.

On the IC platform, more crowded than was usual at that time of day, people stood quietly, all with folded newspapers, none reading them. The coaches, outward bound from town, were still.

At home, George and I, silent from the moment of greeting, turned on the television. Like millions of others, we were hardly to turn it off for the next three days. We left it that first night—again, like millions of others—only to talk on the telephone to absent members of the family; in our case, Red. But what was there to say? Nothing. The national mood was the same as when death strikes a family, and its members find solace in the mere fact of kinship.

Red wrote us a letter the next day, about the Harvard memorial service for the President. His letter was not notable for its content but for its form. He usually typed his letters on any old paper that came to hand, but this one was carefully handwritten on vellum with a printed letterhead. Like everyone else, Redmond felt that a note of condolence should go to *someone*. It was a queer sensation to realize that the "someone" was all of us.

The National Opinion Research Center, in a later poll, said that the assassination was "a public event unique in the lives of contemporary Americans because of the speed with which the news spread." Less than thirty minutes after the shooting, 68 per cent of adult Americans knew about it. Within six hours, the percentage rose to 99.8.

"Never before," the report says, "have the sentiments of the American people been engaged so quickly and deeply by a political happening; the preoccupation with the event was almost universal."

The weekend was grim. Shock and disbelief gave way to sorrow, shame, and anger. Dallas and Washington were the world. Although much of the verbiage was repetitive and most of the tributes were banal, one couldn't leave the television, couldn't do anything but sit there in a stupor of looking and listening and grieving. It was a relief to go out at last, on the day of the funeral, to the University Memorial Service at Rockefeller Chapel.

In April of the previous year, George and I had gone to a state dinner at the White House. This was the second such occasion; the first time had been during the Eisenhower administration. The guests that time had been the country's leading scientists, and the reason was that the United States had finally gotten a satellite into space. The trauma of Sputnik had been acute, and to honor American scientists had been one way of saying that we *too* had good people in research and engineering.

The banquet had been impressive: white tie, fine china, gold plate, more cutlery than I had ever seen at a single place setting, more pomp than I had ever expected to see again. But the dinner had also been strained (and amusing in retrospect) because few of us had ever been at a state dinner at the White House and we had to grope our way through thickets of protocol and ceremony.

This time, when the Kennedys had decided to honor Nobel laureates,* the guests—having experienced the pomp and ceremony of the royal court in Stockholm—were less naïve, and the atmosphere had been more relaxed. In addition, the Kennedys had dropped white-tie banquests; served cocktails before dinner; and substituted round tables seating ten for the formal U-shaped banquet arrangement that the Eisenhowers had favored.

---

* George's Nobel prize had been awarded in 1958, for demonstrating that genes control the biochemical reactions of living organisms.

A newspaper columnist had referred to the dinner as "the President's Easter egghead roll." There had been a goodly number of academicians present, all right, Nobel laureates and others. Milling around in the East Room before dinner, we had seen several university presidents we knew, members of the Cabinet, White House staff, and others whose faces I'd seen in *Time* magazine but couldn't quite put a name to.

George had the same problem. When we found ourselves face to face with the John Glenns and introduced ourselves, George had made polite conversation but had looked a bit puzzled.

After they had moved on, he had said to me, "Who was *that?* I'd have sworn I knew him, his face was so familiar, but I don't think I do know anybody named Glenn."

It had also taken him a long time to realize that the nice Mrs. Johnson who sat at his right at dinner—a charming brunette in a handsome white satin gown—was Lady Bird.

The aides had gotten us all lined up in good time for the fanfare and *Hail to the Chief,* and then they had guided us rapidly past the President and Mrs. Kennedy (Washington style, with husbands preceding wives). There had been time for no more than a "Good evening" and a quick handshake. Thus I had only a glimpse of the fabled Jacqueline, wearing a slim green chiffon gown and pendant emerald and diamond earrings. With her hair piled on top of her head and her splendid carriage, she had looked every inch a queen, and had seemed as distant. The President was both sturdier in build and less youthful in the face than photographs made him appear.

At dinner, I had been astounded to find myself seated at the same table as the President. My place was directly opposite his, a position at a round table that makes cross-table conversation impossible; but it is a good spot for observation.

Each table had a centerpiece of mixed spring flowers, loosely arranged, as if they had just been picked in a garden, and set into small vermeil baskets. When he came to the table, the President reached over, plucked a blue bachelor button from the centerpiece, and slipped it into the lapel buttonhole of his dinner jacket.

The widows of two Nobel laureates—Mrs. George C. Marshall and Mrs. Ernest Hemingway—had the places of honor. (Mrs. Marshall, upon being told earlier by a White House aide that she would sit at the President's right, had said, "Now, isn't that a nice young man?") I sat between the Caltech physicist Rudolf Mössbauer, whom I already knew, and the poet Robert Frost.

Frost was by then a dear old senile gentleman. He refused to serve himself, and ate virtually nothing of what was put on his plate. When the vanilla and mocha ice cream with fudge sauce came around, however, he demanded a second helping.

The President divided his attention three ways. He spoke to the ladies on either side of him, pleasantly but without deep engagement; and, below table level, he read over the notes for remarks he was to make after dinner. At one point, he took out a pen and started revising the text, scratching out big sections of it. I don't know whether it was then that he had the inspiration for his introductory sentence, or whether it was already part of the previously prepared speech, but it was brilliant.

"I think this is the most extraordinary collection of talent, of human knowledge, that has ever been gathered together at the White House," he said, "with the possible exception of when Thomas Jefferson dined alone."

After dinner, there was to be a reading by Fredric March, and then dancing. As we began to rise from the tables, I hovered over Robert Frost, ready to help him get to his feet if help were needed. In consequence, I witnessed a charming by-play. The President paused as he rose, and looked directly across the table at the old man. His eyes, which had seemed gray and rather bleak, became suddenly bright and very blue, and his expression was that of father for child. Then he walked out, the rest of us following.

Rockefeller Chapel is gray limestone, outside and in. The stained-glass windows are muted lavenders, grays, and golds. It can be a somber place. It *was* a somber place on that November day in 1963, during the Memorial Service for John F. Kennedy.

As is customary on such occasions, the Great Bourdon tolled as many strokes as the age of the person who is being memorialized. The President had been only forty-six; but the dirge, with four-second pauses between each stroke, seemed endless. The sound boomed hollowly through the Chapel.

There is a limit to the amount of lamentation that the spirit can take. So I swung my thoughts to any of the happier times when I had seen any of the Kennedys, and of course a recollection of the dinner for Nobel laureates came quickly to mind.

Linus Pauling, the Caltech chemist, had made a Washington day of it: as one of a group protesting atmospheric tests of nuclear weapons, he had picketed the White House in the morning, then had come there as a dinner guest in the evening. The President had been greatly amused; Mrs. Kennedy, less so.

"Why did you do that?" she had remonstrated. "Every time Caroline sees people outside with signs, she says, 'What's Daddy done now?'"

I remembered how Mrs. Kennedy had looked that night, cool and poised in her green chiffon, and how the President's eyes had changed color and warmed as he had bestowed his loving glance on Robert Frost. But the effort at remembrance didn't work. Much more vivid was the mental picture of a dazed young woman in a blood-spattered pink suit, and of a flag-draped coffin on its slow way to a cemetery.

Nineteen

It was a quiet Christmas. Red had decided to work at the newspaper library during his school holiday, and didn't do much partying in his free time. This was the year he became a scholar, and in talking about his classes he taught us a lot about Chinese war lords, the Spartans, and the Salem witchcraft trials. Nevertheless, I was shocked by Harvard's allowing him to take five history courses,* and nothing else.

"But you're supposed to be getting a liberal education," I protested.

"That was last year," he cheerfully replied. "In junior year you have to pick a field of concentration. You'll be glad to know, though, that I'm auditing a couple of courses—just to broaden myself intellectually."

There was a wicked gleam in his eye, but I missed it. "Oh, good," I said. "What are they?"

"American Political History and American Intellectual History."

"Red!"

"Seriously, Mom, if I expect to go on to the Ph.D., now is the time I have to start. Everyone says that the Ph.D. dissertation most often grows out of the thesis you write in

* Among them were courses that Red referred to as "Rice Paddies" and "Mint Juleps"—which the Harvard catalog describes, respectively, as the History of Far Eastern Civilizations and the History of the South.

your senior year at college. So it's sensible to spend the junior year getting as wide an acquaintance with your field as possible. By next year I'll have narrowed things down to a particular country or period. I think now it'll be early nineteenth-century American, but it's too soon to tell for sure."

Redmond was typical of that exceedingly large number of modern college students who then went on to graduate study. Twenty-five years earlier the situation had been quite different; for instance, at the University of Chicago in the 1930's, 80 per cent of graduates of the College had finished their formal education at that point, whereas in the 1960's the same percentage were heading for graduate school and specialization.

This is why the common curriculum and general survey courses of the "Hutchins" College had become fewer each year since the 1950's. It was also the reason that Edward Levi was currently engaged in a marathon of meetings with College faculty and students. They were trying to figure out a plan of reorganization that would satisfy the majority of students who wanted to specialize while at the same time providing a general education for the minority who did not aspire to graduate study.

Although George kept abreast of these efforts, most of his time was going into a problem affecting the development of nuclear research in the Midwest, and it was giving him a headache of colossal proportions. He didn't even seem to speak English any more, so often was his conversation studded with references to MURA or AEC or FFAG or ZGS.

The proper place to begin the tale is, I guess, with the Argonne National Laboratory, which is just southwest of Chicago at Lamont, Illinois. It is owned by the Atomic Energy Commission (AEC) and was managed for the AEC by the University of Chicago. This was a logical outgrowth of research and development work dating from World War II, when the University's Midway campus had been the site of the first controlled release of atomic energy. By the mid-1960's, Argonne had become a whopping big place with an operating budget of around $75,000,000.

Almost from the beginning, there had been difficulties in implementing Argonne's twin purposes: it was supposed to do work assigned or approved by the AEC, and it was supposed to be a regional center for research in nuclear physics. As a regional center, it was to welcome university people who were not on its staff, allowing them to use its facilities for their own research. But as a federal installation it had administrative policies that didn't permit visiting professors to be wholly freewheeling and independent. In its beginnings it also did enough work that was "classified" (for reasons of national security) to wrap in red tape the procedures for getting permission to use its facilities.

In the early 1950's, therefore, a group of physicists affiliated with a number of Midwestern universities decided that a much happier situation would result if they could get the AEC to build another laboratory, one that would function only as a regional reseach center. This group called itself the Midwestern Universties Research Association (MURA). The University of Chicago (as a university) was a member of MURA, even though the University of Chicago (as a manager) operated Argonne for the AEC.

One of the nuclear physicists' basic research tools is the particle accelerator. It is often designed as a circular tunnel into which electrical energy is poured, causing collisions between subatomic particles. As small bits of matter fly off, scientists can gather data about the composition of the scattered bits.

At one time, a 100-million-volt atom smasher had been considered a good research tool, but by the 1960's a machine of that capacity would no longer suffice.* Given more energy and

* Since 1959, the University of Chicago had been trying to sell a 100-million-volt machine once used by Enrico Fermi and other pioneers in atomic physics. It had cost $450,000 to build in the late 1940's; its replacement cost in the late 1950's was around $1,000,000; and the University was offering it for $100,000—all two hundred tons of it, with three hundred tons of concrete shielding thrown in.

Inquiries came in from several American universities and foreign governments, but in the end nobody wanted a secondhand accelerator. In 1964 it was dismantled and such of its components as were salvageable were sold.

bigger tunnels to pour it into (a half mile or more in cir-
cumference), nuclear physicists could probe ever deeper into
the heart of the atom; and of course they wanted to. Hence,
the accelerator of the 1960's was a machine that delivered its
electron volts in *billions*.

One of MURA's main worries was that the unavailability of
a really high-energy accelerator would cause a "brain drain" of
physicists from Midwestern universities to those on the East
and West coasts, where such accelerators were (or soon would
be) available.

MURA had been encouraged by the AEC to design the
atom smasher of its dreams, and in 1958 it asked for $170,000,000
to build FFAG. The initials stood for Fixed Field Alternating
Gradient synchrotron, and it would be a ten-billion-electron-
volt machine. Its distinctive characteristic was not a tremendous
increase in energy over accelerators then available or in the
design stage, but rather its ability to deliver a much higher intensity beam. (That is, it would provide users with thicker
streams of particles to direct toward their targets.)

The AEC, which never funds a project until design studies
have been made and a proposal has been reviewed by a committee
assembled for that purpose, turned down the MURA proposal.

One of the main reasons was that the AEC had, just the
previous year, authorized the building at Argonne of a twelve-
billion-electron-volt accelerator called ZGS (for Zero Gradient
Synchrotron). Its developers said that it needed to be modified
only slightly to do anything the FFAG would do. They also
said that the research frontiers in physics would soon require
very much higher energies than either ZGS or FFAG could
produce, and if the latter were built the Midwest would never
get a more powerful accelerator.

Predictably, MURA disagreed, and continued to press the
AEC for funding.

While this relatively small-scale dispute had been proceeding,
other and much higher-energy accelerators were in the design
stage elsewhere. Lawrence Radiation Lab in California wanted

money for an accelerator that would generate 200 billion electron volts. Brookhaven in New York was thinking even bigger: it wanted an 800-billion-volt machine. The physicists at these labs argued, like many at Argonne, that the next generation of research scientists would need *really* high-energy accelerators.

All this agitation in scientific circles coincided with that period late in the Kennedy administration when Congress was beginning to realize that the federal budget for scientific research had increased fivefold within the previous five-year period, and that it was costing $143,000,000 a year just to support the nine atom smashers already in existence. So the AEC had sensibly appointed a reviewing board to set some national priorities; and in 1963 the panel had given the nod to high energy rather than high intensity. In short, it approved the Lawrence machine, then the one proposed by Brookhaven, then the FFAG.

This was bad news for MURA, because the panel said that funds should be appropriated for the FFAG *only* if its construction would not slow down the building of the other two. If the AEC could afford to build all three atom smashers at the same time, go ahead; but if splitting available funds three ways would delay completion of the Lawrence and Brookhaven accelerators, dump FFAG. Inasmuch as following these priorities would require over $200,000,000 in 1965 alone, it was ridiculous to suppose that Congress would authorize an additional $170,000,000 for the FFAG.

Enter politics.

Midwesterners were already discouraged and angry because California and the Eastern Seaboard states were receiving 75 per cent of federal research and development funds, and great industrial centers had grown up around the academic institutions that did the research. Massachusetts Institute of Technology and Harvard were the nucleus of the vast industrial development along Boston's Route 128; the University of California at Berkeley and Stanford were responsible for a similar concentration of industry in the vicinity of San Francisco; and the presence of Caltech and UCLA in the Los Angeles area had had the same effect in Southern California.

Why, said envious Congressmen from the Midwest, should the federal taxes paid by their constituents be used selectively to strengthen the economy of California or Massachusetts? For example, the FFAG—whose proponents wanted to locate it in Wisconsin—would cost around thirty million dollars a year to operate. Thirty million dollars would be a nice sum to pump into the Wisconsin economy, and nobody realized that better than Wisconsin's Senator William Proxmire.

Proxmire was a member of the Senate Appropriations Committee, and therefore he was listened to when he said to the President's Science Advisor that "failure to approve an accelerator for the Midwest would seriously compromise the prospect for approving [one] on the East or West coasts a few years from now." Hubert Humphrey did his part, too. He had a little talk with President Kennedy and passed back word to the home folks that he was "feeling optimistic" about the MURA proposal.

By late 1963, however, no definite commitments had been made; no reversal of the AEC priorities had occurred; and now it was Lyndon Johnson's baby. He met with representatives of MURA and a delegation of Midwestern Congressmen, expressed sympathy but said he could not override the AEC's decision. This, everyone knew, marked the end for FFAG.

But not for MURA. This time it was Humphrey who carried the tidings to Johnson that the whole national program of research in high-energy physics might be jeopardized if something weren't done to placate MURA (and its congressional boosters). Midwestern universities still needed a place to do basic research, and an atom smasher with higher energy than existed on any campus. The federal government had to find a way to provide it for them.

Aha! The Midwest already had Argonne, and Argonne already had a brand new atom smasher. So why not arrange things so that the MURA physicists got more use of it? (I think it was

Glenn Seaborg, chairman of the AEC, who had that aha! idea.)
President Johnson therefore wrote a "Dear Hubert" letter in
which he said that he had asked Seaborg

> . . . to take all possible steps to make possible an increase
> in the participation of the academic institutions of the Mid-
> west in the work of the Argonne Laboratory . . . I feel
> certain that with the right cooperation between the Govern-
> ment and the universities we can do a great deal to build at
> Argonne the nucleus of one of the finest research centers
> in the world.

This sounded fine, but it put the MURA physicists right
back where they'd been in the 1950's. No guidelines were
offered as to how that "increase in participation" was to be
managed. And in addition to MURA and Argonne, whose
interests must be reconciled, a third group was now involved.
The Association of Midwest Universities (AMU) also wanted
its members cut in on whatever kind of deal was going to be
made. In short, it was a shotgun marriage, with the attendant
problems. This was the point—in January of 1964—at which
George's personal hell began.

The committee representing all the interested parties soon
concluded that the universities who were to use Argonne's
facilities should not only participate in setting its policies but
in addition should also manage it. A multi-university corporation was proposed as the holder of the operating contract with
the AEC. Argonne administrators were horrified at the idea of
management by *committee*, and the University of Chicago (some
of whose faculty also had appointments at Argonne) didn't
want to lose the contract. George's job was to get the proposal
modified so that the University would retain its role as manager.

This was to take virtually all of 1964 and half of 1965.
It involved committee meetings, conferences with individuals,
lengthy phone calls, quantities of memoranda, and the expenditure of so much emotion (because the frustration level was

so high) that George still won't talk about it. But the University *did* remain the manager of Argonne.*

I was expending quite a lot of emotion myself, although in a different direction. The Harper Court Board of Directors couldn't seem to move the Department of Urban Renewal off dead center in the matter of those land swaps that were crucial to the project, nor had it yet recommended to the City Council that the land be rezoned for commercial use. Until that was done and the land reappraised, our estimates of construction costs would be inaccurate. A firm commitment from the Small Business Administration also remained elusive.

But we were in too deep now to assume any outcome but the desired one. And bond sales were going well. Harry Gottlieb had draped his Volkswagen bus with a banner reading HARPER COURT POLLMOBILE, and all through the winter had parked it on Saturdays near the community's shopping centers —with the motor running so the interior was warm and cozy. We invited people to step inside for a cup of coffee and to fill out a questionnaire on the kind of shops they'd like to see in Harper Court. While they were there we gave them a sales pitch on the bonds, too.

By mid-January we had collected $52,000, and by the first

---

* What was finally accepted, in September of '64, was a tripartite agreement proposed by Edward Levi. Decisions affecting Argonne would be made jointly by representatives of the AEC (owner), the newly organized Argonne Universities Association (policy and program), and the University of Chicago (manager). It took until June of '65 to iron out the details, and the actual tripartite contract wasn't signed until 1966. George says that, insofar as he knows, the arrangement is working out well.

Incidentally, the defeat of FFAG was not the end of the congressional campaign to get for the Midwest its "fair share" of funds for nuclear research. The new National Accelerator Laboratory began operation in the autumn of 1971 in Batavia, Illinois (a site that made Everett Dirksen happier than William Proxmire, Hubert Humphrey, or their counterparts in California and New York). Its cost was $250,000,000; its tunnel is four miles in circumference; and it will generate energies up to 500 (and perhaps 800) billion electron volts—more than those proposed for Lawrence (West Coast) but less than those proposed for Brookhaven (East Coast). Some fifty universities are to use its facilities.

of March the total was up to $89,000. We could have quit at that point, but decided that it might be a nice stunt to ask the University to buy *fewer* debentures than it had offered to. Eventually, in fact, we requested the Investments Committee to redeem only $27,000 of its $35,000 pledge. Its members were thunderstruck.

We now had fifteen Board members, a paid secretary, and (as usual) a financial problem. How were we going to get the debentures to their purchasers? Given over four hundred bond buyers, a cost of $1.50 per packet to deliver each bond by registered mail, and you have the makings of a gruesome shock to your treasury. So we made a deal with Hyde Park Federal to keep our securities in its safe for two weeks, and asked our bond buyers to drop in there and pick up their debentures. That got rid of about half of them, and individual Board members finally delivered the remainder. We conducted a benign Sunday morning raid on our still-abed or breakfasting neighbors, and had all debentures in their owners' hands before noon.

By April we even had eight applications from high-rent tenants and seven from artists or craftsmen who wanted low-rent space—among them a little theater group which asked for three thousand square feet and offered fifty cents a foot for it. When we said that our miminum was a dollar-fifty, the manager was upset. "But you're a foundation, aren't you? We were going to ask you for an operating grant, too!" This was not the last occasion when we would have to explain that not all foundations are endowed, and that the Harper Court Foundation and the Ford Foundation were worlds apart.

Spring brought the usual influx of poets, playwrights, musicians, scholars, and political bigwigs. Among them was Robert Kennedy, free at last from the visible weight of grief that had burdened him for months after his brother's assassination. He gave the Law School's 1964 Law Day Address.

As a preamble, he charmed the students by "straightening

out the record" with regard to his appointment to the office of Attorney General:

"For ten years previously I had been employed by the Justice Department," he said in his dry New England voice. "I was on time, sober, industrious, took work home on weekends, got good efficiency ratings, earned my forty-two hundred dollars a year. And so of course"—now the audience was beginning to smile—"it was inevitable, as you young lawyers will realize, that I should have been appointed Attorney General. I commend to you the same behavior and circumstances that resulted in my appointment."

These final words were almost drowned out in the roar of applause. His following speech wasn't very good, and his delivery was wretched, but the occasion was a love feast anyway. There was tremendous empathy between Robert Kennedy and college-age young people. That night, the auditorium glowed with it.

On the other hand, our students didn't know what to make of Everett Dirksen. It was my first close-up look at him, too, and I was struck by the difference between the three-dimensional man and his photographs. In one light his face was soft and pulpy; in another light it was sharp and gaunt. But his hoarse, deep, and syrupy voice was wholly familiar. Sometimes he spread-eagled himself in a heroic stance against the red curtains of the Mandel Hall stage, his voice booming across the auditorium. Sometimes he draped himself over the podium with one arm hanging limply across it, his horn-rims dangling from a finger, and whispered into the microphone. What he said could under no circumstances have been called a speech, but it was great entertainment. I am not sure that the movies and TV are a fair exchange for the Old Time Oratory.

Dirksen told us about his revered mother, who, at the tender age of seventeen, had ventured across the turbulent waters of the ocean to seek the better way of life that this great and glorious Republic offered to the poor and the oppressed of other lands. He told us that the affairs of that great and glorious

Republic were in a perilous condition and that he feared for the future of his grandchildren, nice little tykes aged eight and ten, each of whom had been burdened willy-nilly with a $1,642 share of the public debt. This circumstance made their old grandpappy very sad indeed. Did we not agree that the current degree of fiscal irresponsibility in the tribunals of government was a matter to which patriotic citizens should address their most earnest thoughts and prayers?

This was a general audience, with a wide age span. The younger students were offended by Dirksen's overblown rhetoric, and couldn't understand why the overall attitude of the crowd was good-humored and even affectionate. A girl in the seat next to mine was especially disapproving; she sat and glowered, her lips pressed into a grim line. I tried to explain.

"It's a show," I said. "Behaving like this is his political trademark. Like—uh—like Jack Benny being a tightwad. Dirksen is really a very intelligent and capable legislator."

But her lips tightened further. "Then why doesn't he act like one?" she hissed.

In the question period, a student who wished to point up what a clever fellow he was by comparison with the bombastic old phony on the platform included a quotation from Edmund Burke in his remarks.

Dirksen's reply was as slow 'n' easy as an uncoiling rope in the grasp of a good cowhand, and hit the target with the same snap. "Son," he said, "you got that remark a mite wrong. What Burke actually said was . . ." And then he quoted the relevant passage, entire.

This time, my young neighbor applauded too. She left the hall still puzzled by the older people's respect for Dirksen— as indicated by their indulgent acceptance of his "speech"— but at the same time impressed by his gamesmanship.

It was, on the whole, an uneventful season insofar as student activism was concerned. Some five hundred students took part in a boycott of the cafeteria in one of the student dormitories and marched on our house singing (to the tune of *Battle Hymn of the Republic*)

> . . . The prices are too high and the portions are
> too small,
> And that is why we're picketing this blasted
> dining hall . . .

but there was a rites-of-spring air about it, and the uproar died down quickly.

There was an echo, however, in the office of the Dean of the Divinity School, which had just hired a secretary who was nervous about "campus radicals."

The new Roman Catholic liturgy, with the Mass in English, was making its debut at that time; and a series of demonstrations were being scheduled by diocesan authorities to familiarize communicants and other interested people with the new service. One of these demonstrations was to take place in Rockefeller Chapel.

It therefore came about one day that the new secretary in the Divinity School received a call from a citizen who asked, "What time tomorrow is the Mass Demonstration going to take place at Rockefeller Chapel?"

The lady gasped. This was the sort of thing she'd been afraid of.

"Oh, dear!" she replied. "I don't know. What group is involved? And what are they protesting?"

As June whirled to its climax, a few special events got sandwiched in between the usual celebrations that mark the end of the academic year. The most festive of these was the dedication, at the Law School, of a three-ton bronze abstract sculpture by Antoine Pevsner.

The Law School is a complex of four buildings designed by Eero Saarinen, the central one being a six-stories-high gray glass structure which houses the library and faculty offices. Its immediate neighbor is the neo-Gothic building that was the only one built of the group that Ernest DeWitt Burton had envisioned for his College, and Saarinen took this building as his starting point.

He used the same limestone, chose gray glass to duplicate the tone of the weathered masonry next door, and stressed verticality—but broke the façade of the new building into a series of shallow triangular panels (like the folds of an accordion). There is no time, day or night, when the building lacks visual interest. Clouds and sunset glow are reflected in the multiple prisms of these panels, and at night the pattern of lights inside the building turns the whole structure into a giant black and white abstraction.

This handsome building, and its associated ones, are massed about an open court and a reflecting pool. Saarinen's plans called for a curtain wall of water in one corner of the pool (thrown up by a line of jets installed in a line parallel to one edge); and, offset at the opposite corner, a sculpture. However, at the time the funds were raised for the Law School buildings there wasn't enough money for these finishing touches.

That funds were sought at all at that time—1959—was the height of audaciousness, for it was by no means certain then that urban renewal in Hyde Park-Kenwood would be successful or that the University would survive. But Glen Lloyd, as chairman of the Board of Trustees, and Edward Levi, then Dean of the Law School—both of them Law School alumni—had pulled it off; and in so doing had given a boost to the morale of the whole community. Students had paid their particular tribute to the feat by nicknaming the reflecting pool Loch Levi.

Now a third alumnus, the New York attorney Alex Hillman, had provided the sculpture.

Pevsner called it *Spatial Construction in the Third and Fourth Dimension*. It is a combination of concave and convex surfaces roughly in the form of a three-dimensional X, austere in outline but rich in detail. Different intensities of light, or the wetness, dustiness, or snowiness of its surfaces give it a constantly changing appearance at different times of day or different seasons of the year. The fourth dimension of its title is valid because as you change your vantage point in looking at it you involve yourself with the work not only in space but in time. It sits, all ten feet of it, atop a seven-foot black granite pedestal, and provides a splendid grace note for Saarinen's equally splendid building.

The dedication of the sculpture occurred during exam week, when students ordinarily are neither seen nor heard. Yet, on the morning of the day before the dedication ceremony, rosy-fingered dawn had its counterpart down below. Pranksters had dumped a number of boxes of pink Dreft into the reflecting pool; the jets of the newly installed fountain had done the rest; and mounds of pink suds bubbled gently across the entire surface of Loch Levi.

The Buildings and Grounds men had spent all day and all night flushing out the detergent, but as we gathered for the dedication ceremony I noted that a rosy residue still clung to the edges of the pool. The previous year, some wild ducks—seeing no essential difference between a pool and a pond—had turned it into a bird sanctuary, and local nature lovers had overfed them. I agreed with the Law School wife who said that the pink bubbles were an improvement over the soggy bread that had dotted the surface of the pool while the ducks had been in residence.

Twenty

The academic year peaked in mid-June as usual and then slumped for the summer, giving us a chance to recover our wits and our energies for 1964–65. But, by now, the gung ho spirit of the early years had waned, and we had to keep reminding ourselves that this replay of other Septembers didn't give us the privilege of being offhand about the beginning of *this* September.

The President's Reception, for example, provided a unique moment of personal recognition by the University's top brass to each incoming student—and young Miss Mary Dobbs of Cleveland was not going to see the joke if adult inattention at the start of the receiving line should turn her, at the end of that line, into Miss Cleveland of Dobbs Ferry. So we worked hard at being alert and responsive.

Nor, at dormitory after-dinner discussions, was it conducive to civilized social discourse to let one's manner betray boredom. It was easy to become bored, though, since the questions were so predictable.

One type of question was too specific: "Mr. Beadle, why does the University require a thirteen-meal contract at New Dorm?" All that George could ever reply to questions like this was, "I don't know."

The other type of question was too general: "Mr. Beadle, how is the University organized?" Experience had taught that students had no interest in understanding the corporate structure of the institution, or even the system by which the faculty made decisions on academic affairs; what they really wanted to know was, "Where is the power centered?"

And when George told them that universities are the most de-centralized organizations in the world, that decisions are made after endless talk at a great many levels of the organization, and that "the sense of the meeting" finally percolates to the President's Office and on to the trustees, they didn't believe him.

So he frequently left these dinners feeling like either a fool or a liar, which wasn't good for him—or for the students.

There didn't seem to be any way to swing the talk into the give-and-take of real conversation. From time to time, George would seize the initiative and deliver a short monologue about the University's policies toward admitting and hiring Negroes, or its relationship to the federal fund-granting agencies, or the economics of urban renewal as visible in Hyde Park. But after a moment of polite silence someone in the group would open the question period by asking, "Now, about the bookstore: how come the required texts for the History of Western Civ aren't in stock yet?"

It was a tremendous relief one evening when the first young man to take the floor asked, "Mr. Beadle, what is the University doing about improving the sex life of the students?"

George didn't know the answer to *that*, either.

I kept hoping that someone, sometime, would get George going on his own scientific specialty of genetics, a field which provides dozens of moral and ethical problems of the sort that students (undergraduates, especially) love to argue about. But, no: they did not perceive George as a person but simply as a member of "the administration."

Grosvenor Cooper, a professor in the Music Department, had had the same experience. He and many other faculty members regularly dined at the dormitories and sat around chatting for a while afterwards; and one evening a girl asked him, with great longing and intensity, "Mr. Cooper, how can we get to talk to the faculty?"

"You're talking to me," he pointed out. "And I see Mr. Ginsburg over there."

"Well, sure. But what I mean is how come we never have any contact with the *faculty?*"

This inability to conceptualize—in terms of individuals they knew—such abstractions as "the administration," "the faculty," and "the Board of Trustees" was to become, with the rise of student militancy on all campuses, a formidable barrier between the academic generations.

In October of that year, there was a great pilgrimage to Poughkeepsie of University of Chicago administrators and faculty. The occasion was the inauguration as president of Vassar of one of our own: Alan Simpson, Dean of our College.

Marion Lloyd and I drove East together and made a lovely autumn holiday out of it. The blazing reds and golds of foliage along the way bested even the brilliant show of color in the formal academic garb of the marchers in Alan's inaugural procession.

It is customary for the nation's institutions of higher learning to send official representatives to presidential inaugurations, and among the group at Vassar was a dean from the University of California at Berkeley. What was going on there, we asked him? The campus disorders had been in progress for a month, and according to what we read in the papers, things seemed to be in more of a turmoil than when the protest had started. What was the inside scoop?

"I wish I knew," he said. "The academic senate takes one position and the chancellor takes another. Force has been used and so has mediation. Some of my colleagues say the students are dead right and others say that the whole lot should be expelled.

"Everyone's energy is going into ad hoc committees, and as soon as you get one problem solved—or at least work out some compromise—controversy breaks out about something else. My

God, you never know where the kids are going to pop up next! And some of them are pretty tough to deal with. There's an ugly undertone, an atmosphere of—well, *threat*, that's new in my experience with college students, and it bothers me a lot . . .

"But I suppose everything will turn out all right, eventually."

He was wrong. Between September and December, just about everything happened at Berkeley that was to happen on campuses across the country in the following five years—except violent death. The revolution at Berkeley gave radicals everywhere a pattern to follow; it shocked faculties and administrators everywhere into a state of near-paralysis; and it outraged the general public. In short, it ushered in a period during which university administrators were not joking when they told the joke about the university president who died and went to hell, and it took him a week to notice the difference.

Well, what *did* happen at Berkeley?

In the early sixties, a good many perceptive people had noted that the apathetic, socially uninvolved students of the previous decade had vanished from the scene and that a new generation had taken over. Many students, blooded in the Southern civil rights movement, brought back to the campus both a deep sense of moral outrage and a tactic for dramatizing it; and it was almost inevitable that these should have been extended to the university milieu, since that's where the students were.

The modern big university provides plenty of fuel for its members' discontent. In 1964, over 27,000 students were enrolled at the Berkeley campus alone, and it is no wonder that they found the place cold and impersonal; in the jargon of the times, "alienating." They felt submerged in anonymity and deprived of their humanity by the apparatus of the institution.

California citizens had historically been proud of their public schools, from kindergarten upwards, and were generous in supporting them financially. As a result, UC-Berkeley in 1964 was rated in academic circles as either the best American university or second best only to Harvard. In academic circles, this rating means "best in quality of faculty and research," yet it was a rare Berkeley undergraduate who even saw—let alone talked to—the distinguished professors who were allegedly in residence.

Many of these men had, of course, been lured to Berkeley from other institutions by the assurance that they wouldn't have to teach undergraduates, a ploy that all universities have used at one time or another when they are trying to catch "the big ones." Productive research is a full-time job, and exceedingly important both to society as a whole and to education. One professor at Berkeley recently said, "What we teach today is yesterday's research. What are we going to teach tomorrow?"

People who are good at research often don't want to interrupt it in order to review first principles for great batches of young people who may or may not profit by the instruction. This "careerist" orientation of many faculty members, widespread across the United States, was (and is) resented by students— and also by faculty members who like to teach, or who teach because they aren't very good at research.

In addition to these problems common to most universities with large enrollments, California had some special ones. Berkeley, long considered the most prestigious of the University of California's nine campuses, had recently lost some of its autonomy as a result of a reorganization of the state's system of higher education.

Each campus now had its own administrative head, a chancellor, who was responsible to the president of the entire university, Clark Kerr. It was Kerr's job to synchronize and standardize the workings of all nine campuses, using as advisors the various chancellors and an academic senate whose members were elected from each campus. The recommendations of this statewide body did not always suit the Berkeley faculty, who wanted their standards to be higher than—or, at any rate, different from—those at UC-Santa Barbara or UC-Davis. So *they* felt alienated, too.

Another special factor that made Berkeley ripe for revolution was that large numbers of its students and faculty were already heavily involved in off-campus political activity, and for at least five years had been engaged in a running battle with the administration in an effort to center more of that activity on campus.

University officials had not been unyielding. There had been various modifications of policy, but no one had found a magic formula which met the requirement in California's state constitution that "the university shall be kept entirely independent of all political or sectarian influence" and at the same time satisfied students and faculty who believed that the proscription of political activity on campus violated their civil liberties.

They didn't want their freedom limited to the right to hear speakers who espoused different causes. They wanted to organize action groups which would take stands on issues and attempt to influence events. And they had plenty of experience in doing just that. So it wasn't necessary—as it would have been at, say, the University of Notre Dame—for the Free Speech Movement to build a constituency. It was at hand.

There was also, in the Berkeley area, a large population of non-students: young people of college age who were not enrolled in classes but liked living in a university community, especially one in a pleasant climate where housing cost was low. Some of these "street people" had jobs, but many were being maintained by indulgent parents. This advance guard of the yippie youth culture wanted passionately to reform society, or perhaps just had a gripe against it; in any case, they had the free time to throw themselves into militant activity centered on the campus.

The essentially trivial incident that started the revolution at Berkeley was the university administration's banning of partisan political activity on a university-owned strip of sidewalk just outside one entrance to the campus. Such activity had been taking place there for years, but had been overlooked by university officials because it hadn't been very intense. This, however, was the year of Barry Goldwater, and anti-Goldwater activity *was* intense. Some of the university's regents didn't like that at all.

The area was also being used for recruitment of volunteers and solicitation of funds for other political causes. Since such activity was forbidden on the campus, the dean of students said it must not occur on that strip of sidewalk, either. A large number of students immediately protested the ban; the chancellor of the Berkeley campus refused to revoke it; and the fat was in the fire.

What happened thereafter was a classic case of too many cooks in the kitchen. The actions of the protesting students were responded to at different levels of the academic and civil hierarchy, without much co-ordination, and with different degrees of thoughtfulness or haste. Berkeley's chancellor, the academic senate, the university's president, the regents, the governor of the state—all, at some time or other in the course of that horrendous three months—acted more or less independently in response to the crisis on campus.

The explanation, I believe, lay in both the structure of the university and in the institution's immediately past history of student activism. A university administration is far from being the "monolith" that students like to call it. Each level or division has implicit authority to handle whatever problems fall within its scope, other levels or divisions being involved only if someone at the originating point asks for help or if the authority of that office is challenged. There was no reason, so the dean of students must have thought in the beginning, to take the dispute elsewhere. When it nevertheless escalated to the point where the senate of the student body was petitioning the regents, the chancellor stepped in. And so on up the line, or sideways: as various groups found their interests or responsibilities affected, they got involved, too.

In the early stages of the protest, many officials and groups that were later drawn into the conflict must have assumed that this, like previous skirmishes of a similar sort, would also be resolved by reasoned debate. You don't call a summit meeting of the parties who will be affected by a revolution and try to establish a joint policy or plan of action to keep the peace if you don't know that a revolution is brewing.

A result of this fragmentation, however, was that there were many swings in the official university position. When someone in authority was conciliatory, the leadership of the Free Speech Movement increased its demands. When someone else in authority took a hard line, students cried, "Repression!" At one point the president of the university summoned city and state police to quell the disorders, and at another point he asked the civil authorities to keep their hands off but the governor sent the police in anyway. This action was probably the worst misjudgment of all, for the sight of hundreds of resisting students being dragged out of the administration building radicalized thousands of moderates.

(If you were shocked by seeing on television the behavior of Chicago's police toward militant young people during the 1968 Democratic Convention, you know the emotion. Something deep inside all of us recoils at the idea of adults clubbing young people. This emotion is so strong that it obscures the fact that, at Berkeley and at the Democratic Convention, as on a multitude of occasions in between, the leaders of those young people sought that outcome in order to gain supporters for their cause.)

The Berkeley faculty split into factions: some raised bail for the students who had been hauled off to jail, and joined the FSM leadership in demanding that the university not suspend or otherwise discipline them; others insisted that disciplinary action in both civil and academic courts should proceed. Graduate students and teaching assistants went on strike. The chancellor was fired. The whole place seemed to be coming apart at the seams, and by the end of 1964 Berkeley had become Topic A in academic circles across the country. What if this kind of lightning should strike *us*, university administrators asked each other. What would *we* do?

Mario Savio, leader of the FSM, took to the road in early December, to encourage Leftish student groups at other institutions to engage in Berkeley-style protest, and included Chicago on his itinerary. George breathed a sigh of relief when he learned that Savio would hit our campus during the week before exams, which our students traditionally reserve exclusively for studying. The turnout therefore was small.

This is not to say that we lacked militants. Some of our students had summered in Mississippi, too. But Chicago's student body was less than a third the size of Berkeley's, and therefore the pool of dedicated activists was smaller. In addition, and regardless of whatever else may have been wrong with the University of Chicago, it could by no stretch of the imagination be called a "multiversity." Its emphasis was uncompromisingly intellectual: its science was "pure," not applied; it had no—well, *few*—community service departments comparable to those at the land-grant universities; it did no research that was "classified" for security reasons. Its courses were taught by professors, not by graduate students, and there were quantities of classes small enough to permit the dicussion method of instruction. Student access to faculty members was so easy that only a very foolish reformer would have attempted to make an issue of institutional impersonality. Nor was any sizable segment of the faculty discontented.

So what happened at Chicago for many months after the Berkeley uprising was a lot of talk about revolution and the launching of a number of trial balloons by campus militants in search of an issue that would attract enough adherents to constitute a usable task force. It was by then obvious that the FSM wasn't as interested in free speech as in gaining control of the university's decision-making bodies; and it was this goal that commended itself to Chicago's militants, too.

None of their probes were productive, however, and after each brief flurry Chicago's administrators picked up where they had left off, and tackled other business. Nobody worried about the fire next time. After all, we *did* have a University policy explicitly condemning sit-ins, didn't we?

Twenty-one

There were two memorable gifts under our Christmas tree that year.

One had been ordered by George while under the spell of L. L. Bean's catalog. It was an $8.95 sheepskin rug for the cats to lie on; and they would have no part of it.

George spent weeks lifting them from whatever resting place they had chosen and depositing them on the sheepskin, assuring them that they'd like it if they'd only give it a try. (I could hear echoes of long-ago admonitions to Red: "How do you know you don't like squash? You've never eaten any.") With each encounter, the cats' tails swelled up to twice normal size; they spit at the sheepskin and then at George; twisted out of his grasp and hid under the sofa.

Finally, he gave up. "By now, I should know better than to make an administrative decision without consulting the interested parties," he said.

Naturally, the cats then began to treat the sheepskin as if it were a long-lost relative. During the initial phase of their love affair with it, I thought I might have to serve their meals there. It is still their favorite security blanket.

The second gift, also a success in the long run, was a pair of ice skates for George.

In that section of the Midway which is depressed below street level, the Chicago Park District annually erects a small warming house, installs a custodian, and floods the grassy basin. Given a lack of wind while the water is freezing, the result is a fine skating rink.

George kept fit in the summer by gardening, but his one-time winter sport, skiing, was now well out of reach (Illinois not being notable for its mountains). He had enviously watched children and family groups skating on the Midway, wondering aloud —his Nebraska boyhood being by then some fifty years behind him—whether he could still skate. Now he would find out.

The day after Christmas, he sallied forth at seven in the morning, arriving at the warming house just as the custodian was building the fire in the stove. He scared the man, an old Negro, half to death: who but someone up to no good would enter the place at that hour?

"Don't you try nothin', now!" the old man said, holding his poker at the ready.

George thought it a nice switch on the more usual pattern of black/white confrontation.

Learning to skate again was no breeze. I spied on George from an upstairs window. Morning after morning, the dogged solitary skater over on the Midway fell down, picked himself up, wobbled off, fell again, hauled himself upright, and so on until his thirty minutes was up and he came home—discouraged, disgusted, and sore. But, as with the cats and the sheepskin rug, the moment of breakthrough finally arrived; and from my window I was able to admire a grand display of swoops and turns executed by an exhilarated sixty-two-year-old Nebraska schoolboy.

Aside from the physical benefits of exercise, it provides psychological relaxation. And this George needed more than the other. The Argonne-MURA fight, because many of the people were deceitful in their dealings, continued to bruise his spirit. George is not made for political in-fighting. The never ending round of trips and conferences that filled his office calendar and the never ending round of evening engagements that filled our social calendar also depleted his (and my) psychic energies. This was not because they were unpleasant or unproductive—frequently they were just the opposite—but because they *were* never ending.

George had rarely been ill, and had never been a patient in a hospital, yet he was beginning to develop a history of ailments that suggested lowered resistance to infection or less emotional resilience than had been characteristic of him before we came to Chicago. He'd had shingles, a nasty case, in 1963; a brief bout with an inner-ear disturbance that makes one woefully dizzy, in 1964; and now he began to have frequent massive nosebleeds. We got a humidifier, which poured so much moisture into the bedroom that the wallpaper came loose, but the nosebleeds continued.

One evening, after forty minutes of first aid at home had failed to stanch the flow, and his face was beginning to take on the color of putty, I persuaded George to go to the hospital's Emergency Room for treatment.

That was an experience: the admitting intern had never heard the name of the President of the University of Chicago and George was damned if he'd pull rank, so we found out firsthand how the Emergency Room serves the indigent poor. (It provides excellent medical attention, most impersonally dispensed.)

While I was waiting for the staff to finish George's nasal cautery, a campus cop on duty there recognized me and joined me in the bleak waiting room. Like many of our security people, he was a city policeman moonlighting on his day off; and he made me feel better about the Emergency Room services when he said, "You know, if I ever get into a shoot-out and am hit in the belly, I sure hope they bring me here."

"Why?"

"Because they really *care* about saving life. I've come in with enough emergency cases to know."

So it seemed small-minded to be cross because George didn't get VIP treatment for a nosebleed.

I was having troubles, too—intestinal ones. Inasmuch as my GI tract has always been, so to speak, my Achilles heel, I thought it likely that I was just having another round of suppressed emotionalism (as turned out to be the case).

There was worry about George, for one thing. And worry about Harper Court, for another. We blithe spirits on the Board of Directors had gotten ourselves 'way out on a limb, and the view was scary.

In December, because the contractor had workmen available and using them then would save us money, we had broken ground for the first of our buildings. The only thing wrong with this decision was that we didn't have title to the land. I would have had an ulcer, instead of diffuse symptoms of heartburn, if I had realized then that all three buildings would be nearly completed before we would own the land they stood on.

Of course, we knew that no one else would get it. A friendly City Council had reclassified it for commercial development by a not-for-profit corporation proposing to build a shopping center catering to artists and craftsmen. Who but the Harper Court Foundation could meet the specifications? So it was not surprising that ours had been the sole bid.

Nor were we sure of the Small Business Administration loan. Our great hope there was the new Administrator, Eugene Foley. It was said that he wasn't a typical Washington bureaucrat, and that things might move faster if we could only capture his full attention. Bruce Sagan comforted us by saying, "The longer the SBA lets us go on publicizing their encouragement of the project, the less able they'll be to renege." But in January of 1965, certainties would have been more calming to the nerves.

Nevertheless—or maybe because of the as yet unresolved "details" of our project—we planned and executed the equivalent of a ground-breaking ceremony, and called it a "bricklaying."

We used the Harper Theater, an old movie house adjacent to Harper Court, which Bruce had bought and was converting to an off-Broadway type theater. It was a shoestring operation, still in its first stages at that time: there was no drop curtain for the stage; the seats were secondhand ones reclaimed from a school auditorium; and the fixtures in the coffeehouse had been salvaged from Finnegan's Drug Store at Fifty-fifth and Woodlawn when it became a victim of urban renewal.

But the place acquired an ambience that January afternoon which no amount of luxurious fittings could have bestowed. I still tingle as I recall it; it was one of those rare times when an occasion builds a mood of its own, envelops the participants, and sends them home feeling uplifted.

The program was simple enough. We asked eight people, representing various agencies or groups which had had key roles in the project, to place bricks in a form which later would be mounted in a tower that stands between two of the Harper Court buildings. Among the bricklayers was Fax Cone, for the University of Chicago; Nancy Gist, the pretty sixteen-year-old daughter of a Harper Court Board member, for the bondholders (because we wanted a young 'un, someone who might still be around in 1990 when the debentures would mature); and Mayor Daley, for the city. In addition to the Midwest directors of such federal agencies as the Urban Renewal Administration and the Small Business Administration, the heads of these agencies—William Slayton and Eugene Foley—had popped into town from Washington at the last minute. Thus on one stage: youth and age; black and white; community, city, and federal officials—all united in one enterprise.

This was nice symbolism, but was not in itself responsible for the afternoon's magic.

We had asked various groups to sit together, and had affixed labels to the theater seats to indicate groupings: Harper Court Board members, here; people who had worked at tenant selection and recruitment, there; and, in other sections, those tenants who had already signed leases; members of the Hyde Park-Kenwood Community Conference's Community Planning Committee; members of the Community Conservation Council; and so on. The master of ceremonies asked each group to stand, in turn, and that was impressive enough; but when he asked all Harper Court bondholders to get to their feet, and almost everyone in the theater stood up, *that* was the electric moment—especially for Mayor Daley and the visitors from Washington.

They knew that Harper Court was a community venture; but "community" is an abstraction and these masses of people were not. It had now been two years since we had started the project, and it made *my* eyes sting to see this living witness of faith in a visionary idea with nothing more to commend it than the slight improvement it might make in the quality of urban life.

Everyone there seemed to feel the special warmth that the afternoon had generated, and went home in great good humor. In contrast, Harper Court Board members expended their share of cheer right there in the theater, and had to draw on their reserves. As we were tidying up, we discovered that the labels we had affixed to the theater seats—the kind that are supposed to pull off easily—would neither peel off nor wash off. Dousing them with cleaning fluid worked better, but it also removed the varnish from the seat backs. We finally scraped the labels off, quarter-inch by quarter-inch, with our fingernails. It took almost two hours. George and I had a dinner date that evening, and I wonder if my hostess really believed me when I told her why I was wearing Band-Aids on the tips of both thumbs.

The euphoria induced by the bricklaying was not so total as to prevent our having observed that Eugene Foley had been enthralled by the experience. Of all that I have learned as a result of the Harper Court venture, the most important discovery is that administrative decisions can determine the fate of a project which depends for its success on governmental agencies. No enabling legislation can be precise enough to eliminate the need for interpretation, and this is the point at which an administrator's "yes" or "no" can make or break you.

The section of the SBA program for which we thought Harper Court could qualify allows construction loans to individual small business men, but it required an administrative decision to determine whether a corporation like ours wishing to build a facility *for* small business men could qualify. When Gene Foley decided once and for all that it could, and passed the word down the line to expedite matters, things began to hum in both the Washington and Chicago offices of the agency. There would be hundreds of difficult hours ahead, as the SBA staff and our manager wrestled with the problem of putting twenty-seven different loans into one package; but the will found the way.

It was a better-than-usual spring for intellectual and esthetic delights. Richard Lippold of the marvelous wire sculptures visited the campus, and so did Shirley Jackson. (I entertained her at luncheon in a spirit of abject hero worship.) The biologist Roger Sperry, an old friend from Caltech, gave a lecture in which he equated free will with anarchy. And Tyrone Guthrie, physically as towering a presence as he was in the theater world, provided down-to-earth advice for Chicagoans who were trying to get a repertory theater established here. ("The stupid rich and the stupid poor have identical tastes in entertainment. Count on neither. Experiental theater will be supported, if at all, by the intellectually eager—and this will always be a small group.")

It was a spring in which the Quadrangles rang with new and unfamiliar music. An Anglican Jazz Mass made its debut at Rockefeller Chapel, and I still can't find words to describe what a wailing saxophone did to the *Angus Dei* or wild percussion and a piercing clarinet to the *Te Deum*—except to say that I thought it was as suitable as any other kind of music for praising the Lord. There was also a very special concert in the year-long series that the University's new Contemporary Chamber Players had been giving, an all-Varèse program.

The Contemporary Chamber Players, led by the gifted composer-director Ralph Shapey, had been funded by the Rockefeller Foundation. Its purposes were twofold: to provide a hearing for modern music (since the average symphony-goer disdains it to such an extent that any music director who programs much of it risks his job); and also to give musicians a chance to play it.

Contemporary music is often so spare that it pitilessly reveals any flaws in the musicians' technique, and the musicians who accepted Shapey's invitation to play in his ensemble did so in a spirit of self-testing. Their utter concentration gave the concerts a unique aura of professionalism that could be appreciated even by someone as naïve about modern music as I was.

I had attended a great many of the CCP concerts, primarily to accustom my ears to this kind of music. Leonard Meyer, the head of our Music Department, said that I could consider myself a member of the inner circle when I was able to recognize the humor in it; and he assured me that modern music is not devoid of humor. But the only time I had been amused during a year of listening was when I had attended a concert of electronic music in which no human being had been on stage, and a full hall of aficionados had enthusiastically applauded two amplifiers.

The all-Varèse concert in May was especially affecting because Edgard Varèse himself was there. (He was then eighty years old; yet his "modern" music is still fought and feared by the majority of music lovers!) The program that evening included *Déserts*, which sets taped sounds—mostly from industrial sources—against the sound of wind instruments, percussion, and piano; and *Poème électronique*, which combines natural sounds with electronic distortions intended to heighten their effect. And indeed they did: at one point when the audience was being assaulted by something like shrieks, shots, and sirens—clearly a commentary on urban life—I found myself sitting with clenched fists.

I had often been emotionally stirred by traditional music, but had never before experienced this strange combination of pain and pleasure as sound penetrated to some inner core and rasped the nerves. Professor Edward Lowinsky of the Music Department was sitting beside me, and at the conclusion of *Poème électronique* he said, with a slight shiver, "The only times I'm frightened are when I read my newspaper and hear music like that."

By the spring of 1965, three of the proposed four sessions of Vatican II had been held, and those people from the University who had attended as observers were by now ready to comment publicly on this historic event. Their reports—whether presented in the role of diarist, journalist, or interpreter—made a feast of listening.

The press had so stressed the significance of Vatican II, and the weightiness and deliberation of the proceedings, that it was easy to forget that the participants were human beings and that there is more to life than prayer. A sweet and revealing glimpse of Pope John came from Barnett Blakemore, Acting Dean of Rockefeller Chapel, who said:

> There were seventy Protestant observers, and nine of us brought our wives along. The Pope received us all in the Sistine Chapel, but in addition he held a special audience for the wives. The red brocade had recently been removed from the walls of his private apartments and replaced with mauve velvet, a change about which some in Rome were doubtful. So, cannily, the Pope chose these rooms as the setting for his ladies' party—knowing that within hours after its conclusion, a detailed description of the furnishings would be all over town. And of course he was right. The women spread the word that His Holiness had impeccable taste in wall coverings.

And why should the religious be cheerless? Jerald Brauer, Dean of the Divinity School, reported that Vatican II had spawned a whole series of jokes, some of them good for a chuckle anywhere, others best savored by those on the scene.

During the year that Barry Goldwater ran for President of the United States, for example, Vatican Council delegates had told each other that the Protestant observers were going to leaflet the participants with fliers combining a picture of Martin Luther and a caption reading, "In Your Heart, You Know He's Right."

Or, for those who appreciated the bitter feeling that had developed between the conservative Curia, as exemplified by Cardinal Ottaviani, and the liberal German and Dutch churchmen, the wits offered this imaginary dialogue:

Delegate, to Ottaviani: "The Germans are after your head."

Ottaviani: "Fine. They can use a good one up there."

And yet Vatican II *was* basically a solemn affair, both in procedures and import. Jerry Brauer also said:

When Pope John opened the windows, a lot more blew in than anybody had anticipated. When we went for the first session, we didn't know why we were going, and neither did anybody else. By the second session, those who wanted renewal began to be heard, and a real battle began. By the third session, the progressive voice was dominant and the conservatives were on the defensive. Imagine! the key theologians at Vatican II were on the Index ten years ago . . .

Nobody knows where the fourth session will come out, but even if they can't avoid the headlong clash between the liberals and the conservatives that seems likely, changes have already occurred that will have a great impact on society. The new emphasis on a shared priesthood, for example: the old idea of a clergy surrounded by a passive laity seems to be gone for good.

And from Paul Tillich, a thoughtful summation:

Pope John didn't desire so much to approach Protestantism as to find a proper relationship to secularism, which threatens all religious institutions today and is therefore driving them in convergent directions. Secularism didn't fall from heaven or arise from hell; it is an autonomous creation of the human spirit, the outcome of the churches' failure to provide for the spiritual needs of all people. This empty space has been filled by quasi-religions—Communism, Fascism, liberal humanism—which rule the modern world as religion never did.

The real problem of our time is to find together how relevant is any religious message for those who live in secularism —and of the Western religions the Roman church is doing a far better job than the Protestant churches. The World Council of Churches at this moment cares far more about whether the Episcopalians will unite with the Presbyterians than about the fate of religion itself.

Whenever I count my blessings as a university president's wife, the first item on the list is always "intellectual stimulation." I am grateful beyond measure to George's office for exposing me regularly to the fruits of other people's inquiry and reflection. I learned things that I would never under my own steam have investigated, and expanded sensibilities that would otherwise have remained undeveloped.

Of course I often wanted to dodge the opening banquet of some group having a national or international symposium at the University, events that we attended because George was supposed officially to welcome them to the campus. But that was mainly because my feet hurt from the night before. I discovered very early on that even the dullest-sounding conference often produces a keynote speaker of surpassing interest; and once I was there, I was delighted to have come.

At such events that year, for instance, and before the ideas propounded had had any public exposure to speak of, Edward Schwartz of our School of Social Service Administration explained the rationale behind proposals that the poor be given a guaranteed annual income, and sold *me*.

I also heard a persuasive argument by the anthropologist Sherwood Washburn to the effect that we are making an ecological mess of the planet because man's emotional responses to the circumstances of life are still those of his ancestors of twenty thousand years ago. ("Even if primitive man's emotions had not been wholly engaged in coping with the problems of the present, there would have been no point in being concerned with the future, for he couldn't control it. But *we* can. It is well within our power to determine what life on earth will be like a century from now. Yet we are not moved to exercise this ability. I can think of no reason other than that we are a species incapable of future-oriented action.") Heady stuff!

Nevertheless, there can be too much of a good thing, and the spring months of 1965 remain in my mind as half bliss and half nightmare. In addition to the delights I have been chronicling, there was a round of visits from the Washington staff of the Small Business Administration; a spate of civic banquets, dreary affairs that in four hours can take a week off your life; and, of course, all the usual end-of-the-academic-year activity.

One morning in May, having left the house before nine o'clock to take some clothing to the dry cleaner and mail some packages, I returned home at a dead run, thinking ahead to the tight schedule of the day. As I galloped through the kitchen, Mrs. Galloway handed me a prettily decorated and ribbon-bound scroll that some ladies who wanted me to attend a luncheon had left at the door.

"They told me to put it on your breakfast tray," she said.

I stopped dead, took the scroll in my hands, turned it over lovingly, wondered what it would be like to have breakfast in bed—and broke into tears.

The morning's mail brought a letter from Redmond noting that he had not heard from us in three weeks and inquiring after our health and welfare in exactly the pointed terms that parents use when reproaching their children for not writing. So I wept again.

That was the day we had our annual cocktail party for the University's important donors. The caterers, upon going to the auxiliary freezer in the basement to get extra ice cubes, discovered that it had ceased to function some days earlier and was now full of water, melted ice cream, and spoiling meat.

In the evening, there was a special meeting of the Harper Court Board. The city of Chicago's Building Department has a nasty habit of approving building plans "subject to final approval in the field," and now that our buildings were two-thirds done, the electrical inspector was insisting on changes in wiring and meter-box installation that would add three thousand dollars to the cost. I came home, very late, exhausted, and still angry.

So of course it was then that M'zelle came pounding up the stairs making the peculiar keening sound that signals a cat's having caught something nice and juicy.

I slammed the bedroom door, wakened George, and yelled at him, "I will not, positively will *not*, have that cat in here dumping another half-dead mouse or cockroach at my feet. DO SOMETHING!"

George, however, was befuddled by sleep and M'zelle was not, so she simply came 'round to the bedroom by another entrance, deposited her catch, and sat there beaming.

It was a large, moist black olive; I suppose she had fished it out of some corner into which it had rolled during the afternoon's cocktail party.

So I dissolved into a fit of giggles which bordered on hysteria, and didn't get to sleep until 2 A.M.

That day, fortunately, was not typical. But there were enough days that approached its pattern to create a household that, by mid-June, was positively awash with emotion. It was a relief to everybody when George and I left town.

What a joy, what ineluctable joy, it was to attend a college commencement for which we had no responsibility. The Puseys had to shake the hands; all *we* had to do was to drift with the stream of parents that swept from Mem Church to the Yard and back to Lowell House.

It was perfect June weather, marvelous for sitting outdoors in the torpor generated by ceremonial speeches and warm sun, and I did what every other mother does when celebrating one of the milestones of a child's life: mused on the past, recollected the stages and problems of the growing years, and viewed the product through a mist of sentimentality and pride. Red would return to Harvard in the fall with a graduate prize fellowship which carried a stipend so generous that George (in his role as a university president) had sighed enviously, and said, "Gad, it must be wonderful to have an endowment of a billion dollars."

But Harvard has more than money to give it singularity. Even those students or visitors who are most grossly insensitive to tradition, or are repelled by it, cannot wholly escape awareness that a company of scholars has been a presence in that spot for over three hundred years. It is a subtle thing, this seeping of the past into the bones of the present, and I wished then and now that the University of Chicago's history stretched back even half so far.

Twenty-two

"What you'll need, of course, is a couple. The wife as a cook, the man as butler and chauffeur."

"Think twice before you hire a couple. One of them is usually capable and industrious, and the other one drinks."

Both pieces of advice, given early in 1961, had been useless. Even if I had wanted a couple, I couldn't have found them. For that matter, it was a miracle I found anybody—given the reputation of the South Side of Chicago as an urban jungle, and the scarcity of trained people. They might go crazy with loneliness out in the swank suburbs, but at least (they thought) they would be *safe*.

I thanked my lucky stars for Mrs. Galloway and Mrs. Carter, both of whom did their jobs superbly well, but there *were* gaps. Who would shovel the snow? Answer the door at odd hours? Change the bulbs in all those lighting fixtures that were twelve feet from the floor? Carry the extra chairs up from the basement when a big party was planned? Act as occasional bartender? Run errands on days when my schedule was packed to the hilt with University activity? Help with clerical chores?

The answer: a series of part-timers. For the first few years, we had hired graduate students who came in for several hours a day and did assorted odd jobs. But by the mid-sixties, as students too joined the affluent society, that source had dried up. We finally found James Coleman, no longer a young man but still with enough energy to work nights at one job and put in ten additional hours a week doing some of the heavy work at our house. The faculty club loaned me bartenders. I could call on a secretary in George's office for help when sending out invitations to large parties, and could have used her as a real secretary if I had taken the time to work out a schedule and train us both to each other's ways. But I never found the magic formula, and ended up doing a great many things that wisdom argued I should have delegated.

By 1965, the pattern was set. All things considered, the household functioned very well. The only aspect of its management that I minded was the keeping of records; and this I minded to the point of hatred. George's desk and bureau drawers always look as if a windstorm has just passed through, yet his records are meticulously kept. I am a tidy housekeeper but am always having to call the bank to ask to whom check number 3426 was drawn and for how much.

Three of the people who worked for us were on the University payroll, but in different categories. Mrs. Galloway, who "lived in" and worked weird hours, got a monthly check. Mrs. Carter and Mr. Coleman got their checks bi-weekly, but record-keeping procedures were different because Mrs. Carter worked forty hours a week and was therefore on the "regular" payroll whereas Mr. Coleman's ten hours a week put him on the "part-time" payroll. I had to keep cumulative records on all three, in order to qualify them for vacation pay, sick leave, or raises.

We also had a laundress who came one day a week to do George's shirts and the table linens. Although the University reimbursed me for a portion of what I paid her, she was our private responsibility and I therefore had to record her hours and make contributions on her behalf to Social Security. The three waitresses who came regularly to help us serve large parties sometimes also fell into this category (depending on number of hours worked in any three-month period).

Aside from records of expenditures for service, I was required to get and keep receipts for all other outlays for which I in-

tended to ask reimbursement—new glassware, the cost of cleaning draperies, repair of appliances, flowers for the house, and so
on; as well, of course, for food. The University was an enlightened employer: I was never given an "entertainment allowance,"
nor was any expenditure for which I sought reimbursement
denied me. Nevertheless, the Comptroller—with the Director of
Internal Revenue looking over his shoulder—needed some assurance that we were discriminating between personal needs and
those connected with official University business. For example,
what proportion of each pound of coffee did we drink as private
individuals, and what proportion was consumed by the household staff and official guests?

Because I had become so distraught when it was first proposed that I attempt to estimate such percentages for all the food
served in the house, the Comptroller took pity on me and worked
out a fancy formula of cost-sharing. I kept monthly records of
how many guests had been given food or drink, how many meals
had been served to the staff, and how many meals George and I
had eaten at home. Twice a year, the Comptroller's Office added
up the "business" meals; calculated what percentage they were
of all meals served; and set that percentage as the amount of
household food cost that I could claim as "business" expense
for the following six-month period. (Incidentally, these percentages were remarkably consistent over the years. On the average,
60 per cent of our food cost was for official University entertaining.)

These semiannual reviews were audits. I sent to the Comptroller a huge file folder stuffed with all my receipts, plus the various
books I kept, and in due course they were returned with neat
little check marks after each item and a formal report attesting
to the fact of the audit. This almost always revealed errors in
simple addition or subtraction, and the poor dears who composed the covering report could never certify my records as correct but had to say something like, "Adequate records were
maintained and most expenditures were substantiated by documents that appeared proper." These reports always plunged me

into a fit of blue gloom. Why, after all the years I had been trying, should the product of eight times nine continue to elude me?

In late June of 1965, under the guise of participating in one of those symposiums on the future of the American university that foundations love to fund, we'd had a relaxing holiday in Aspen. But because we hadn't returned home until the second week in July, I was late with my semiannual report. Doing it in a hurry made me all the more cross.

So George picked a poor time to look over my shoulder and say, "Have you kept a record of the number of stamps you use for personal mail and those you use for University business?"

I sat up straight and my lips tightened. He recognized the danger signals, since we'd been over the same ground many times before, and quickly changed the subject.

"What's the head count this year?" he asked.

"Guests? Let's see: two thousand eighty-two. But we're slipping. Look here. I've just added up the totals since 1961, and although we've entertained almost ten thousand people since we came, the pattern is changing. This year we didn't have anything like six hundred guests in any one month, and we used to do it all the time. I think I'm running out of steam."

He patted me comfortingly on the shoulder, and went out to work in the garden.

Watching him turn the soil under the crabapple trees we'd planted made me recall one of the big parties we annually gave, a reception for foreign students (who were one in six of the University's enrollment). It was always a rather formal affair, with printed invitations and a receiving line, because students from other countries are nowhere near as casual about being received by the president of a university as Americans are.

The previous autumn, as the people in the receiving line inched toward us, I had noticed an Indian student drop out of the line. He had such a stricken look on his face that I thought he must have had a seizure of some kind. As soon as I could, I asked the head of International House to check on the young man's well-being, and when he came back he was smiling broadly.

"That young man," he reported, "is a medical student who walks past here on the way to the hospital at seven o'clock every morning. For three months now, whenever he has seen your gardener at work, he has been extending a kindly greeting. America being a democracy, you know, one speaks to the working classes. But I'll bet he's been damn condescending about it.

"Anyway, the reason he dropped out of line in such a fright is that, when he got close enough to see Mr. Beadle, he realized just who your gardener *is*."

We had established a new practice that year, as much as anything to show (we hoped) that small-town morality *can* flourish in a city. George had, over the years, turned our garden into a showplace, and now on the weekends we simply left the gate open and placed a small sign outside inviting passersby to come in and stroll around.

I could watch the gate from my study window, and it always amused me to see the cautious approach: the pause at the entrance, the head stuck in first to see what the catch might be, the tentative first step inside the garden, the signal to any companions that it looked safe inside, the subsequent and slightly self-conscious "stroll."

During the several years we were to do this, none of our garden visitors—who were as varied a lot in terms of cultural and economic background as one could imagine—ever picked the flowers, stole the cushions on the garden furniture, or defaced anything. They all seemed to be stunned into a pattern of Victorian respectability by the unfamiliar sight of an open door in an inner-city community whose residents routinely lock and bar everything.

One day, when I answered the phone, a curiously tight young voice asked if it would be possible for him to "borrow" our garden for half an hour some day that week.

"*Borrow?*"

"Yes. For private use. Because it has the fence and those

shrubs. I've looked all over the campus and can't find any other place that will be right for us."

"*Us?*"

"My wife and me."

He sounded about fifteen years old.

"What do you want it for?"

"Our baby has just been born." Pause, and an ingathering of breath. "*Still*born. And we want to have a memorial service for it." Another pause. "I mean, for *him*. Somewhere outdoors. And *private*."

We set a date and a time, and when they came they were accompanied by the girl's mother and by an adult leader from the Chicago Ethical Society. The young couple were a pair of flower children who couldn't yet have been twenty years old.

I showed them into the garden, where I had already placed a pitcher of lemonade and some cookies. (There are no social precedents for an occasion of this sort, but some kind of refreshments seemed to be in order.) Then I stood in the dining room, out of their sight, and watched the service begin.

The pastor—I think one could call him that—seated himself in a chair facing the young couple; opened a book and began to read. The husband and wife sat apart, as stiffly as children at a dancing school, their young backs so straight and their chins so determinedly high that my heart ached for their youth and vulnerability.

Then I turned away from the window, and gave them the privacy they had sought in asking for the use of the garden. I don't know how long the service lasted, or when they went. But I'm glad they came.

All through the summer, we had our usual informal dinner parties in the garden, swung around the carillon concerts, as well as one formal party that turned out a bit differently than I had expected it to.

In August, we were informed that His Imperial Highness Prince Takahito Mikasa, youngest brother of Japan's Emperor, would be visiting the University on September 15. His wife,

Princess Yuriko, and his daughter, Princess Yasuko, would accompany him. The prince's special academic interest was the history of the Middle East, hence a stop at our Oriental Institute had been included in the royal family's four-week tour of the United States.

September 15! It is frequently so hot in mid-September in Chicago that one longs to spend the whole day standing in a shower, and here I was faced with having a black-tie dinner in a house that held heat like a well-insulated oven.

I called an immediate conference with the head of Buildings and Grounds, who obligingly installed three window fans in the house and moved in four high-powered standing fans. For two weeks before the dinner we practiced various patterns of pulling cool night air into the house or ejecting sluggish air that was already in the house.

Then, to make certain that some part of the evening would be pleasant, I asked Dan Robins to play a special carillon concert for our visitors. However hot it might be that night, the garden would be fresh and cool.

The other major problem was that the guest list stood at twenty-two, one more person than I could possibly seat at the dining room table. I was brooding about this dilemma one morning when Red dashed by me on his way to class—he was taking a cram course in German that summer in addition to working at his newspaper library job—and a sudden recollection of the "children's table" at long-ago family holiday dinners flashed into my mind.

Princess Yasuko was twenty years old and a university student majoring in English literature. Why not assemble some young people her own age and put them at a separate table? So we invited several faculty children and Red's Harvard roommate, Joe McKeon (a Chicago boy), who knew so much about T. S. Eliot that he alone could keep the conversation going if all other gambits failed.

That idea turned out to be inspired. The young people had a fine time together, and whenever the slightly stiff and labored conversation at the adults' table died down we could hear the lively chatter in the next room.

Our table looked lovely, laid with the longest of our fine old hand-hemmed damask cloths (although the only patch in it *had* turned up at Prince Mikasa's place); and the food was delectable. We served Lake Superior whitefish, partly because it's a regional specialty and partly because I had correctly guessed that the royal party would have had beef or chicken everywhere else in the United States and would enjoy something closer to a Japanese menu. Prince Mikasa was so enthusiastic about it that he trotted out to the kitchen after dinner to thank Mrs. Galloway in person.

There was just one hitch. It was "cool and fresh" in the garden, all right: the outside temperature at nine o'clock was fifty-five degrees. It was unthinkable to herd a group of people in evening gowns and light wraps into the garden for a thirty-minute carillon concert. So I prepared to phone Dan Robins, sitting up there in his eyrie awaiting my signal, to cancel the program. But the prince would not have it that way. He had never heard a carillon, he said, so he preferred that the evening should proceed as planned.

Not wishing to be remembered as the hosts who had induced pneumonia in three members of Japan's Imperial Household and their retinue, we did the only sensible thing. We went upstairs and grabbed anything warm that we could quickly lay our hands on.

The prince wound up wearing an overcoat of George's, so much too large that he had to turn the sleeves up in order to use his hands. Princess Yuriko found herself swaddled in a pink blanket. The majordomo who traveled with them acquired the parka that George wore when skating on the Midway, an old one with a wolf-fur trim that made the Japanese dignitary sneeze.

The young princess looked so funny with her lavender kimono and white orchid peeping over the top of a fuzzy Hudson Bay blanket patterned in gaudy stripes—in fact, *everyone* looked so funny—that all of a sudden the party came to life and became a party. The Scarlatti sonatas sounded marvelous in the crisp night air; our guests lingered on afterwards in animated conversation; and their "thank yous" on departure were far warmer than polite convention requires.

The next day, Buildings and Grounds retrieved all the extra fans; and the following week, when the usual September heat wave struck, I wished I had them back.

The Harper Court buildings were finished that summer, and we had a dedication complete with bands, balloons, oratory, and fireworks—an event so successful that the crowds trampled to death all the fresh-laid sod and it had to be replaced. By the end of September, several of the stores were open, and most of the space was leased.

It had taken so long to bring the project to completion that hardly any of the community's beloved artists and craftsmen were tenants. They couldn't hold out long enough, and had re-established themselves elsewhere or had given up. But we did have tenants who would offer many of the same services, and so, with fingers cautiously crossed, the Harper Court Board decided that at long last it could schedule its meetings at six-week intervals.

In October, Redmond returned to Harvard to begin his graduate studies, and George and I settled once more into the opening-of-the-academic-year routine. The year itself would not be routine; none ever was. What would give '65-'66 its distinctiveness was the launching of a mammoth fund-raising campaign for the University; a great community fight about a new high school; and a sit-in that marked the end of fun and games in the student militancy movement.

Twenty-three

Before he had reached his thirtieth birthday, William Rainey Harper was one of the hottest properties on the American academic scene; and all because he had beguiled thousands of people into the serious study of ancient Hebrew. His audiences may have been the pious young students of Chicago's Baptist Union Theological Seminary, or the older citizens, bent on self-improvement, who flocked to summer conferences at Lake Chautauqua in New York; but whenever Harper lectured on the Prophets, there was standing room only. Many thousands more bought his mail-order courses and subscribed to *The Hebrew Student* or *Hebraica*, which he edited.

Yale University raised two million dollars (a stupendous sum in 1885) to endow a professorship for Harper and to house and administer his correspondence school, his institutes, and the publications and societies that had spun off them. It was not enough. In fact, no amount of money would have been enough. Harper's goal in life was not to revive general interest in the Semitic languages and literatures but to establish America's first complete university. And this he did—in Chicago, of all places, a site that a distinguished Baptist theologian had dismissed with the words, "I would as soon think of building a university in the Fiji Islands as in Chicago."

Harper was an incredible man.

He was an intellectual genius: he got his B.A. at age thirteen and his Ph.D. at nineteen. He was a scholar so dedicated to the truth that he was accused of heresy when his research revealed certain discrepancies between what was actually said in the original Hebrew of the Old Testament and what Baptist fundamendalists thought it said.

He had tremendous energy. The multitude of activities in which he was concurrently engaged makes one think of Edna St. Vincent Millay's candle burning at both ends—only in the case of William Rainey Harper, it must have had seven branches.

He was short and pudgy, with thick-lensed spectacles, and had a staccato style of speech that was not especially pleasant to the ear, yet he was one of the great spellbinders of all time. In *Young Man in a Hurry*, a short biography of Harper, Milton Mayer says:

> Will Harper could sell anybody anything. Once he walked into a smoking-room on a train between Chicago and New York. There were four men sitting there, none of whom knew each other. By the time the night was half over, the four had pledged a total of $50,000 for archeological research at the University of Chicago.
>
> Harper's own correspondence discloses that Miss Helen Culver wanted to give the city of Chicago $50,000 for an art museum; after a three-hour conversation with Harper, she found she wanted to give the University a million dollars for biology instead.
>
> And Charles T. Yerkes, the coldest plunderer of his time, never suspected himself of harboring a latent interest in the search for truth until he met the President of the new University of Chicago.*

There is also a story, perhaps apocryphal, of a wealthy old lady whose children had arranged for Harper to call on her. But when he arrived, she balked. "I won't see him. I won't,

* Culver Hall, on the campus, and Yerkes Observatory, in nearby Wisconsin, are still productively in use.

I *won't,*" she said to the maid. "If I do, it will cost me two hundred thousand dollars!"

Harper was also as shrewd an entrepreneur as John D. Rockefeller. He was shrewder, actually, because he let Rockefeller come to him; waited until Rockefeller was convinced that he would have no one but Harper as president of the nice little Baptist college he proposed to found; then refused to head anything less than a full-fledged university.

"The first step will have been taken," Harper told a friend, "when the University has $50,000,000."

But he didn't tell America's Oil King that. He gratefully received a $600,000 grant from Rockefeller, and escalated it over the years to $35,000,000—simply by keeping the University perpetually in the red while at the same time developing in The Founder such pride in the institution that he continued to make good the deficits. A 1911 *Life* cartoon by Harry Grant Dart shows a dray wagon, heaped to the top with bags of money, arriving at the University of Chicago. The shipment is labeled, "The Rockefeller Weekly Endowment."

It is said that Rockefeller finally stipulated that he would hear the annual report from Harper in person (as was their custom) on condition that Harper *not* inform him of any deficit that might exist that year. Harper readily agreed. However, during "the moment of prayer" with which these two devout churchmen began their meeting, Harper told *God* all about the deficit—and John D., with a sigh, once more wrote a check to bring the budget into balance.

Harper's secret weapon was his absolutely unshakable conviction that the educational innovations he would and did institute at the University of Chicago would dramatically change the course of higher education in America. In this belief he was quite correct; for perhaps forty years after its founding, Chicago by both its boldness and its excellence set standards for all others. Inasmuch as donors like to back a winner, its endowment grew accordingly. Nevertheless, the institution has always sailed close to the wind financially. The University's money managers after Harper were more prudent than he, but none has ever really been afraid of a deficit—perhaps because, as Milton Mayer says, the University of Chicago is still "the lengthened shadow of William Rainey Harper."

By 1965, then, although the endowment stood at almost $280,000,000, the University had so many obligations and aspirations that "the first step" this time was set at $160,000,000. That sum was to be raised within three years. In the following ten years, the target was another $200,000,000. Total: $360,000,-000. When the Campaign for Chicago was announced, it was the largest fund-raising effort ever to have been undertaken by an American university. William Rainey Harper would have been pleased.

How does a university go about raising money?

The activity is continuous, of course. It is a major responsibility of the institution's president, and I feel sorry for any candidate for the office who is naïve enough to believe any chairman of a board of trustees who is mendacious enough upon hiring him to de-emphasize this aspect of the job.

Deans of academic divisions are expected to raise money, too; perhaps from foundations whose interest is in the research specialty of a particular academic division, perhaps from individual donors who would rather see their names over the door of a hospital or an art gallery or attached to a professorship in a particular academic field than emblazoned upon a general facility such as a dormitory or gymnasium.

Presidents and deans especially cherish those assemblies of women who organize themselves into Boards or Friends or Guilds, and raise money by the thousands and sometimes by the millions in support of university hospitals or research institutes or scholarships.

A university's alumni on the average provide something like 20 per cent of each year's income from gifts. (The University of Chicago is not so lucky in this respect as, say, Harvard, because so many of our alumni are teachers—and teaching is not one of the best-paid professions.)

Trustees and other individual friends of the university frequently make annual contributions, too. A few of these even go out and actively *hunt* for money for the institution.

Bequests are also an important source of income, but cannot (for obvious reasons) be budgeted. Most of them come from people who have been generous donors during their lifetimes, but once in a blue moon a sizable bequest will come to a university from a wholly unlikely source or in unusually dramatic circumstances; and this is a heady experience indeed.

One of the biggest gifts in the University of Chicago's history, for example, came from Louis Block, an industrialist who grew worried in the early 1950's because he felt that the United States was not keeping pace with Russia in the training of scientists. He decided quite independently (he was on no University of Chicago list of prospective donors) to bequeath money to the University for that purpose. Within days after making his will, he died of a heart attack; and a stunned University of Chicago learned from his attorney that the bequest would total fifteen million dollars—*if and when his executor found the original copy of Mr. Block's will.* That had been quite a cliff-hanger, because it took weeks of searching through Mr. Block's effects before the will turned up.

Another donor of note was Stanley R. Pierce. He had been one of Stagg's boys, a Chicago grid star in 1911–14, and when he died in 1959, he had left his estate to the University for the construction of a building which would bear his name.* All seemed routine to his executors until they had found a slip of paper bearing a combination to a safe. They had finally located the safe in an old outbuilding, and inside it (on the back of a blank check) they had found this note:

> Dig down under iron pipe on north edge of
> Bartlett Pear tree located rear So.W. Corner
> of house (surveyor's pipe and hard to find).
> Dig hole about 2 ft. deep. Also dig in tool

* Pierce Hall, a men's dormitory, now memorializes him.

house in So.East Corner under paper bag hanging
from rafters. Also dig under barb wire and big
chain S.W. Cor. tool house.

The bank trust officer who was in charge had felt exceedingly foolish as he dispatched a crew to dig for buried treasure on a suburban estate in Mt. Prospect, Illinois. This, after all, was the twentieth century. But not to the romantic Mr. Pierce: the diggers exhumed over six thousand "double eagles"—twenty-dollar gold pieces in mint condition, their face value just over $121,000, their market value to collectors about twice that.

Happily, Uncle Sam had decided that the gold was a "collection" rather than a "hoard," and permitted it to be sold and the proceeds added to Mr. Pierce's approximately one-million-dollar estate. Months later, after the executors had finished their job, it was learned that Mr. Pierce's library had contained a great many books on the appraisal and collecting of diamonds. Consequently there are those today who are haunted by the belief that Mr. Pierce's land should have been excavated more thoroughly.

And then there was Miss Myra Virginia Smith, a Chicago high school French teacher who in a sentimental moment bought D'Evereaux Hall, one of the grand old ante-bellum mansions in Natchez, Mississippi; spent a lifetime restoring it; and nursed her other assets into a half-million-dollar estate. In 1961, most of this, along with D'Evereaux and eleven acres of property near Bat Cave, North Carolina, was left to the University of Chicago. I kept trying to get George to go on an inspection trip to the University's just-acquired Stately Home down South, but we never made it; and it has since been sold.

On the whole, however, money for the support of private institutions of higher education must be specifically sought. Some people believe that the customary technique is to sneak up behind a prospective donor, wining and dining him or her and otherwise conducting what amounts to a courtship, the money then being extracted while the donor is temporarily out of his or her wits. Nothing, in my experience, is further from the truth.

It's true that I gave a lot of parties whose guest lists included possible donors, but many of them were also on the list because they were people of consequence in the city, people whose good opinion of the University was just as important to it as their dollars. Once anyone thought that any of these people might make a substantial donation to the University, no reliance was placed on the indirect social route. Someone went to the prospective donor, during business hours, and *asked*.

One learns quite easily to identify the rich person who is making a career out of dangling the carrot; of being fawned on by institutions eager for his (or, more often, her) money. It is not very productive to "cultivate" them. I associated with many, and developed great compassion for rich people who suspect that they are in demand only because they are a potential source of income to some cause or institution. Whether it's true or not, their suspicions isolate them from all save a handful of old and trusted friends, turn them sour, make it difficult for them to accept new friends at face value, and leave them with little attraction *other* than their money. This is a good example of a self-fulfilling prophecy, and among the things I am grateful for is that I will never have enough money to wonder whether people like me for myself alone.

One also hears tales of honors or positions bartered for financial contributions. Some institutions cannot be as principled as others; it all depends on how much they want a new science building or auditorium, and how many prospective donors they have to choose from. A strong and well-endowed university like Chicago can be principled. It has not, so far, exchanged an honorary degree for a benefaction; and the one instance I know of personally when a prospective donor indicated that he would like to become a trustee in exchange for a sizable gift of money backfired. A member of the Board told the others that God had made the gentleman in question out of cheap dust, which disposed both of him *and* the possible donation.

I cannot recall a major gift to the University of Chicago during George's administration that was not obtained as a result of making an appointment with the prospective donor for the purpose of presenting a specific proposal—all in a perfectly straightforward, businesslike way. Tremendous amounts of work went into the preparation of those presentations: a study of the prospect's interests; sufficient knowledge of his resources and his giving patterns so that the amount asked for would be realistic; assembling people he already knew (or would listen to sympathetically) to make the actual presentation; preparation of drawings or charts to reinforce the spoken word; and a plan for following up the presentation, if he preferred—as donors usually do—to "think it over for a week or two." It can take a year to get such a presentation together; it can be very costly; and the donor is as likely as not to say "no." Some of our gloomiest evenings followed the days when George brought home word that a prospective donor had said "no."

All of the things one normally does to raise money are done in extra measure during drives with definite dollar goals and definite time limits.

Chicago's campaign, partly because it was hoped that the Ford Foundation would start it off with a sizable grant, required an in-depth examination of the University's activities and expenditures for the ten years preceding 1965 and an equally detailed prospectus of what the institution would need during the decade just ahead. Prudence required that everyone involved look very deeply and carefully into the crystal ball. One cannot return to people who have been extra-generous because of the special nature of a campaign of this sort and say, "Ooops! We miscalculated. We need more."

During this self-examination phase of preparation for the campaign, the University's administrators had discovered that Chicago should have shut its doors during the early 1950's. The only reason it didn't was that nobody had then dug deeply enough into its financial affairs or had closely enough checked the health of the institution's various academic units, *taken together*, to realize how precarious the University's position had been. Under close scrutiny, however, it became perfectly obvious what the expenditure of $29,000,000 for purposes of urban renewal had done to the University. In the words of Edward Levi, at the June Convocation in 1965:

> The income on money spent by the University [for neighborhood improvement] would be sufficient to pay every member of the faculty $12,000 in each ten-year period, or to establish a fellowship program [that would award] 230 top students each year a stipend of $5,000. The $29,000,000 would have given us the projected new graduate library, the restoration of Cobb Hall, new facilities for Chemistry, a new science library, new quarters for the Music Department, and possibly a much-needed new theater. If anyone thinks I speak with feeling concerning these matters, as one concerned with academic budgets and the academic strength of this institution, he is not far wrong.

And so, one rainy mid-October day in 1965, the University formally launched its Campaign for Chicago. The very audacity of the immediate goal—approximately a million dollars a week for the next three years—was enough to draw to the announcement luncheon the city's most important citizens, from the mayor on down. I got a lump in my throat as I watched them pour into Hutchinson Commons: they knew they were going to be asked for money, and they came anyway.

I felt a different emotion—awe, I guess—as I listened to Fax Cone preside. He was absolutely matter-of-fact as he said, "It is inconceivable that we will not raise the money." At no time, and from no speaker, was there a begging note. The general assumption was that the money would be forthcoming because it was needed in order to do important and exciting things that only the University of Chicago could do. When Fax finally announced, so casually that it was really a throw-away line, that the Ford Foundation had laready given $25,000,-000, one's reaction was not "Wow!" but "Of course!"

Neither then nor later did George seem daunted by the prospect ahead of him (although *I* was). I still remember his later asking the Development Office for an interim report, a conversation that he concluded by saying, ". . . not necessarily exact. Just round it off to the nearest million." The Nebraska farm boy had traveled a long way from home, but the University he headed was still behaving as it had at its birth.

George was out of town a great deal from 1965 onward, primarily for the purpose of making presentations to foundations or corporations. He was usually accompanied by Fax Cone or another member of the Board of Trustees, and perhaps by a dean or a department chairman if their presence would help to convince the prospect that his money would do more good at the University of Chicago than somewhere else.

Once, such a team found itself making a pitch to the head of a company in the Southwest who turned out to be the chairman of another university's board of trustees. He was funneling his company's philanthropic funds into that university, but was curious to see how the University of Chicago went about this kind of solicitation.

Alumni clubs were added to George's traveling agenda more often than in the past. I accompanied him, sometimes. I remember with particular amusement a meeting for San Francisco area alumni that was held at the swank and exclusive Bohemian Club. Noting the exceptionally large crowd, I mentioned to an alumnus ('60) that the huge turnout was a touching tribute to my husband. The young man was not yet good at dissembling. "Well, yes," he said, "but then, too, the Bohemian Club isn't ordinarily open to women, and all our wives wanted to see it."

Trustees, administrators, faculty members, alumni: all had a role to play in this massive effort, and I wish it were possible for me to pay tribute to all who "brought every ounce of vital energy into the service of the canvass." That's a quotation from a memorandum by Frederick T. Gates, secretary of the Baptist

Education Society in 1890. Gates, in the company of Dr. Thomas W. Goodspeed, had raised for the University of Chicago the money necessary to match John D. Rockefeller's initial pledge. His advice (as sent to a friend about to embark on a similar enterprise) was just as good in 1965 as when he had first applied it, and it remains just as good today—for anyone wishing to raise money for anything. Here are excerpts:

> Dress well. Put on your best clothes and let them be costly. Let your linen be immaculate. See that your boots are polished, and also that your hands are kept clean and your hair well brushed, not only in the morning, but kept so throughout the rough and tumble of the day . . . People are judged by these apparent trifles of personal appearance far more than is often supposed, and the streets of Chicago soil the person hourly.

> Keep absolutely and serenely good humored. Mark, I say good humored, not gay. Enter the room in genial and radiant good nature and allow no lapse from this for an instant under any provocation.

> On entering, go straight to your subject without palaver. Do not press your work without consent but do not allow the impression of the first sixty seconds to be that you are in for a long talk. On the contrary, awaken the happy anticipation that your stay will be brief without being abrupt.

> If you find [your victim] big with gift, do not rush him too eagerly to the birth. Make him feel that he is making the gift, not that it is being taken from him with violence.

> Appeal only to the noblest motives. His own mind will suggest to him all the more selfish ones, but he will not wish you to suppose that he has thought of these.

> It is of the highest importance that you have a companion in your canvass . . . Your victim will, himself, unconsciously and instinctively decide with which of the two he

prefers to talk. Let him make his choice. There is wisdom underlying Christ's sending forth his disciples in pairs.

Never argue with a man; never contradict him. Never oppose anything which he says, that you are not absolutely bound to oppose by the very essential nature of your mission. In all else yield.

Never tell a man how much you think he ought to give . . . You can say to him, you will be glad to tell him what others are giving, if he desires to know, but that you cannot presume to name any figure for himself.

It is a good plan never to allow a man to give a final no or to commit himself in words definitely against your cause. If you see it coming, excuse yourself before the fatal word has come out and withdraw so as to give yourself an excuse for coming again.

Before entering on your canvass, meditate long on the downright merits of the question and do not ask a man for a dollar until you are in the depth of your soul satisfied that your cause fully justifies all the gifts and sacrifices you ask.

Canvass every day and all day, going rapidly from man to man, rain or shine. Read nothing, write of nothing, think of nothing, so long as your canvass continues, but the canvass. Speak publicly on that subject only, bringing every ounce of vital energy, every moment of waking time into the service of the canvass . . . This rapidity of movement keeps one's self in tension to do his best work. It brings the success, small though it may be, that tends in the aggregate to keep up courage. Gradually the work gathers volume, force, breadth, momentum until at last it becomes irresistible and rushes on to a successful culmination.

The records kept by professional fund-raising firms indicate that almost half the money given to colleges and universities during major campaigns comes from individuals, and that perhaps two-thirds of that amount comes from the relatively few donors who can write checks in six or even seven figures. This was to be Chicago's experience, too.

Eighteen months after the launching of the campaign, it would be announced that $79,000,000 had been raised—and $52,000,000 would have come from only seventy-four donors. Not that anyone would sniff at the $27,000,000 which would come from another fifteen thousand people (an average of $1,800 each); or would fail to greet with gratitude the smaller amounts from an even larger total number of donors as the campaign got down to the grass roots toward the end of the three-year period into which the initial push was concentrated.

I do not know how faithfully the fund raisers of 1965–68 followed Mr. Gates's 1890 precepts. But the work did "rush on to a successful culmination, and the $160,000,000 was to be in hand within the three years set for its accumulation.

Twenty-four

If George hadn't been so occupied with fund raising, he *might* have been able to play a more decisive role as a peacemaker in the great high school controversy which erupted in 1965. My own feeling is that the situation was so nearly hopeless by the time he got involved that it would have taken someone as canny as Lyndon B. Johnson in his Senate Majority Leader days to have effected a workable compromise.

Those people who felt strongly about the community's schools did so for the best of reasons: the quality of education offered to middle- or upper-class children is a key element in their parents' willingness to live in a given neighborhood. Every large city in the United States has new housing projects intended to draw suburbanites back to the center of town, and many of these projects have successfully done so—but the people who occupy them tend to be childless, or parents of grown children, or young couples whose children are not yet of school age. In contrast, the conservators of Hyde Park-Kenwood were determined to keep the complete-community character of the place, which meant that it had to be attractive to parents of school-age children *too*.

Almost from the founding of the University, its School of Education had operated a laboratory school—in the beginning, under the direction of John Dewey, the father of Progressivism —whose purpose was to try out new ideas in lower-school education. In due course, University High School was added. These schools give preference to faculty members' children but also admit others, and over the years they have evolved into private schools not very different from private schools elsewhere whose object is to educate bright children from middle- and upper-class backgrounds. Tuition is steep but the quality of education is worth it. Whether one's child will be admitted to the Lab School or U High often determines a prospective faculty member's acceptance of a University appointment, or whether a local doctor or lawyer will stay in the community.

At dormitory dinners, George and I sometimes argued the "morality" of the University's operating these schools. As the more idealistic students saw it, the University should close its private schools because such a move would force their pupils into the public school system. We wholly agreed that the public schools needed the brighter and more highly motivated children whom the private schools creamed off, but we did not agree that closing the Lab School or U High would accomplish the purpose. All that would happen, we told the students, would be the loss of these families from the community. It is simply a fact of life that academic or professional families are in general oriented toward private school education.

The exceptions are people who prefer public schools for a social rather than an educational reason: because their children will there associate with children from more diverse backgrounds than their own (which can be an exceedingly enriching experience), and hopefully at the same time acquire the academic skills that are the main business of any school. George and I, during our years as the parents of a schoolboy, had belonged to this category. Red had been educated in the Pasadena public school system, and we had never had cause to regret it.

For fifty or more years, people who lived in the University area had been fortunate in having both alternatives. In addition to the Lab School and University High School, there were other private schools in the neighborhood (including several run by religious groups). There was also a good public school system.

However, as the percentage of poor blacks had begun to rise during the 1940's and 1950's, the public schools had not only become overcrowded but in addition had been profoundly affected by the multiple social problems which the incoming children brought to school with them.

Large numbers of middle- or upper-class parents (white and black) had therefore decided that this kind of milieu was in no sense "enriching" for their children and had withdrawn them from the public school system. To fill the empty seats, the Chicago Board of Education had widened the boundaries of each school district, thus admitting more lower-class children from adjacent slums, which in turn had reinforced their cultural impact upon the school and made it less desirable to the parents of the middle- and upper-class chidren.

"I am *not* going to send my six-year-old to a school where she can see fornication on the playground," one mother said to me; and although she may have been overstating the problem there nevertheless is sufficient variation in the behavior patterns of children from the slums and those from professional homes to create conflict—even if the behavior pattern in question is that of language usage and not precocious sexuality.

This dismal chain of events might have been averted in Hyde Park-Kenwood (and elsewhere) if the Board of Education had poured extra funds, extra teachers, and extra programs into schools in "changing" neighborhoods; or if a quota system had been established to maintain a viable balance of middle-class/lower-class children (which in practice meant a racial quota, and civil libertarians would immediately have attacked such a "discriminatory" course).

The Chicago Board of Education, however, did nothing. By 1961, there was only one public elementary school left in Hyde Park to which middle- and upper-class parents would willingly send their children, and the changes in all the others were beginning to be reflected in the local high school. By 1965, the process was nearly complete: the number of middle-class white pupils was down to less than 7 per cent, plus nobody knows how many middle-class black pupils, and only a miracle could by then turn the school's population into a truly diverse social and cultural mix. Nevertheless, a sizable number of adults in the communities served by that school set out to work the miracle.

Hyde Park High School, once one of the city's "elite" public schools, still had a corps of exceptional teachers and a fine academic program. For years, more of its graduates had continued through the nation's university system to the Ph.D. degree than those of any other Chicago public school. It produced more Merit Scholars than most of the others. It functioned, in the classic mode of the American Dream, as a way "up and out" for children of minority groups—in large part because of the pace set by children of the majority group.

But its plant was obsolete, and instead of the 2,600 pupils it had been built to accommodate it had an enrollment of over 4,200, with some six thousand expected to be in its district by 1970. Physically, the high school was in Woodlawn, the community just south of Hyde Park (and one that had been indistinguishable from it when Hyde Park High School had been built). But Woodlawn had turned from nearly all-white to nearly all-black during the five years between 1950 and 1955; and from predominantly middle class to a mixture of lower-middle and lower. The filthiest, most blighted, and most dangerous section of Woodlawn was at its east end, and this too was where the high school was located.

The prospective saviors of Hyde Park High said that the way to do it was to clean up the vicinity via urban renewal; modernize and enlarge the high school plant; and further strengthen the academic programs. They proposed an "educational park," a system of school organization that had been successful in some other cities but had not been tried in Chicago.

As proposed for Hyde Park High, it would split six thousand students among four individual high schools on the same site. All students would leave their "own" schools and "own" faculties to share such facilities as science and language laboratories, the library, and the cafeteria. The educational park enthusiasts claimed that this kind of institution would provide greater educational opportunity for its academically less-able students without affecting the program offered its "honors" students, and at the same time would be easier to run than Hyde Park High School as it then was.

But the main advantage of their proposal was a social one. The experience of pioneering a new concept in education, in rehabilitated or new buildings among decent environs, would be exciting enough, they said, to hold the middle-class segment of the district's school-age population. If those students went, there went the school.

Middle-class black families in Woodlawn, who highly value education, were especially alarmed at the prospect of the high school's academic decline if the Hyde Park-Kenwood contingent were to be lost. (In 1965, 80 per cent of pupils in the "honors" program were residents of Hyde Park or Kenwood. Without them, the program would surely fold.) And middle-class blacks dislike the behavior patterns of lower-class blacks as much as middle-class whites do.

The opposite proposal was that a new high school be built in Hyde Park or Kenwood. Its supporters argued that even if the educational park plan were put into effect on the Hyde Park High School site, the racial composition and socio-economic background of the families in its jumbo district would be such that the middle-class students would be swamped out and they'd leave the school anyway.

A school built to serve a smaller and more heterogeneous population had a better chance of enduring as an integrated (racially and culturally) high school. If built to accommodate 2,500 or 3,000 students, it would eliminate overcrowding at Hyde Park High School; and if Hyde Park High's physical plant were at the same time modernized, its adjacent Skid Row eliminated, and extra effort expended on innovational programs, it could continue to offer a good education—although to an all-black student body.

The educational park proposal* was backed by the South East Chicago Commission (once damned by the liberals in Hyde Park for not having a social conscience); by The Woodlawn Organization, a community group whose membership reflected the aspirations of the Woodlawn middle class; and by assorted smaller groups whose primary interest was in equality of opportunity for minorities.

The separate-school proposal was backed by the Hyde Park-Kenwood Community Conference (once damned by conservatives in the community for not being sufficiently "realistic" about race relations); by Bruce Sagan in his role as publisher of the local newspaper; and by Chicago's (then) superintendent of schools, Benjamin Willis. This latter endorsement alone was enough to discredit the separate-school proposal among the area's militant civil rights groups, to whom Willis' name was anathema.

The Woodlawn people were solidly behind the educational park proposal but the Hyde Park-Kenwood citizenry was badly split. Half the people at any morning "coffee" or evening dinner party were for the educational park, half were for the separate school; and *passionately*.† Most dramatic evidence of the split was the vote taken by the Hyde Park-Kenwood Community Conference Board, the vote that determined endorsement of the separate school. It was 14–13, the chairman's tie-breaking vote being the deciding affirmative one.

And each side in the controversy wanted the University of Chicago, as the most powerful institution in the area, to support its proposal.

This, the University—as a corporate body—refused to do. The Board of Trustees said that intervention in the physical renewal of the University's own environs had been essential to its educa-

* As well as several alternatives, whose sponsors felt that it was socially or morally imperative to hold middle-cass whites at Hyde Park High School.

† Nearly a year later, when I was seeking recruits for a neighborhood improvement project and called a woman who had been actively involved in the school fight, she said, "NO! Whenever I hear the words 'community action,' I feel like screaming!" Then she burst into tears, and slammed down the receiver.

tional purposes, because neither faculty nor students can pursue
an education in a blighted neighborhood with a high crime rate.
The University also had in the works, through its School of Education, a proposal to the federal government for funds to establish an experimental school on the edge of Woodlawn—to be run
in co-operation with the public school system and with a structure and program so innovative that it would draw a racially
and culturally diverse enrollment from all over the South Side.
To do this was compatible with the purposes of the University,
said the trustees (or most of them; it was by no means a unani-
mous opinion), and such social engineering as might result
would be a by-product. The University had no business engaging
in social engineering for its own sake, which was the core of
both high school proposals.

But many people did not believe that the University's official
position was its *real* position. The South East Chicago Commission was "the action arm of the University," wasn't it? And
hadn't its executive director, Julian Levi, come out strongly
against the proposal for a separate high school in Hyde Park or
Kenwood? So far as I know, Julian represented only his own
Board of Directors; the danger inherent in the ambiguous relationship of the SECC to the University was never more clearly
demonstrated than on this occasion.

Between trips to Washington to plan a White House Conference of which he was chairman and trips to Dallas and Houston
in search of oil money for the University, George hosted meetings at our house. He hoped that some alternative plan might be
worked out to which both the educational park people and the
separate-school people would agree. No luck: upstairs in my
study, I could hear our guests shouting at each other.

The local Democratic ward committeeman, an old pro, was
wiser. He had also cast himself in the peacemaker role, but
faded abruptly out of the picture as soon as he realized—which
was at the first meeting he called—that everyone was already
too polarized for negotiation to be possible.

And George, the rational man, soon found out that *he* was not at his best when caught between evangelists. Edward Levi was right when he advised George not to attempt to mediate the dispute because, whatever its outcome, the losing side would assign responsibility to "the interference of the University."

Before the outcome was known and while "the University" was still "interfering," Bruce Sagan lost his temper—which, when he does so, he performs *fortissimo con brio, prestissamente*. He published some of the nastiest anti-University editorials in my collection of attacks on the institution.

Rumors flew like leaves in a gale. Have you heard that the University is offering tuition-free education to white children if their parents agree to oppose the separate school? Have you heard that The Woodlawn Organization is assembling a group which will march on Hyde Park and loot and burn if the separate school is approved?

A group of faculty members tried to convene the University Senate in order to get a faculty endorsement of one proposal or another, but the executive committee of the faculty Council refused to call the meeting. It didn't matter; the faculty would have split eight ways, with 10 per cent abstaining.

Some two hundred separate-school boosters had a rally in the chill November rain and marched on the President's House, singing (to the tune of *Wave the Flag for Old Chicago*)

> . . . So shame, shame on you, Chicago
> Your tricks are out of hand. . . .

And they in turn were picketed by a group of fifty supporters of the educational park plan.

Meanwhile, the Chicago Board of Education kept saying, "Will you people out there please make up your minds?" They hinted that if the warring factions in District Fourteen couldn't reach an agreement, the school board would use its money for other districts in the city whose constituencies *did* know what they wanted.

The most sensible reply came from Ray Marks, chairman of

the Hyde Park-Kenwood Community Conference's Schools Committee, who said, "*You* decide. One can't have a consensus on all issues. Sometimes it's necessary to have an outsider decide."

So the Board of Education decided. In January of 1966, it voted to build a new high school in Kenwood; to rehabilitate Hyde Park High School; and to channel into the latter a "saturation program of compensatory education to equalize learning opportunities for those below average in achievement."

The president of The Woodlawn Organization said, "The approval of a separate high school in Kenwood is a vote against the black children of Woodlawn."

The executive director of the Hyde Park-Kenwood Community Conference said, "This action insures the continued existence of Hyde Park-Kenwood as an inter-racial community."

They were both right. As of the time I write this, the new Kenwood High School is the only integrated school in the city which, the last time the racial head counts were made, had an *increase* in the number of white pupils enrolled. Many of the academic and professional families in the community do send their children there in preference to a private school.

But there have been no Merit Scholars from Hyde Park High School on the lists published during the past three years.

Twenty-five

We had a new cat, Buster. Named for his sire, he was Mary K's last litter in its entirety. He had been born—that is, dropped and abandoned—on an evening when we were away from home, and when I stumbled on him he looked dead. But he was a tough one, and when he had been brought to his mother's attention she had cared for him well. He grew big and strong but, for a cat, was singularly graceless. Where M'zelle was silent and sinuous and Mary K minced, Buster tramped around flat-footed, like a bear.

He had Mary K's big round eyes and a perpetually startled look at, rutted ice to walk on, cars that won't start, coughs that or cabinets and had to stay in them for *ages* before someone heard his raucous wails and let him out. He never understood that he was not supposed to prowl across the kitchen counters, dump over wastebaskets, or sit on top of the icebox and glare at Mrs. Galloway. He got himself tangled up in Mr. Coleman's mop; asserted his territorial rights over Mrs. Carter's vacuum cleaner; and ambushed George and me whenever we came up the stairs. In short, he livened things up a good deal during 1966 (and has continued to do so).

One can use diversions of this sort in Chicago in midwinter. It is a hard time: there is nothing but masonry and dirty snow to look, perhaps because he found himself so often locked in closets won't stop. People on the street walk all hunched up, chins buried deep in their collars, and it doesn't make the native feel any better to realize that he's not as uncomfortable as that poor Indian girl who just went past in a too-thin coat over a sari whose hem is sodden with dirty slush.

I disliked our house more in winter than in summer, and for the same reason. I couldn't get it cool enough. Enormous steam pipes coursed through the basement, and their residual heat alone was enough to raise the temperature in the rooms above to an uncomfortable eighty degrees. That's why passersby on bitterly cold days sometimes saw open windows in our house, and wondered what kind of a fresh-air fiend the President of the University was.

That's why, too, I kept a window open in the basement storeroom which we used as a wine cellar. I adjusted the opening to the vagaries of the weather, and thus kept our wine in suitably cool storage. Except once, during a four-day sub-zero spell, I forgot that the window down there was open; went into the room to get some wine for a dinner party; and discovered a frightful shambles.

The spirits were all right, but much of the wine had frozen in the bottles, with corks extruding. The soft drinks and mixers had just plain exploded, and the floor of the room was thick with splintered glass and gobbets of frozen ginger ale. Horrified, I rushed to the phone to ask George what to do.

"Did you shut the window?" he asked.

"Why, certainly," I answered, with some asperity. How stupid did he think I was, for heaven's sake?

"Well, go right down there and open it again," he commanded. "Wide! When is Mr. Coleman due to arrive? Three? Okay. Tell him to keep on his coat and gloves, and have him clean up the mess while it's still cold in there. It'll be much easier to sweep up frozen ginger ale than to mop it up after it's melted."

The recollection of a summer sign on a neighborhood store window suddenly flashed into my mind: WE SELL BOTTLE POP ONLY IN THE CARTON'S WE DO NOT SELL LOOSE POP. That store may have been in the University community but (at least in matters of syntax) was not *of* it. The same was true, in reverse, of George. He was indeed an ivory tower type, but the practical farm boy was right below the surface; and Mr. Coleman was grateful to be spared the handling of loose pop.

In some respects, the winter months in Chicago are more pleasant than the others. Because the weather is unpredictable in its details but almost certain to be bad, there is much less scuttling between city and suburbs from January to April. People tend to sit by their own hearths with only a handful of neighborhood friends to keep them company. The slower pace of life in general plus the effort it takes to fling yourself out into the storm in order to go anywhere create a mood of heightened sensitivity: one savors the talk or the music more than if they were heard at some other time of year, and one's emotions become more deeply engaged in the small dramas that are always being played out wherever human beings congregate.

I minded the "nut calls" less at that time of year. There was a perfectly sensible-sounding woman who telephoned every few months to report that the interns at Billings Hospital had "transistorized" her brain, thus enabling them to "tune in on" her thoughts, after which they "taunted" her with their knowledge. There was a male alumnus who called—prepaid, from California —whenever he was drunk (which was fairly often) to say that the University would never get a penny from him so long as that bastard Hutchins was its President. And there was the mother of a former student (who had flunked out at least in part because of what could only be called persecution by his mother) who wanted me personally to check on the welfare of the boy, from whom she hadn't heard in several years. She, too, was afflicted by drink; although *she* said, "I'm not really an alcoholic, I'm just passing as one."

It was always entertaining to shop at the Co-op Supermarket (which also serves Hyde Park as a communications command post), but during the winter slowdown I had time to park my cart between the English biscuits and the Polish hams and have a really good chat with chance-met friends.

"Why, hello, Bettie. It's been ages since I've seen you. Have you been away?"

"In a sense. I've been on jury duty for three weeks."

"Interesting?"

"Dreadful. There were thirty of us who spent all day sitting on uncomfortable straight chairs in a big, noisy, smoky room. I was used once; called and excused twice; and the rest of the time I just sat."

"What a terrible waste."

"Well, not wholly. I got fairly well acquainted with another juror, and she gave me two marvelous cookie recipes."

Or:

"Hi, Mrs. Beadle. Had you heard that Kay Clement and Adele Halkin and John Hawkinson finally got acquitted?"

"They did? I'm glad to hear it."

(These three tree-lovers had, the previous summer, stationed themselves between an old elm and the city workman who was supposed to cut it down; and had thereupon been arrested under an ordinance forbidding collecting in a crowd for unlawful purposes.)

"Yeah. Guess why the magistrate directed a verdict for acquittal? He said he couldn't accept as fact that three is a crowd."

Usually, there were fresh controversies to hear about, too. The Co-op itself was often in ferment, since some of its members saw it as a social-action institution and were always forbidding its manager to buy South African lobster tails (because they disapproved of apartheid) or kitchenware from U. S. Steel (because its local plant was ruining the ecology of the Indiana sand dunes).

Those who championed such causes were balanced by the conservatives in the Co-op membership who could be counted on to rise at a meeting and bellow, "What the hell relationship should there be between Verwoerd's morality and our operating *a grocery store?*" And there was almost always someone shopping at the Co-op who could give me a blow-by-blow account of the latest crisis in member-management relations.

Failing that, there was infinite pleasure to be derived from looking at the advertisements on the bulletin board ("Young woman needed to help English teacher grade themes"; and, in a different hand, below: "This is not a complete sentence.") It was fun, too, to scan the titles available in the Family Reading Center. (*Hot Rodding* to *Forbes*, *Astrological Digest* to *Karate*, *New Statesman* to *True Romances;* and the whole black spectrum from *Tan* through *Sepia* to *Ebony* and *Jet*.) A very intellectual community, ours: I once eavesdropped while a young mother gave her six-year-old an anatomy lesson, using the organ meats as her visual aids. ("See? Your heart looks just like this.")

Another large notice board holds announcements of coming events at the community's various churches or clubs. In the winter of '66, for example, the Unitarian Church was offering five Sunday meetings on "the new morality," and among the topics were abortion, homosexuality, and pre-marital sexual experience. The woman standing next to me as we read the notice murmured, more to herself than to me, "Oh, dear. I'll have to go to all of them so that nobody will know which one I'm really interested in."

The Unitarians were always raising someone's blood pressure. A black family from Kenwood had recently moved to Kenilworth (until then a lily-white suburb), and its residents were sharply divided on how to behave toward the newcomers. At a dinner party there, a friend told me, he had overheard someone say that the Kenilworth pro-integrationists were "either Unitarians, have some connection with the University of Chicago, or have marital problems."

And back in Hyde Park? A controversy was raging about five town houses that were being built so close to an adjacent building that its owner would be unable to repair or maintain one wall. The owner, a widow, had obtained a court injunction to halt the building of the one town house that would most affect her property, but she lacked funds to fight a prolonged legal battle. So a neighborhood committee in support of her cause was organized, and had a series of money-raising benefits. The final, and most successful one, was a showing of *King Kong* in the social hall of the Unitarian Church.

One of the town house developers said to me, ruefully, "We started the project three years ago, and with each year of delay the price of the houses has gone up 15 per cent. If we get 'em done next year—*if*—we'll be at the limit of the market, or maybe beyond. We ought to have a movie benefit, too. Do you suppose we could get Rodfei Zedek to screen *The Bride of Franken-stein* for *us?*"

Two distinguished visitors were scheduled to visit the University during the winter quarter of 1966: Vice-President Hubert Humphrey, and Prince Philip of Great Britain. One of them didn't make it, and the other was with us for ten minutes—but both occasions were memorable.

The Vice-President was to speak to a student assembly at three on a Friday afternoon. The University was told that a several-block-square area around the auditorium must at that time be completely clear of both parked and moving cars, so NO PARK-ING signs were posted on Thursday. In accordance with hallowed urban custom, there were generally ignored; and, therefore, on Friday morning the police began a colossal tow-away operation. They hauled cars by the dozens to an impound area which is many blocks distant from the University. To reclaim such cars, one has to pay the towing fee *and* a fine *and* (if one parked the car in gear) very likely a repair bill on a wrecked transmission.

That's why a good many people would have been hot under the collar even if Humphrey had arrived; but he was delayed en route and never made it to the University. I suspect that one more small piece in the growing student resentment against the Establishment was set in place that day—for the Vice-President *did* make it to Chicago in time to appear, that evening, at a hundred-dollar-a-plate banquet in behalf of a fellow Democrat.

A couple of months later, on a particularly dreary March day, Prince Philip came to call. He has long been interested in the

work of the International Variety Club, one of whose philanthropies is La Rabida Children's Hospital, just south of the University. To visit it was on his schedule; so, on his way back to
the city, why shouldn't he have a look at the campus site where a
bronze sculpture by England's great Henry Moore was to
memorialize the first controlled release of atomic energy? The
twenty-fifth anniversary of that event would occur in 1967, and
the sculpture had already been commissioned for installation
then.

The prince would do no more than pause briefly for a look at
the plaque marking the spot where Enrico Fermi and his team
had built their first "pile," and the time of his arrival was sufficiently uncertain so that it was announced only as "late afternoon." In curious contrast to the security measures that had been
in effect for Vice-President Humphrey, an extremely small area
was kept clear; there were no police in evidence until fifteen
minutes before the prince arrived; and they allowed onlookers to
stand quite close to the official party.

University of Chicago students, who had been eager to hear
and see Humphrey, adopted a tone of lofty disdain toward Prince
Philip's visit. They were very populist about it: good red-
blooded Americans simply don't flip over royalty. In fact, the
students whose curiosity overcame their scruples were particularly grubby. They looked as if they'd deliberately avoided shav-
ing that day, or had worn their oldest and dirtiest clothes to make
the point that they weren't paying homage to an outmoded
institution or to a particularly glamorous representative of it.
Happily, however, none of them showed up with picket signs
insulting the Crown.

When the small cavalcade, led by a shiny black Rolls, arrived,
George stepped forward to greet our visitor. The rest of us—
myself, Mrs. Fermi, several scientists who had been in Fermi's
group, and the people on the Moore sculpture committee—were
loosely lined up along the curb, and George introduced us in
turn.

My total conversation with Prince Philip consisted of "How
do you do?" But there was abundant opportunity to observe that

he was as handsome as his best pictures show him—tanned and fit, lean rather than tall. The effect of tallness, I expect, is due to contrast with the Queen, who is petite, when they are pictured together. There was no sign whatsoever of his alleged abruptness, and considerable evidence of his famous charm.

After looking at the plaque (scoured and polished that morning after unknown vandals had daubed it with paint) and having the site of the Moore sculpture pointed out to him, the allotted ten minutes had passed and the visitors prepared to depart. But the prince delayed a moment to speak to a cluster of male students who were lounging behind the restraining ropes.

I had noticed them earlier: a sullen-looking lot, with expressions just this side of a sneer, and as the prince paused beside them I held my breath in anticipation of some coming rudeness.

"What are you specializing in?" the prince asked them.

"Chemistry, sir," one of them replied.

Sir!

"So am I," said another; and a third said, "Mathematics."

"Are you good at it?" Prince Philip asked him.

"This is the week I find out," the boy answered. "We're in exams now."

"Good luck, then," said our royal visitor, with a smile and a slight wave of his hand.

I was spellbound throughout this exchange. The students had not only stood up straight as soon as the prince had addressed them and had been as polite as if they were ten-year-olds at a wedding reception but had also acquired expressions that could only be described as awed. (*Imagine! Prince Philip of Great Britain is speaking to ME! Wait'll the folks back home in Columbus hear about THIS!*)

What I often forgot about students, especially undergraduates, is that surface appearances are misleading. Most them are at base as conventional as Presbyterian deacons.

March was also enlivened by the city's annual St. Patrick's Day parade. Dozens of pounds of green dye are dumped into the Chicago River; a green stripe is painted down the center of State

Street; and shamrock-emblazoned flags fly from the light poles. There are over eighty thousand foreign-born and first-generation Irish in Chicago, and twice that many with sentimental ties to the Old Country—including Richard J. Daley. So it is no wonder that St. Patrick's Day brings out the finest of the city's marching bands, decorated floats, and delegations from every group that is or ever expects to be beholden to the mayor for a favor. In fact, as many Krskas and Kucharskis as Ryans and McDuffys turn up in green ties for the march along That Great Street, which is relabeled O'State Street for the day.

Mayor Daley, even if standing in a snowstorm or a sleety rain, beams at the TV cameras, pronounces the weather "nearly perfect," and steps off briskly at the head of his fifty thousand Sons (however temporarily) of Old Erin. Parade buffs like me stand and shiver on the curbs, waiting to see if the Pioneer Total Abstinence Society will be in the line-up this year, or what device the United German-American Societies will use to bridge the gap between Von Steuben and St. Patrick. There is never any doubt about the presence in the parade of the Bridgeport Mothers' Club, the Sweeney Senators, the Chicago Police Wives' Association, the Asbestos Workers' Union—and every city employee who can possibly be spared from his desk that day.

All in all, the St. Patrick's Day parade is a great folk festival; and I was always delighted if I then happened to be entertaining a foreign visitor on a first trip to the United States. (As I was, on March 17 of '66.) Parades of this sort are uniquely American: amusing, yes, but with that valiant innocence and vigor that lie close to the American bone. No foreigner can fully appreciate our national character until he has stood in a street crowd and watched the marching bands and drum majorettes, the ethnic sodalities, the trade unions, and the neighborhood improvement associations pass in review.

Despite its size and affluence, Chicago has been unable to establish and maintain a repertory theater—but it is not for want of trying by a small group of enthusiasts. The 1966 version of this perennial effort was an alliance between the Goodman School of the Theater, which is run by the Art Institute of Chicago, and the University. Edward Levi was the impresario, the wherewithal being supplied by the Rockefeller Foundation, and the object was to see whether Chicagoans—whose usual fare is a road show of last year's Broadway hit—would take to a professional production of a classic drama.

The Goodman's director, John Reich, settled on *The Misanthrope*, and hired a company headed by George Grizzard and Barbara Baxley to perform it. The "theater" was the University's Law School auditorium, which has a tiny stage, no footlights, no curtain, and no dressing rooms. On the eve of opening night, it seemed likely that there would be no audience, either—so poor were the advance sales (and twenty-nine performances scheduled!). Yet *The Misanthrope* turned into an SRO hit.

Joseph Maronek's set, an elaborately detailed and gold-washed drawing room which at first glance looked authentically baroque, turned out to be a collage of washboards, pie tins, pot lids, and other twentieth-century "found" objects. Richard Wilbur's translation had a lively contemporary sound, yet in no way violated the original. The actors also managed to give a gloss of here-and-now to their delivery and their actions. Yet the drama was costumed and played as a period piece. It was, in short, a stunning performance, and people who had never heard of Molière and couldn't have defined "minx" flocked to the Midway to see a seventeenth-century man grapple with the same problems *they* had.

The initial question was therefore answered affirmatively: Chicagoans would pay to see a really good professional production of a classic drama. During the post-*Misanthrope* euphoria, there was a lot of talk about a permanent alliance between the Goodman School of the Theater and the University of Chicago, but nothing was to come of it.

The city's ordinarily rather stuffy musical Establishment also found itself in an innovative mood that spring. The Chicago Symphony was celebrating its Diamond Jubilee with a series of special events, and the most festive was a dinner dance held in Orchestra Hall itself. Like our Law School auditorium, the building had not been designed for the use that was made of it, but turned out to be wondrously adaptable.

The audacious ladies who masterminded the party simply had every other row of seats on the main floor removed, replacing them with narrow shelves at table height, and served dinner on them to people sitting in the facing seats. These counters were laid with avocado green felt and garlanded with pink satin ribbons caught up into nosegays of fresh flowers. Pastel felt banners hung from the railings around the balconies and boxes; tiny pink lights twinkled in a swag of greens which swooped across the rear of the stage; and the steps and edges of the stage were banked with ferns. In the cool ivory and Wedgwood blue setting of Orchestra Hall as it was then decorated, the scene was a visual treat of high order.

After dinner, there was dancing—brisk modern music on the stage, waltzing to a string ensemble in a second-floor foyer. The Symphony's conductor, Jean Martinon, added the final fillip by both conducting the strings and playing his own violin. A man who was so austere in his behavior at the regular concerts that many Symphony-goers never did warm to him,* Martinon that night was swinging and swaying in waltz time, with a broad smile on his face, and I thought it a pity that the general public never saw him thus.

In sum, March and April were that year's merry months—for me. For a good many students and administrators at the University, they were just the reverse, and May was a nightmare for us all. . . .

* He has since returned to France.

Twenty-six

Because a C student at a very selective and demanding college may have done far better work than an A student from a college with lower standards, sophisticated employers and graduate schools began, a long time ago, to ask colleges to "rank" their students. There are various formulas for doing this, but one way is to say that "Joe Doakes has a grade-point average of 3.5, which places him in the upper 10 per cent of his class." However such rankings are computed, they are a more accurate measure of academic achievement than grades alone.

One of the tragic side effects of the Vietnam war was that, during the 1960's, the colleges and universities of the United States held—in the same sense that jails hold prisoners—a large population of young men who were enrolled primarily because they could thus avoid serving in a war they considered to be both senseless and immoral. The interest of such students in scholarship was minimal, but so long as their colleges certified that they were "in good standing" they were almost without question deferred from military service.

Nevertheless, since the young are idealistic and at present are thoroughly egalitarian as well, many of these students felt guilty about being members of an elite group which was allowed to sit out the war while men of the same age but without the student deferment were being drafted. What drove the knife deeper was the knowledge that it wasn't some anonymous other person who sent the non-college man off to war; it was you, yourself, the person who had asked for and been given a 2S deferment.

Even some students who *were* interested in scholarship felt this way. It was a heavy burden on the conscience to know that while you sat in Music 101, some contemporary—as "worthy" of a college education as you were, but one who had been denied the opportunity because he was poor, or black, or both—was getting his head blown off in Vietnam. Many students believed that such inequity was wrong, but couldn't bring themselves to redress it personally by refusing the student deferment. It's a dreadful combination: to act for self-protection yet at the same time to loathe oneself for acting that way.

In March of 1966, a change in Selective Service policy further exacerbated an already emotion-laden situation. Draft boards were instructed to consider the *quality* of a student's work when deciding whether to defer him. This meant that he would be wise to produce a grade record when requesting deferment, although he was not required to. He also had the option of taking an examination administered by Science Research Associates for the Selective Service, and to submit whichever grade record was better.

Nothing about the draft is equitable, and this scheme was probably no more inequitable than any of the other devices which have been used over the years to enable the armed forces to take some but not all of those in the manpower pool. Nevertheless, this version did create an elite category *within* the elite, and made the best students feel that they were not only sending unknown black brothers out to die but in addition were doing the same to good friends on their own campuses. The better their grades, the more they felt like executioners.

And on May 12 of that year, the issue of comparative academic achievement as a yardstick for draft deferment exploded into violence on the University of Chicago campus.

For two months beforehand, students and administrators had been meeting in an effort to find a solution to the problem. George, who was spending much of his time asking people for money for the University, was at that point little involved. The job had fallen to the Provost, the Dean of the College, the Dean of Students, the Committee of the Council (the executive committee of the faculty's ruling body), and assorted others; and they were all gray with fatigue long before the battle was officially joined.

As in all such intramural controversies of the 1960's, it was not a simple case of the old in closed ranks against the young, for the student point of view was supported by some faculty members and by some administrators. And in this particular case, there was little argument among the disputants as to whether grades *do* reveal the extent to which a student possesses the qualities or skills for whose development the Selective Service postpones drafting him. Instead, the argument swung around the role of the University in providing grade records—specifically, rank-in-class—to draft boards.

Providing such information makes the University an active agent of Selective Service, the protesting students said. You must stop co-operating with the draft boards.

The University isn't co-operating with the draft boards, the administrators replied. It is co-operating with its own students. It has been our long-time belief that a student's grade record is *his* property, to use as he sees fit. When he asks us to send a transcript to a graduate school or to a prospective employer, we do it as a service to him. That action can't conceivably be interpreted as supporting the interests or activities of the other university or of the firm with which the student is seeking employment. The University's relationship to a student's draft board is no different.

Well, then, the protesting students demanded, eliminate comparative grade records when you know that the report is going to a draft board. The use of rank-in-class as a basis for deferment is morally wrong, and the University should take a stand against it.

But what if a student *wishes* us to send a comparative grade record to his draft board? the administrators countered. It's his legal right to do so. Many would think it just as immoral for the University to deny a student that right as for Selective Service to use his grade record as a basis for deferment.

Wrong, the students said. There is a higher morality that demands your withholding this information. Besides, providing it will corrupt the educational process. Students will be forced to work for high grades alone, and to get them will be limited to the easiest courses and the easiest professors. The faculty won't be able to grade objectively, knowing that they are judging not only the student's course work by also his right to live or die.

Will corrupt the educational process? replied the administrators. Grade records were given to draft boards during the Korean war, and the educational process wasn't corrupted then. As for grading objectively, no single grade determines a student's grade-point average; that depends upon *all* course grades. Many exams are not even scored by course instructors. So there's no reason for a professor to feel that the grade *he* gives will condemn a student to "live or die." As for the grading system itself, we agree that there's a lot to be said against it. But it continues to exist, and both faculty and students have managed to live with it, because it serves purposes that are considered to be useful. Grades can determine whether a person remains in college, or gets a certain job; and these consequences of the system can have at least as great an impact on a person's life as his qualifying or not qualifying for draft deferment. So, if an awareness of those consequences hasn't fundamentally impaired the grading system, it seems unlikely that Selective Service guidelines will do it.

Then, the students said—and almost eight hundred of them said it—drop *my* record from the total that you use when computing the rankings.

If we do so, the administrators replied, the rankings will be statistically meaningless. And wouldn't such a course be a great disservice to other students? Such statistics explain the significance of the grade record to outsiders. How else can you make the point that a C+ average is such a good record in our College that it places its holder in the upper half of his class?

Oh, hell! said the students. There just isn't enough time left in this quarter to discuss the issue fully. Why don't you postpone the formation and dissemination of class rankings until next October? That'll give all points of view a chance to be really *heard*.

Nothing doing, the administrators replied. We know as well as you do that draft deferments are granted during the summer. We are quite willing to discuss at greater length the issue of academic achievement as a basis for draft deferment. Perhaps some changes in University policy might result. General conclusions or recommendations arising from such discussions might (just possibly, although we think it unlikely) affect national Selective Service policy. But we are not in the meantime going to deny their grade records to students who have gone through this school year with the expectation that such information will be available to them during the summer. It makes a particular difference to seniors who will want to ask for deferment in order to go on to graduate school in the fall.

What else can you expect of administrators? the protesting students then asked each other. They're a bunch of desiccated old men. Let's take this to the faculty. *They* think straight. *They* understand us.*

So the postponement proposal went before the faculty Council. The Council turned it down and endorsed the University's current policy—of sending grade records to draft boards, at a student's request—but offered to consider changing the policy in the fall after the desired "fuller discussion" had occurred.

The Council also arranged for an immediate open meeting at which all the facts about the draft laws would be discussed; called a full-scale, nationally based conference on the draft, to be held the following autumn; instructed the President of the University to ask the Association of American Universities to

_____

* One of the curious mental blocks among university people (and not just students) is that they distinguish so sharply between "administrators" and "faculty"—even when, as at the University of Chicago, all administrators with responsibility for the academic side of the institution are also members of the faculty.

initiate a study of ways to make the draft laws more equitable; and appointed a faculty-student committee to study the University's own policies and report their findings and recommendations by June 7.

It should be mentioned at this point that there is a Student Government organization at Chicago, its members being elected in accordance with principles of representative government. I have already noted that the faculty Council is similarly selected. However, both students and faculty often bypass their own representative bodies (at Chicago and elsewhere) in favor of setting up ad hoc committees.

In May of 1966, consequently, some faculty members refused to accept the decision of their Council, and both the already-organized Students Against the Rank and other students ignored Student Government's endorsement of the official University policy on computing and distributing grade records. Among the latter were some three hundred students who called themselves the Ad Hoc Committee for a Free Choice, but they couldn't think up anything more dramatic to do than sign a petition affirming the right of a student to decide for himself what use should be made of his grade record. They were a comfort to the administrators, however.

By the second week in May, then, it was clear to the Students Against the Rank that they weren't going to get what they wanted by using the appropriate channels for effecting change. So, okay—if you can't persuade, you coerce. Only they didn't put it that way. When four hundred of them moved into the Administration Building they said they "deeply regretted having to do so but had been driven to it because all attempts to rationally and openly change [the University's policy on ranking] have been thwarted. The only channel left open is direct action."

The desiccated old men in Administration—and many of them did feel old by that time—were thoroughly exasperated, not least because they knew that "direct action" (such as asking the police to clear the building) was not a channel left open to *them*. More correctly, it was a last resort. By now, there had been enough sit-ins around the country for university administrators and police riot squads to have gotten acquainted with each other. And the police assured the academics that one had to provide four police officers for each student if one were to carry them out of a building—kicking, screaming, and biting every step of the way—without the use of nightsticks or the other visual symbols of force which so enraged the uncommitted moderates that they became radicalized. Thus a force of sixteen hundred police officers would be needed to handle the four hundred students in the Administration Building; and Chicago's administrators knew full well that the mere arrival on campus of that many cops would radicalize everyone anyway.

So they fell back on the tactics they had used during the 1962 sit-in. They did nothing. But they did it more conspicuously: the top administrators simply vanished from sight, and neither students nor faculty could find them. George worked at home part of the time, but where he holed up elsewhere I don't know. He and Edward Levi and the others whose responsibility it was to "run" the University met every morning to evaluate information provided them by deans and the University's own security people who were in contact with the sit-inners. Anywhere from half a dozen to seventy faculty members were invited to join these meetings, partly for their own education and partly so that the administrators could seek informal counsel from them.

Each morning the question was the same: Shall we take any action today? The administrators usually came to yesterday's conclusion, which was that inaction might not be the right course but that other proposed alternatives seemed definitely wrong, so they'd stick with inaction.

I can understand why the students didn't figure out what this stall was in aid of, but I am still astounded by the obtuseness of the press. Here was a university with an explicitly stated policy banning sit-ins or similar "disruptive and coercive acts" as a means of settling disputes. But here too was a policy which was unenforceable because there was no penalty for non-compliance.

Compliance could be obtained via public opinion. If, for example, a majority of faculty and students believed that a sit-in is such a gross offense against the common good that one simply doesn't do it (in the same sense that one doesn't do murder), disaffected groups would be unlikely to defy the sanction.

Or compliance could be obtained in a more legalistic way, by imposing a penalty such as the suspension or expulsion of those who participate in sit-ins.

The administrators were convinced by weeks of meeting with the protesting students that their leaders were not really interested in the class-rank issue except as a tool for gaining greater control over policy making within the University. Looking ahead, therefore, the administrators could see innumerable repetitions of the same pattern. The issues would be different but the outcome would be the same; and neither the adults who had to deal with the students nor the University itself could stand repeated disruptions of this kind.

Students have more energy than administrators. They can manage with less sleep. They can skip classes that professors have to prepare for. They don't have a multitude of private or professional responsibilities outside office hours. Furthermore, they can recruit fresh troops each year. The administrators quailed at the prospect of a future filled with emergency sessions of ad hoc committees or ruling bodies, drafting of statements, reading of statements, exclusion from their own offices, extra expenditures for security, repair, and clean-up of buildings; and, worst of all, the attendant emotionalism. You can't think coherently, or do so only by expending a tremendous lot of extra energy, in an atmosphere full of turmoil. And thinking is what a university is all about.

So they decided to postpone action on *this* sit-in in hope that it might be the last. Perhaps faculty and student opinion would coalesce into something resembling a true sanction against coercive acts of this nature. Perhaps a legalistic penalty would be imposed. But for either development to occur, it was necessary to wait. Some of the faculty, for example, weren't even aware that a sit-in was in progress until it had been under way for two days and the New York *Times* reported it. Those of the faculty who did know about it had a range of opinions from total disinterest ("Let the Administration handle it") to total involvement ("I'm going over to the Ad Building tonight to talk some sense into/give my support to those kids").

Now, who were the Students Against the Rank?

Among the leaders were a handful of rebels (mostly, members of Students for a Democratic Society) who believed that the United States had become so rotten that it was beyond reform. Their long-range goal was revolution; only by tearing everything down and starting fresh, they thought, could one create a truly decent and democratic society.

I have never understood why they tried to start the revolution by taking over the universities. It should have been self-evident that the net result of success would be to close the universities but leave the nation unaffected—at least, for quite a long time. Nor do I find it easy to believe that the rebels, as intelligent as most of them were, seriously expected that they could keep the universities alive as corporate bodies, once they had control of them, if they made the fundamental alterations in organization and role that they proposed to.

However, they *acted* as if their goals made sense, and they convinced a great many of their fellow students. They themselves were more interested in strategy and tactics than in issues, and they were very good at the art and science of campus confrontation politics. One of this type who was a leader in the Chicago sit-in of 1966 was a girl who had come to campus fresh from the Free Speech Movement at Berkeley. The staff people who watched her in action said that she was a marvel at crowd control and manipulation.

Then there was a group of idealistic militants, kids who really were exercised about the class-rank issue, the morality of the

Vietnam war, the University's alleged sell-out to the military-industrial complex, and all the rest of it. They didn't think logically, couldn't argue worth a darn, and were incredibly gullible—but they could (and did) *feel*. If they thought of revolution at all, it was not in realistic terms. Bloodshed, hunger, imprisonment, and death had no place in the romantic vision of the world they wanted to live in.

They hated the hypocrisy of adult society, the rigidity of its political institutions, the impersonality of its bureaucracies. They sought to create a society that places human values before materialistic ones, that has a little less head and a little more heart, that is less dominated by self-interest and loves its neighbor more. And they were persuaded that group protest of a militant nature would advance those goals.

But again, why pick the university as their target? It is among the freest of society's institutions, the one that places human values highest. Ah, but the students didn't know that. At Chicago, as at any university, it is always easy to find examples of bureaucratic rigidity and indifference to professed ideals. To realize that these are few and transitory requires experience with the world "outside" and development of the ability to make comparative judgments—which twenty-year-olds haven't had and can't do. Perhaps they wouldn't have in the 1960's, anyway, theirs being a singularly Puritanical college generation.

The administrators were not only well aware of the imperfections in the University but in addition saw in these high-minded young people the ghosts of themselves in earlier days. Hadn't they joined Moral Rearmament in the 1930's? Resigned their ROTC commissions as a protest against pre-Pearl Harbor "involvement" in the European war? Grieved over Hiroshima and Nagasaki? That's why they were patient with the idealistic militants long beyond the time that the public wanted "all those longhairs" tossed in jail. Many of them were so fundamentally *good* that the adults on campus couldn't lightly let them acquire the criminal records that would haunt them all the rest of their lives.

Finally, there were the hangers-on, students who became involved in the movement—any movement—because it was emotionally satisfying. At Chicago, there are few activities in which "everybody" participates, and the lack is especially felt by the younger undergraduates. A sit-in can fuse them into a fellowship of "we" against "them." It packs them into a hot, steamy mass of singing, chanting, touching bodies. It encourages such communal acts as sharing a blanket and eating from the same jar of peanut butter. It is not surprising that they come out of it—a few days of it, anyway—feeling that they have had something akin to a religious experience.

Some of the University dormitories will pack bag lunches for students in lieu of a meal in the dining hall. One of the funny products of the '66 sit-in were the coveys of freshmen girls, bag lunches in hand, skipping off to spend the night in the Administration Building—having first, in strict adherence to the rules, entered their destination in the dorm's "sign-out" book. To them, the sit-in was the equivalent of those Girl Scout overnights they had enjoyed so much when they were thirteen.

One can easily forget how very young many of our students are, they talk so well and are so bright. After the sit-in had been in progress for three days and it was obvious that those faculty members who were their mentors did not represent a majority of the faculty, many of the student protestors paid calls on other faculty members in an attempt to convince them of the righteousness of the cause.

One professor later told me about his visitor. She was a girl, he said, who "had a shiny quality—the sort of thing you don't want to destroy by being scornful or hostile or 'adult.'" So he listened to her exposition of the points at issue, and murmured noncommittally at appropriate moments. Then she told him how wonderful it was to be part of the sit-in, how uplifting to the spirit, and ended by saying, ". . . and another thing. From the fourth floor of the Ad Building, you get a simply beautiful view of the tulips in the Quad. I'll probably never have a chance again to see them like that."

Nevertheless, when several hundred of these innocents—plus others who were much less so—gathered into one compact group, they constituted a mob. And as such they were potentially dangerous. What if they got into fights among themselves (as they were beginning to do by the third day of the sit-in), and some were badly hurt? What if they set fire to the building? The University's officers, in their morning sessions, worried a good deal about questions of this sort.

Fortunately, the campus cops were allowed in the building. (As "workers," their presence was acceptable to the students.) The administrators knew they could rely on these men to head off real trouble inside the building, or to organize its evacuation in the event of physical danger. The security force also kept an eye on offices and files which had been locked when their legitimate users had left, or been thrown out of, the building. Not that the campus cops could have done much to prevent looting had the sit-in taken that turn. Perhaps the University was lucky to have lost nothing but typewriters, stationery, and similar supplies from the unlocked Registrar's Office.

Late one evening, on his way home from yet another marathon meeting with student representatives, George observed that the light in his office was on. Envisioning the sit-inners gleefully pawing through his files, he called the security office to find out why the room was lighted.

The officer on duty checked and called back. He said, "Sorry, Mr. Beadle. One of our men went in to water your plants—remember, you asked us to?—and forgot to turn out the light when he left."

By 1966, the rhetoric of student activists had become more intemperate than in earlier years. The administrators were determined to keep cool; yet this was difficult to do when some stripling said (as one did to Edward Levi—Edward, of all people, who holds the University as dear as if it were a blood relative),

"The welfare of the University? That's secondary to the just-ness of our cause. The hell with the welfare of the University!"

Or not to feel one's hackles rising when a dinner meeting, one of many held by the executive committee of the faculty Council in order to save time when conferring with student spokesmen, was publicized by the latter as "an attempt to buy us off."

Or to remain calm when obscenities were whispered into one's ears at 3 A.M.; at least, that's the time the callers chose to telephone *us*.

(Off-campus calls could be controlled at the University's main switchboard, but not calls originating within the internal system; and we didn't dare disconnect our phone in case it was necessary to somebody who *ought* to be able to reach George in a hurry.)

On the fourth day of the sit-in, a Saturday, the mass of students vacated the Administration Building. They left a small "occupation force" but announced that they would "per-mit free access to and operation of the building by the Ad-ministration, so long as they act in good faith." They were genuinely surprised, on Monday, to find that no one had come to work; and they were appalled to discover that no one would be coming to work—most notably the President and the Pro-vost—so long as any of them were there.

By now, all save the hard core wanted out. But they wanted some token victory, too. After the Monday-night meeting with the students' spokesmen, George came home nearly in tears, and told me that the students were in the same state.

"*Please* give us some promise, something concrete, some con-cession that we can use to convince the others that it hasn't all been for nothing," one boy pleaded.

But Edward and George were unable to do more than reiterate the standing offer: wider and fuller discussion, aimed at re-consideration of the University's policy on drawing up and distributing records of class ranks—once the atmosphere was free of coercion.

Some time after midnight, the remaining students left the building.

But that wasn't the end of it.

For George, there was a mountain of correspondence to be acknowledged. Many of the letters were abusive ("Do you have so little character that you cringe at the thought of standing up to those creeps?"). A few were amusing ("Don't turn off the electricity because then the kids will light matches, but do turn off the water. After the first flush the johns won't work, and that'll be the beginning of the end"). And some were supportive ("Congratulations! Had you called the police you would have placed yourself on the same level as the protestors in that you would have resorted to physical coercion"). A sufficient number of letters, even those written in the heat of passion, showed such deep concern for higher education or for the problems of young people of draft age that George felt he should respond. During the next few weeks he signed close to a thousand letters.

He also had to prepare a statement for an upcoming meeting of the faculty Senate. This was an extraordinary session, the University's statutes providing for only one meeting a year of the entire faculty (usually in November, when the President gives his annual report). Upon petition by a certain percentage of the faculty, however, the Senate may be convened—and such a petition had been circulated during the sit-in. The hoped-for moral sanction against sit-ins did not seem to be sprouting from the grass roots, so the Council was going before the full Senate with a recommendation that "in the future any student who engages in such an act shall be subjected to appropriate disciplinary action, not excluding expulsion."

Other administrators had to oversee the clean-up of the building; replace stolen supplies; repair damaged equipment; set up procedures for advancing emergency funds to especially hard-pressed employees among the five thousand whose paychecks could not be drawn during the period when the building had been occupied; and work out overtime schedules aimed at catching up on this and similar clerical work. (The cost of all this came to something like $100,000.)

The proposed "fuller discussions" had to be gotten under way. There were several, some open to everyone, some restricted to particular groups of faculty and students. And, of course, planning for the Draft Conference in the fall was going forward.

Student Government sponsored a referendum which allowed students to indicate their opinions on a variety of options having to do with the use of grade records for draft deferment, and the Students Against the Rank did their cause no good by urging fellow students to boycott the referendum. They gave as their reason that insufficient time for full discussion had elapsed, but students who had been opposed to the sit-in from the beginning interpreted this position as foreknowledge that the vote would go against the protestors. As it did: 924 voted for continuing the "free choice" policy until a possible reconsideration of it in the fall, 322 for withholding grade records over the summer.

Nor was it sound strategy for an offshoot group to move into the faculty club and start a hunger strike there. This move brought the controversy to the attention of far more faculty members than might otherwise have become interested in it, and annoyed them so much that it generated a strong bloc against the student "cause."

On May 27, George went off to the meeting of the faculty Senate with some trepidation. Would they approve the Council's recommendation that penalties up to expulsion should be the future consequence of participating in a sit-in? And if they didn't, would he resign his office? He hadn't decided: he was too tired of receiving ultimatums from students to give himself one, but the prospect of going through more such altercations was unbearable. He had lost fifteen pounds during the past month, and was exhausted. So were those University officers who had been on the front lines even longer.

He told the Senate that day:

By the restraint of our action and by our continued willingness to confer, we hoped to reaffirm, as nothing else could, the belief of our University in the process of rational discussion and decision. But I am not prepared to say that the University's response to future extra-legal actions can be of this same nature.

The backing of the faculty is extremely important, and for two reasons: one, the knowledge of that backing will itself diminish the chance of a recurrence and thus make disciplinary action unnecessary; and, two, if despite this backing there is a recurrence, your administrators must be in a position to act as promptly, decisively, and effectively as the integrity of the University requires.

About half the members of the Senate came to the meeting. They approved the Council's recommendation by a vote of 268–46, with 130 abstaining. Many of these latter, I dare say, took issue with some small point of phraseology or procedure; academics are great nit-pickers. Other abstainers, having kept their distance from the firing lines, didn't believe that "such a stern measure was called for"—but they couldn't quite bring themselves to vote against a recommendation strongly advocated by colleagues whom they respected.

Among those who voted "no" were faculty members who believed that the end justifies the means, and those who had been arguing all along that the kids were "so sincere" that their cause should be supported. George heard several of them say this again as they left the hall.

"Imagine!" he exclaimed when he came home to tell me about the meeting. "Full professors! Men who are supposed to be teaching the students how to think! And they believe that disputes can be settled on the basis of someone's *sincerity!* Good God!"

An interesting postscript to the sit-in was provided by Richard Flacks, a young sociologist on the Chicago faculty. Because he had been a founder of the Students for a Democratic Society, and was still close to the current student generation in age and outlook, he was in a good position to use the sit-in for scholarly purposes. He interviewed a sizable number of militant activists at Chicago and other institutions, as well as their parents, and compared them to an equal number of students who did not engage in protest activities, and *their* parents.

He found that the militants had the superior academic records. (This has generally been found true in all similar studies.) Their parents were affluent, professional-class people, both mother and father highly educated, both likely to be politically active themselves. Many of them had been Left-leaning in their youth, and still felt guilty about having compromised their ideals in order to gain status and financial security. Such parents therefore supported their children's radicalism as much for reasons buried in their own phyches as for the reasons given by the students. (The Chicago political theorist David Easton has called this "the cat's paw effect.")

Certainly this profile fitted the family of one boy who had been among the leaders of the 1966 sit-in at Chicago. He was an intelligent boy, honest and responsible; he and a few others like him had played key roles as middlemen between protestors and administrators, and it was due to their efforts that the withdrawal from the Administration Building had been effected with some dignity.

But when he went home for his summer vacation, his father's greeting was, "So! You sold out!"

Twenty-seven

Happily, I never had to attend one of Mayor Daley's Prayer
Breakfasts, to which the city's "leading citizens" were bidden
from time to time. George went, and said they weren't bad,
but I still shudder at the thought of a thousand people getting
together at 7:30 A.M. in a hotel dining room for purposes of
spiritual uplift.

Nor did I feel obliged to attend the parties that business
firms were always inviting us to, in order to introduce new
regional managers or launch new products or plants. ("United
States Steel Corporation cordially invites you to the official opening of the World's Largest Five-Stand Cold Reduction Mill
at Gary Sheet and Tin Works. . . .")

Despite these omissions, however, a formidable lot of civic
banquets and ceremonies remained. They ranged from celebrations of Chicago's being named the Cleanest American City
(!) to welcomes for foreign trade delegations and astronauts.
Most of them were like a drink mixed with soda that has gone
flat, doubtless because many of the guests were present for
reasons of duty rather than pleasure. Conversation is not very
sprightly when one's attention is centered on the unspoken
question, "When will this be over?"

And one's memory of the details dims quickly, too—except
in rare cases. One of these was a testimonial dinner for the

retiring superintendent of schools, Benjamin C. Willis; and I recall it as the quintessential civic banquet of our experience.

As I indicated in an earlier chapter, Ben Willis was extremely unpopular with the militant civil rights groups, who accused him of drawing school district boundaries to perpetuate segregation. The reverse of that same coin, of course, was that whites of the type we have since come to call "hard hats" gave Willis the credit for keeping black children *out* of their children's schools. This conflict added a thick overlay of emotionalism to problems of public education which, under the best of circumstances, would have been difficult to solve.

Illinois starves its public schools. Chicago isn't really sold on them, either—perhaps because so many citizens send their children to parochial schools and can see no reason for taxing themselves to improve the public schools. In addition, both the teachers' union and the city's political machine put self-interest above the schools' welfare. As a result, Chicago's public schools in the 1960's were educationally mediocre, unresponsive to the citizenry, and spiritless. Or so they appeared to me. This indictment may be too harsh, since I have never been more than an onlooker; but, given the bad public relations policies that characterized the period, I don't see what other opinion a newcomer to the city could have formed.

When we arrived in Chicago in 1961, fresh from a California school system which did everything it could think of to promote co-operation between the citizenry and the schools, I had been appalled by the Chicago policy which actually forbade a parent to have the telephone number of his child's school. I had myself once spontaneously taken an out-of-town visitor to see the physical layout of a Chicago high school, and had been appalled all over again when we were stopped and challenged by an assistant principal, who made it clear that we were trespassing. And I was amazed by the policy that kept most public schools locked up tight after school hours, thus denying the use of these facilities to neighborhoods that were in dire need of recreational and cultural centers.

Such barriers between the schools and the citizenry may have been necessitated by inadequate funds or the rising hostility of the black community, but I can recall no sustained efforts by the school system to counteract their chilling effect. The responsibility to do so lay with the Board of Education, of course, but that body resembled a team of horses half of which were pulling in one direction and the other half in another. Besides, the public isn't very clear as to the relationship between policy makers and the people who implement policy, so Ben Willis became the target for the disaffected. He grew increasingly defensive as the 1960's wore along, and his public personality became increasingly abrasive. All in all, it was a messy situation; and by June of 1966, Chicagoans were pretty well polarized as pro or con Ben Willis.

Within the school system itself, I am told, he had provoked a similar polarity. There seems to be no doubt that Willis was a fine bricks-and-mortar man. No revelations of graft or similar scandal marked his regime, and in Chicago that in itself is a notable accomplishment. However, it is a huge system—half a million pupils, some six hundred schools—and a thoroughly bureaucratized one. The young, the liberals, and those of an innovative bent felt stifled and frustrated by it, and blamed Willis. Those who had made their peace with the system and were moving along via prescribed channels approved the order and efficiency that Willis had established and maintained. Among this group I am sure there were many who were truly sorry to see him retire, and they came to the banquet in his honor with a genuine desire to pay tribute to a man they admired.

But there were inevitably present at that function many teachers and administrators in middle-echelon jobs who had never even seen Willis, and who were there because their principals or supervisors had made up a table and had "asked" them to buy tickets. Under these circumstances, anyone who knows which side his bread is buttered on buys a ticket.

Finally, there was the category to which George and I belonged. We had nothing to gain or lose personally by attendance, nor did we have emotional ties to the guest of honor. We attended the banquet simply as a salute to the office he held. Representatives of other colleges or universities were on hand for the same reason.

And as soon as we had seated ourselves at Table Number 206 and glanced through the program, we realized that this was going to be a long and difficult evening for all but the truly faithful.

"Good grief!" I involuntarily exclaimed. "There are going to be ten speakers. Even if they limit themselves to five minutes each, that's fifty minutes right there. And they won't, of course."

A nun sitting across from me caught my eye and smiled. She represented a women's college in one of the suburbs.

"It might be interesting to time them," she ventured.

She had a mischievous sparkle in her eye, and she gave me an idea.

"Don't you imagine that the rhetoric will be on the flamboyant side?" I asked.

She nodded.

"Then suppose *I* keep a record of the clichés?"

She nodded again, and we both got out our pens and laid them neatly beside our programs.

The banquet was in McCormick Place, Chicago's huge exhibition hall, and although there were some three thousand of us in it, the room dwarfed us, the American flag over the entrance, the head table set for twenty-eight, and the gold banner behind it which said, in letters four feet high:

A SALUTE TO DR. WILLIS

COURAGE   CANDOR   COMPETENCE

After the occupants of the head table had entered in procession, to a standing ovation, a Monsignor gave the invocation and the master of ceremonies welcomed "this magnificent outpouring of friends" for a man "who has been a source of inspiration to us all." Time: two minutes. Clichés: two.

Then we ate our chicken.

The program began with the School Opening Ceremony that Dr. Willis was said to have instituted. The City Cadet Corps Staff and Color Guard (ROTC) marched in with Old Glory and the city of Chicago flag. We all pledged allegiance and sang the National Anthem. Time: four minutes.

Then the master of ceremonies introduced all the guests at the head table—among them, Mrs. Willis, who had "stood with her husband in storm and sunshine." He also introduced six relatives of Dr. Willis, who were seated at a table on the floor of the hall; those members of the current Board of Education who were not at the speakers' table; and members of earlier Boards of Education who were at still another table. Time: eleven minutes. Inasmuch as it had been "a privilege and an honor" for the master of ceremonies to welcome them, and those who were or had been school board members were "unsung heroes," my list was growing nicely.

Mayor Daley led off. Time: four minutes. He said his "heart-felt thanks" for Dr. Willis' "dedication and devotion," and the master of ceremonies thanked him for his "meaningful tribute." Clichés: three more.

The mayor had, of course, spoken for the city of Chicago. Now came Samuel M. Brownell, Detroit's superintendent of schools, who spoke for the Great Cities of the United States. The master of ceremonies described him as "a tower of strength." He himself was not only "honored and privileged" to pay this "well-deserved tribute" to Ben Willis but in addition praised Willis' "insightful leadership," which had been "given without stint." This was the richest harvest yet: five clichés in only four minutes.

Next, Ray Page, Superintendent of Public Instruction for the state of Illinois, was introduced as "a stalwart supporter" of Dr. Willis. He used his five minutes to say, in part, that the guest of honor had been "a source of inspiration to educators everywhere" and that he had been "fearless in the face of adversity." Three more.

Now there was a musical interlude. The 150-voice All City High School Chorus sang *America the Beautiful* and *Three Hungarian Folk Songs;* and the All City High School Band played *A Tribute to George M. Cohan* and *The Knightsbridge March.* The nun forgot to clock them.

Next came a civic leader, introduced as "a man of vision and accomplishment." He mumbled into the microphone, and I caught only a few phrases. These included "second to none," "the challenge of the future," and "God bless you and your lovely helpmate." Inasmuch as he spoke for eleven minutes, my tally would undoubtedly have been larger if I could have heard him. But four wasn't a bad increment.

The Hon. Roman C. Pucinski (Democrat, Eleventh District) then spoke for the Congress of the United States. Time: seven minutes. I may not have heard him correctly, but my notes clearly say that *he* said, "Dr. Willis is now going on to a new plateau. His departure is a loss to Chicago but a gain for America."

Someone, of course, had to speak for The Students. The young man who did so had the style of a debater and took only three minutes. I was so pleased by both the brevity and the crispness of his presentation that I ignored his assertion that Dr. Willis had swept away cobwebs and brought about a vibrant regeneration of the school system. It was hearsay testimony, anyway: when Dr. Willis had been doing all this the speaker had been in kindergarten.

Nor was I quite sure how to categorize a definition of the parent-child relationship as "a beloved union, set to the words 'Mom' and 'Dad.'" This was a contribution from the master of ceremonies when he introduced "a lovely Mom" to speak for The Parents. She thanked Dr. Willis for "having planted seeds in the minds of our children," told him that "the world is a little better for your having been in it," and conveyed to "our beloved Dr. Ben a multitude of thanks from the deepest recesses of thousands of grateful hearts." Time: five minutes. Clichés? Let's be kind: four.

Another musical interlude then intervened. This time the All City High School Chorus and the All City High School Band teamed up for *The Battle Hymn of the Republic*, and the diners joined in for group-sing at the end.

The tribute to Dr. Willis from The Staff was delivered (time: nine minutes) by an associate superintendent. According to him, the guest of honor had "never compromised with mediocrity," had "improved everyone's insights," and was leaving to the staff "a very rich heritage." He also pledged that they "would keep faith with our young people." Four more.

The president of the Board of Education, who was said not to be very fond of the superintendent, concentrated on good wishes for the future. Time: five minutes. Clichés: *none*.

But, since the dinner committee apparently wanted to program a really enthusiastic tribute from the Board of Education, one of its pro-Willis members was introduced next. She gave a twenty-two-minute eulogy. She not only spoke too rapidly for me to keep my tally but was such fun to watch that I surrendered myself to her spell; she was as good as Aimee Semple McPherson. She wound up with an expression of gratitude for "the beneficent destiny that brought dear Dr. Ben to Chicago and that has given us the privilege of touching the hem of his garment." She got a standing ovation.

Now it was time for Dr. Ben to respond. He managed an appreciative sentence or two for each of the speakers who had preceded him, made a few hopeful predictions for the future of the Chicago schools, and said that his years here had been "rich and rewarding." Considering the example that had been set for him, to speak for twenty-five minutes without perpetrating more than one cliché was remarkable, and my applause for him was totally unforced.

The benediction over—this time by a black Baptist bishop—we tottered out of the hall. Time at table: four hours and thirty-five minutes. As we left, aides were collecting from each table the sheets upon which every person present had been instructed to write a word of appreciation to Dr. Willis, said sheets to be later bound into a portfolio. I have often wondered if that gentleman has ever read it. Imagine plowing through three thousand echoes of that evening's rhetoric!

One of the most delightful of all the amateur theatricals that occur in University of Chicago circles is an original revue presented each January by the faculty wives for the faculty wives. The following year I was asked to parody a typical Commencement speech, one of those graceful time-killers that is all air and no substance. It was easy. All I did was to refer back to my notes from the Testimonial to Dr. Willis. The audience loved it. Now at last I can give credit where credit is due. To Dr. Ben and his devoted friends, I herewith proffer a multitude of thanks from the deepest recesses of my grateful heart.

Twenty-eight

If Charlie Fox has ulcers, Harper Court is probably to blame. He worked for a real estate management firm and had successfully managed much larger shopping centers, so he had reason to believe that this one would be easy. Ten hours a week, say? Alas, *this* one was full of artists and craftsmen who didn't think of themselves as businessmen—and behaved accordingly.

One tenant, owing three months rent, packed up his merchandise in the middle of the night and did a moonlight flit. Another endangered the safety of an entire building because he personally reinstalled his shop's gas meter. (In its original position, it clashed with the decor.) One tenant forgot to get a cash register when she opened her shop; another refused to have one because cash registers are "crass and commercial"; and a third regularly overpaid or underpaid his rent because he couldn't remember how much it was.

The Harper Court Board of Directors had made a serious mistake when it did not require all tenants to be members of a merchants association. (A title, incidentally, that our first lot of tenants rejected, calling themselves instead The Harper Court Guild.) Because only half of them participated and only a quarter of them paid their dues, they had no money for advertising or promotion. This may have been just as well, because if a group of merchants can't even agree on what business hours they will keep, what chance is there that they'll be able to agree

on the copy for an advertising campaign? Nevertheless, their
inability to organize themselves was hurtful to their business in-
terests.

The indestructible innocence of some of our first-time shopkeepers drove Charlie wild. ("What do you mean, you want to
see the insurance policy on the glass in my shop windows? That's
your worry, not mine; they're your windows. The lease? It
does?") But at the same time they worked so hard at making
their shops attractive and displaying their goods appealingly that
he—and the Board of Directors to whom he reported—developed great sympathy for those with problems, and we weren't
able to maintain a truly impersonal businesslike relationship with
them.

Our first full year's financial report showed that our operating
costs had exceeded income by six thousand dollars. Most of this
deficit was due to slow-paying, delinquent, and bankrupt tenants
and to difficulties in renting still vacant (or recently vacated)
space. Nor did it help to know that much of this trouble was of
our own making. We were the good guys, the saviors of the
community's artists and craftsmen, the benefactors of fledgling
businessmen who had this great idea, see, which deserved a
try-out. Therefore we had told Charlie to go easy on this
tenant because the community greatly needed his services (and
he had, after all, paid half of his rent last month), or to postpone once more an eviction notice for that tenant because his
prospects looked good and he *was* trying.

Charlie was, thus, doubly damned. Not only did he have to
deal with a high percentage of novices among the tenants, but in
addition he was working for a landlord (our collective selves on
the Board) of comparable inexperience. Not that we lacked ex-
perts: we had Fritz Neugarten and Ira Marks, both of them in
retail businesses in the Loop. But we either overrode their advice or persuaded them that Harper Court was "different."

That difference was also causing difficulties with the Small
Business Administration. Eugene Foley had gone; and with his
departure the agency had lost its enthusiasm (never very great)

for high-risk ventures. Given this attitude at the top, you can imagine the nervousness of the new people in SBA's Chicago office upon realizing that they were not only stuck with a huge loan to the Harper Court Foundation but in addition had loaned thousands upon thousands of dollars to Harper Court merchants —several of whom had already failed or were on the verge of bankruptcy.

So the agency's rules began to be interpreted with great strictness. For example: our buildings weren't yet ready for a formal certification of completion, and until we got to that point, the SBA wouldn't pay out the last $35,000 of the loan. We were forced to borrow it elsewhere, which further ran up our costs.

Parking was a problem, and even those of our Board members with demonstrated political clout couldn't prod the City Parking Authority into faster redevelopment of the lot that was to serve Harper Court. The merchants were being plagued by petty thieves, and the courtyard was becoming a hangout for unsavory-looking loiterers who scared the suburban matrons who came to shop there. Young people liked the courtyard, too, and used it as a picnic area. The noise of their bongo drums, the litter they left in their wake, and their uninhibited behavior *vis-à-vis* each other caused more conventional Hyde Parkers to cringe. I began to get anonymous letters whose writer objected to the association of "white school girls" with "black dope fiends" in Harper Court.

But there was some light in the gloom. The majority of our tenants were *not* in financial trouble, and a couple of the novices among them were making spectacular successes of their businesses. We were also going to be able to add the fourth building that we had envisioned from the beginning of our venture. When we had learned that the Hyde Park Co-op wanted to open a Scandinavian furniture store somewhere in the community, we had begun negotiations to exclude a portion of our land from the SBA package so that we could rent it to the Co-op instead. Its management would construct a building there and pay a share of Harper Court's taxes and maintenance cost. There was every reason to believe that this new store would generate shopping traffic which would spill over into the other shops in the complex. (As it has.)

Idealism and civic virtue may have been responsible for Harper Court Board members' joining that body, but what kept us going was the atmosphere of suspense. Will the new manager of the art gallery owned by forty artists be able to persuade its most talented members to exhibit work in their own shop? *Are* dope sellers active in the courtyard? When, if ever, will the mason come to repair the brickwork? What's the word this month from the City Parking Authority?

Hot weather usually breeds tension, but that year was worse than usual. By midsummer, a sense of menace hung over the neighborhood; the old-timers said the atmosphere was like that of 1952. The reason was not crime *in* the community, this time, but crime on its borders. What had happened within the past six months was that the South Side street gangs had been consolidating themselves into much larger units, and were now on the warpath against each other and middle-class society in general.

Street gangs are as old as cities. They arise in communities whose residents (to quote a psychiatrist who has studied gang members) "live in a common ocean of despair." Their primary function is to provide social support for their members: to give a sense of status to young people who have no effective ties to family, church, school, or any other social institution. A kid who is afloat in the aimless chaos of an urban ghetto can find a mooring of sorts in the crude but simple social structure of a gang. Fighting, crime, or vandalism may or may not be part of gang activities; even when they are, sociologists have found, they are only occasionally indulged in, to bolster the reputation of a gang leader or to provide kicks for the members.

Over the years, both Chicago social agencies and the police (despite radically different approaches to "the street gang problem") had managed to exercise some kind of control over the city's numerous but small and very localized teenage gangs. During the 1960's, however, as the civil rights movement became more violent, the South Side street gangs grew larger and became more violent, too.

The Blackstone Rangers, whose turf had been a ten-square-block area in Woodlawn, started to affiliate with gangs on its periphery and eventually achieved a membership of what has variously been estimated as five hundred to fifteen hundred youths. The East Side Disciples, a gang based in Englewood (some miles west of Woodlawn), were doing the same thing, and by 1966 the two groups were involved in a power struggle. Its by-product was extortion of local merchants; intimidation of boys who didn't want to join a gang but were forcibly impressed; and random violence that terrified the stable householders of Woodlawn and adjacent areas.

Not much of this guerrilla warfare actually occurred in Hyde Park or Kenwood, but it had its effect there. A sudden shortage of newsboys (most of whom were twelve years old, or thereabouts, and lived in Woodlawn) indicated parental refusal to let their youngsters venture out alone into the pre-dawn dark. The cleaning women who came daily into Hyde Park homes brought with them tales of neighbors who had sent their children "to safety" with relatives in other cities; of friends' purchases of guns "for self-defense"; of pursuits and beatings and shootings that chilled the blood.

At the bank one day (George and I banked in Woodlawn), I heard one woman tell another, "Hones', honey, they come through the alley like race horses. The boy in front he was a-yellin' as loud as he can, 'I don' know nothin' about nothin'. I jes come from down South. And, man, I'se goin' back there quick as I can!'"

Billings Hospital was full of the wounded. Admitted on the *same* night were: a fourteen-year-old boy shot in the lower back while entering a grocery store at Sixty-fourth and Woodlawn; a seventeen-year-old shot in the chest outside his house at Sixty-first and Greenwood; a sixteen-year-old shot in the right arm while sitting near a window in his cousin's apartment at Sixty-second and Calumet; another sixteen-year-old, shot in the left arm while standing on the corner of Sixty-first and Woodlawn. Those who were already in the hospital were receiving telephoned threats against their lives—"We're going to finish the job when you get out"—and the University had to hire two armed guards to watch over the wards where the victims of gang shoot-outs were convalescing.

All of this, piled atop the incidence of "normal" crime in the community, created a very nervous populace. The facts were bad enough, but rumor expanded and elaborated, and it got to the point where one didn't know whether there really had been a rumble at Fiftieth and Blackstone or whether a bunch of grade-schoolers had been playing at cowboys and Indians with cap guns and water pistols. The social agencies' street workers said that the wild tales of gang activity were much exaggerated—to the benefit of the gangs, which thrived on scare publicity and rumor —and they were probably right. Nevertheless, I didn't deliver my usual "welcome to the community" speech to the new medical school wives with quite my customary air of confidence that summer.

We dedicated the handsome and much needed Silvain and Arma Wyler Children's Hospital in August, swinging around it a symposium on child development that made me wish I could begin all over again.

In early September several thousand delegates to an International Congress on Human Genetics arrived in our midst, among them a geneticist from South Africa who had been in graduate school with George. He was at a cocktail party at our house when we heard that Verwoerd had been assassinated. Tears came to his eyes, and he excused himself. The next morning, he flew home. I had forgotten that there are two sides to most issues.

October brought a welcome addition to Rockefeller Chapel. I had sometimes amused myself during University Convocations by imagining ways to get more color into that dull gray interior; but it was Earle Ludgin, a trustee, who did it. In memory of his wife, he bought the forty-four liturgical banners originally made by Norman Laliberte for the Vatican Pavilion at the 1964 World's Fair in New York, and gave them to the University.

Wrought-iron brackets were installed at clerestory height in the Chapel, allowing the display of sixteen banners at a time. Each about fifteen feet long, they are made of wool, burlap, or felt with the designs appliquéd or embroidered and then trimmed with buttons, bells, beads, and assorted other found objects. The great Bible stories and parables are all there, looking as if a Cubist had designed them and a Pennsylvania Dutch housewife had executed them, and the overall effect is both modern and medieval. With their introduction to the Chapel, a cascade of color rolled down the length of the nave, lightening and brightening it, and enhancing greatly the ecclesiastical symbolism of the structure.*

In November, I scheduled a reprise of the teas for faculty wives which had inaugurated my entertaining at Chicago. Our tally of guests, since 1961, now stood at just over eleven thousand; and I wouldn't have added another eight hundred within one month if I hadn't known that half of them had never been in the President's House. I had kept my original file-card index of faculty wives up to date, each year using cards of a different color to record the newcomers' names. I was well aware that academic people move around a lot, but it had been startling that fall to see that there were now as many coral, blue, green, and yellow cards as there were white ones dating from 1961.

And so, off we went again: the kitchen full of fragrant cookie smells; the hallways full of coat racks; the ground-floor rooms full of chattering women; the cats, locked in our bedroom, full of wrath.

At the second of these teas, on an exceptionally cold day, I was interrupted in the middle of a smile of greeting by a warm

* Not that (as usual) all viewers agreed. George got a number of letters of protest from individuals, and also from a group calling itself the Committee on Artistic Unity. It argued that modern art tapestries were an anachronism in a Gothic building as "authentic" as Rockefeller Chapel (c.1929) is.

splash on the back of my neck; and then another. Shortly, a small but steady trickle of brownish water was dripping from the middle of the ceiling into the middle of my tea party, and I was receiving guests in company with a green plastic bucket set just behind me.

The house had been behaving very well that year, so it was about time for something to fall apart. The worn-out member in this case was a pipe leading to the radiator in my upstairs study. All that Buildings and Grounds had to do was to turn off all the heat in the house; tear up the carpet and flooring in the study; replace the pipe; replace the flooring; replace the wallpaper on the ground floor across which part of the leak had leaked; and repaint the ceiling across which the rest of the leak had left its rusty traces. B and G comes on strong in an emergency. They finished the downstairs part about thirty minutes before the next day's tea guests were to arrive, and the sound of hammering upstairs didn't matter because the ladies' high-pitched voices masked it.

The final tea in the series was on a Saturday, for the benefit of any faculty wives who were employed and couldn't come during the working week. Not many accepted, so I had supplemented the guest list with acquaintances in the community: fellow veterans of the Hyde Park Centennial celebrations, members of the Kenwood Open House Committee, women who had sold bonds for Harper Court, others I had come to know because we had worked together on civic projects.

They lingered on and on—because they were having such a good time, I thought, and I guess they were; but they were also being polite. Finally, one of them came over to me and said, "Will you be making the announcement soon? I must be going, and I don't want to miss it."

"The announcement? What announcement?"

"About the drive. Or the cause. Or whatever project you're going to ask us to help with."

Bless them. And they had come, anyway.

Late that same day, I answered the door myself and found a

male student there. He looked angry and beseeching at the same time.

"Will you sell me two eggs?" he blurted.

"Whatever for?"

"I'm making a cake," he explained. "And the recipe calls for two eggs. I went to a couple of stores and none of them would sell me two eggs. Will you?"

"Come in. Heavens, I'll *give* you two eggs."

He departed at a lope, his two eggs cradled in a box filled with cookies left over from the tea, and I suddenly realized that I hadn't asked him why he was making a cake. On top of that came the realization that I hadn't been a bit surprised because he had been determined not to buy six eggs when he needed only two.

A couple of weeks later, in the early evening, I answered the phone and heard a young male voice—one that obviously wanted to scream or cry and was being kept under control by the smallest of margins—ask for George. I said that he was out of town, but could *I* do anything?

I could indeed. It seemed that a crew of men from Buildings and Grounds had appeared at his dorm that afternoon and had hung Christmas decorations which he found offensive because he was a Jew and these were Christian symbols and he had spent hours calling Deans of Students and Assistant Deans and the Director of Residences and he either couldn't reach them or they wouldn't do anything about it. DIDN'T ANYBODY AROUND HERE CARE ABOUT MATTERS OF PRINCIPLE?

I knew somebody who might care: a warm-hearted, cool-headed young man named Jerome Frese, who was an instructor in the College and a part-time assistant to the Provost. I telephoned him. Would he call the distraught youth? He'd do better; he'd go see him.

He did, and two hours later the student called me again to thank me for producing Jerry and to say that he had withdrawn his objection. Jerry, like me, had envisioned a dormitory lounge plastered with manger scenes and madonnas, and had been surprised to discover that the actual decorations depicted Santa Claus and reindeers. I doubt that Jerry, Jesuit-trained and something of a religious purist, considered these "Christian symbols." Whether he used that argument with the student I don't know, but in any case he defused the young man's ire—and without disputing his fundamental concern about bigotry.

Principles. It was nice to live among people who had them.

Twenty-nine

In late 1966, the headlines *twice* trumpeted: NOBEL PRIZE TO U OF C PROF. It is uncommon for any university to harbor even one Nobel prize winner; for two of its faculty to receive the prize in the same year is a rarity; and when both of them have done their research at that same university the situation is almost unique.

One of our two was Robert S. Mulliken, whose prize in chemistry could equally well have been in physics: Mulliken is *the* authority on the paths that electrons follow within molecules. The other was Charles Huggins, an M.D. with a taste for biochemistry, whose prize in physiology/medicine saluted his discovery that prostate cancer could be controlled by withdrawal of male hormones or by administration of female hormones.

Both had been on the faculty since the late 1920's, and it was this length of tenure that accounted for much of the joy that swept the campus. After all, when your children have grown up together . . .

The University had a great civic banquet in their honor, which at some point in the proceedings was transmuted from a civic banquet into a real party. It was one of the bright spots in an otherwise dreary December.

Another was Red's Christmas visit. He no longer spent his summers in Chicago, and was by now quite independent of us financially. He looked well that year, was in buoyant spirits, and entertained me with thumbnail sketches of eccentrics who had figured in the temperance movement of post-Colonial America. He had received his M.A. the previous June, and was now launched on studies for the Ph.D. The only thing that caused me worry was his silence about whatever he did when he wasn't studying. My lecture on the necessity of his living a fully rounded life—meaning, "Do you have a girl, and if not, why not?"—was courteously received but its implied question was delicately parried.

I complained to George that Red might as well be in a monastery, that the direction his life was taking struck me as frighteningly narrow, and was there anything we could do about it?

"Just relax, honey," George said.

I wonder if *he* knew about Suzie? He says not, and I can understand why Red didn't wish to share with us the beginnings of a romance that for all he knew might never flower. When *I* want something very much, I tend to propitiate the appropriate gods in private, too.

As we came into the New Year, there was little joy in it. I had unwisely gotten myself involved in an anti-litter campaign, which hadn't gone well from the beginning but to which I was now committed. I was also the co-chairman of a committee to acquire sculpture for the new neighborhood parks, a project which was moving with infuriating slowness. Both hung over me as if they were threats rather than opportunities. In January, I got the flu, a long, dragged-out case; and passed it along to George. All this, plus the bleakness of the season, made me feel like a dying horse that was still on its feet only because it was being flogged.

It is often asserted that Chicagoans are a vigorous breed because only the strong can survive the weather. And it's true that the weather is extreme, changeable, and unpredictable: temperatures can drop by twenty degrees within an hour and vary by forty degrees within a day; a rousing northeasterly wind can (and often does) turn a reading of just below zero into the equivalent of forty below; and in midsummer the city can swelter in hundred-degree heat or shiver in fog, with thermometers at fifty. It is tornado country, subject to high winds, torrential rains, and thunderstorms of unmitigated fury. But it is also a city of blue skies alive with racing clouds, of balmy summer and brisk autumn days that match in their perfection anything that gentler climes can offer.

And it has a great benefactor in its lake. I never quite shook the habit, left over from our years in California, of referring to Lake Michigan as "the ocean." And no wonder: it's a hundred miles wide, three hundred miles long, nine hundred feet deep at its deepest, and has some 22,000 square miles of water surface. Although given to raging squalls that sink even large boats and toss spray far enough inland to make the shore drives unsafe for cars to travel, Lake Michigan makes life in Chicago much easier overall than life in those Midwestern cities that lack a great thermal reservoir on their doorsteps.

The lake retains the cold temperatures of winter well into the summer, and the warm temperatures of summer well into the winter, and transfers these to the passing winds. In winter, the warmed air over the lake holds moisture until it gets to the cool land mass of Michigan, whereupon it dumps its moisture as snow. Chicago, therefore, is both cooler in summer, warmer in winter, and far less snowy than the cities across the lake.

But that is not the same thing as saying that to winter in Chicago is a lot of fun, and in late January of 1967 George and I were feeling sufficiently wretched to accept with delight an invitation to spend a week with friends in Palm Springs. We had seats on an eleven o'clock plane on January 26; and were pleased rather than apprehensive to discover, upon arising that morning, that it was snowing heavily. The prospect of soon being in hot California sun was all the more delectable.

The forecast was for clearing by midafternoon. So, as I closed my suitcase on the cotton sundress I had packed last (for easy availability when we arrived), I suggested to George that he check with the airline and shift us to a later flight if—as seemed likely—the morning flights weren't going to take off. He did; reported that O'Hare *was* temporarily closed; and that we were now scheduled for a late afternoon flight.

St. Christopher had his eye on us, I think, for we nearly tried to make it. At three, the snow was still falling as heavily as it had been in the morning, and the wind was now up to fifty miles an hour and was blowing the snow into drifts. But the streets looked passable, and the forecast still predicted that the storm would end "soon." If we had left the house, it is virtually certain that we would have ended up stuck in a snowdrift on the expressway, or snowbound for three days at the airport itself.

It's odd that neither we nor anybody else realized the danger. Perhaps it was simply because snow had been falling heavily all day and traffic was moving nevertheless that caused everyone to assume that man and machine would prevail. Instead, a critical point had already been reached. The snowfall was so heavy that the plows couldn't keep ahead of it, and now drifts were building up even on the expressways.

It took only a few old cars or bad drivers to start the chain reaction that eventually paralyzed the city. A car would plunge into a drift, falter, and stall, forcing cars behind it to slow or stop and then to ease into an ever narrowing channel—with the snow piling higher all the time and the diminished flow of traffic less able to mash it down.

By nightfall, streets and highways were clogged with thousands of stopped or stalled cars. Their drivers, noting the undiminished force of the storm and deciding to hike to whatever haven was nearest, simply abandoned their vehicles where they stood. Buses, which might have managed to force a passage, were blocked by cars skewed every which way in their path; and the same barrier closed the streets to snowplows. But, by now, *they* were faltering too. Their crews had been at work since dawn and were exhausted; relief crews couldn't get through the storm to report for work; and the machines couldn't be refueled.

Fires could still be reported, but even if the fire engines made it to the street they didn't always get to the scene of the fire, and there they couldn't find the fire hydrants, buried as they were under six- to ten-foot drifts. Stores were broken into and looted, but the police couldn't stop it because they couldn't get their cars through, either. In nearby Gary, which was as hard-hit as Chicago, the authorities called out the National Guard to help both with snow removal and to control civil disorders, but only fifty out of six hundred Guardsmen were able to reach the armory.

It was cold. Power lines iced and fell, cutting off electricity to thousands of buildings. Trains jumped the tracks as switches froze, reducing further what little rail traffic had managed to keep going through the day. Airport runways were too deep in snow to permit takeoffs or landings, even if the weather had cleared, but that was immaterial because flight and maintenance crews couldn't get there anyway. The thousands of passengers who were stranded at O'Hare couldn't leave because parking lots were buried in snow, and the roads outside were impassable. . . .

And the snow kept coming. All told, twenty-four inches fell within a period of twenty-nine hours. If that doesn't sound like enough to account for the havoc it wreaked, think of it instead by weight: twenty-four million tons.

By Friday morning, the storm was over and an eerie silence had replaced it. Where was the distant hum of traffic on the Midway and the closer sound of cars and trucks on streets immediately adjacent to our house? The wail of sirens on fire engines or police cars, or of ambulances bound to Billings Emergency? All had been stilled. There wasn't even the crunch of footsteps on snowy sidewalks. In fact, there weren't any snowy sidewalks; the whole landscape was a vast expanse of white as unbroken as if men had never laid a grid of pavement upon it.

The calls from students had begun to come in early. Would there be classes today? George could tell them only that if both professors and students could make it, he assumed so. The men of Buildings and Grounds—those who had been trapped on campus overnight and still had enough energy to push a shovel or a snowblower—were already cutting a few paths in the wilderness of white.

Then we heard that the hospital was running out of linen because snow had caved in the roof of the laundry building, and its employees couldn't get there anyway. So we began to suggest to students that they skip class and volunteer to wash diapers in the makeshift laundry that had been set up, or run dishwashers to relieve hospital employees who had been on the job for something like twenty hours and were dead on their feet. The kids turned out in droves, bless them.

By Saturday, the city snowplows had cleared a single lane along the Midway and a route was open to the hospital's Emergency entrance. A massive tow-away program had begun along the expressways, but it would be days before the job was done. The stores ran out of perishables like milk and meat and bread, and members of a generation that had never had to eat Spam suddenly found slices of it on their dinner plates—if their mothers had managed to break a footpath to the supermarket early enough in the day to buy anything before the shelves went bare.

The prisoners at O'Hare weren't freed until Sunday.

By Monday, people were able to get to work via public transportation, the normal rhythms of the city were becoming reestablished, and the sense of common crisis that had sustained good humor and human charity during the storm was already passing.

Among those who felt put upon was a woman who, upon arriving at her office, complained at great length about the inconveniences to which the Superstorm had subjected her—among them the necessity of walking eight blocks to a bus line that morning.

A much older employee finally silenced her with a recollection of another storm.

"I remember a snow we had in nineteen thirty-two," he said. "It was terrible. We must have gotten four inches, and I had to walk through it for two miles to get to work."

The woman said, "*Four* inches? But that's nothing!"

"But in thirty-two," he replied, "I had holes in my shoes."

It was weeks before ordinary city streets were free of buried cars, the Superstorm having been followed by a lesser one a week later and then by a flash blizzard called a "snowburst," which dumped seven inches of snow on the city within an hour. Perhaps no tale of that period is more poignant than this one, related in a newspaper story by a Good Samaritan who should have passed by on the other side of the road:

> I was coming home from church when I saw a man trying to move his '62 Chevvie out of a drift, and offered to give him a hand. The two of us almost had it out when three other men appeared and also offered to help.
>
> After the driver had started the car and got it rocking by rapidly shifting from first to reverse, the four of us gave it a mighty push toward the ruts in the middle of the road—only about six feet away. As we did, we heard a snap and the wheels stopped spinning. He had blown his transmission.
>
> One of the men told the driver that maybe only the forward gears were shot, so why not put the car into reverse and rev the engine? He did, and we all pushed. It moved about a foot, and both of the rear wheels fell off. One of the men said that he must have busted his rear axle, too.
>
> The three men who had come on the scene after I did shrugged their shoulders and left. I told the man I was sorry, and also left. What can you tell a man when you destroy his car?

All during February the snow-removal crews shoveled up the ice-crusted and sooty remains of the Superstorm. But twenty-four million tons of snow isn't easy to get rid of. Tons went into the Chicago River, tons were piled on vacant lots, and there were still more tons awaiting disposal. Finally, someone had an inspiration: export it. The result was a series of rail shipments—five hundred coal hoppers and gondolas full of used snow—to places like New Orleans and Fort Worth. It melted as it went south, and no one was happier than the shippers when the cars arrived empty.

But even into spring there were echoes.

In March, when drivers who had been ticketed for moving

violations in February would normally have thronged to Traffic Court, the place was deserted, and the judges got what amounted to a fortnight's holiday.

In early April, with leaves in bud and crocuses in flower, the weather bureau announced that the season's total snowfall had set an all-time record: 65.4 inches. And then, on April 23, we got another three inches.

There were even to be echoes into the following year. On January 26, 1968, the president of a club to which I belong looked out the window at snow flurries which had begun while the meeting was in progress and said to me, in a nervous whisper, "Do you think we should adjourn early?"

Thirty

For a few hectic weeks that spring, the University became the mother of a bride. I'm sure that Loraine Percy was just as busy as *we* were, but her activities were the more traditional ones of dealing with caterers and florists and dressmakers, whereas the University's problem was to adapt for the wedding reception a building that hadn't been designed for that use, to make sure that a glut of traffic could be accommodated in the area, and to provide security for the horde of distinguished visitors who would be coming.

There was good reason for Sharon Percy and John D. Rockefeller IV to have chosen Rockefeller Chapel for their wedding. Without the first John D. ("The Founder"), the University would never had come into being. He also gave the Chapel. The second John D. gave its carillon, and was for many years a member of the Board of Trustees. The fourth John D. (Jay, the bridegroom) would soon join his uncle David as a member of that Board. The Percys' links with the institution, although not of such longevity, were equally close. Chuck Percy—Horatio Alger's kind of boy, one who had progressed from genteel poverty to the presidency of a great corporation before he was forty and then on to the United States Senate—was not only an alumnus of the University but a trustee as well.

The Rockefellers and the Percys controlled quite a few millions of dollars, too; but this was not the main reason for the interest that the Wedding of the Year provoked. It was partly due to respect for the two families, who are much in the public eye yet always behave with great rectitude. And it was partly due to the charm and good looks of the bride and bridegroom. I myself had felt like a doting aunt ever since the engaged couple and their parents had visited the University to decide upon it as the site for the wedding, and had lunched with us.

My second-floor study window commanded a good view of the Chapel and its grounds, and it was fun to watch the acceleration of activity there as the wedding day, April 1, approached. The University's groundsmen put in a full week cleaning litter out of tree basins and flower beds on the Chapel lawns and chopping away piles of dirty snow. At the same time, I knew, the painters and cleaners were finishing up a refurbishing job in the rooms at Ida Noyes Hall (across the street), which would be used for the reception.

The great surprise was the out-of-season appearance of the city's Department of Streets and Sanitation sweepers plus an army of men with brooms. They curried the Midway as if it were a prize horse, something that hadn't happened since the 1959 visit to the city of Queen Elizabeth. (I doubt that Mayor Daley was all that fond of either the Percys or the Rockefellers, but he was very much aware that Mayor John Lindsay of New York would be a wedding guest.)

On the day before the wedding, a telephone company truck with a snorkel-like attachment topped by a seat moved into the parking lot behind our house. The whole apparatus rose high enough for a dispatcher to observe traffic flow in nearby streets, and co-ordinate parking and retrieval of cars. A corps of men with walkie-talkies would act as lieutenants at ground level. NO PARKING signs were also posted throughout a four-square-block area, and extra cops were assigned to see that the ban was observed.

From noon on, they also took up posts at the entrance to the Chapel itself. An amazingly large number of people suddenly felt the need for private meditation on that particular day, especially as the time for the wedding rehearsal approached. They all pretended to be surprised by the presence of guards, then strolled casually around the Chapel, surreptitiously trying the locks on all the other doors.

Spencer Parsons, Dean of the Chapel, came back from lunch on Friday to find that a crew from *Life* magazine had installed a great battery of floodlights there. He blew his top, and ordered them dismantled. Ordinarily an even-tempered and benevolent man, Dean Parsons was tiring of the tendency of assorted technicians and expediters to treat the Chapel as if it were public property. In fact, one of the University's main problems that day and Saturday was to keep tabs on all the people who were making independent decisions. The head of the catering firm was issuing one set of orders; the florists were issuing others; and there was one zany moment, over at Ida Noyes, when a crew of workmen was found to be moving furniture from the lounge into the gym and another crew was moving the same furniture from the gym into the library.

Saturday morning dawned everywhere except in Chicago. At eight o'clock, the sky was midnight dark and a cloudburst of impressive ferocity slashed down on the city. At ten, in pouring rain, the marquees outside the Chapel went up. By two—rain or no rain, although by now it was intermittent—the wedding-watchers began to assemble, and the streets were thick with police. By three the first of the long black limousines had begun to pull up under the Chapel's porte cochere to discharge members of the bridal party.

The bridegroom, I learned later, was momentarily refused entrance to the Chapel by a guard who failed to recognize him. The tight security precautions paid off; the inevitable phone call to the police saying that the caller intended to throw a bomb into Rockefeller Chapel that afternoon required no additional protective measures.

The Chapel will never again look so lovely. The chancel end is a mass of lacy Gothic stonework, and its base had been turned into a floral bower. Potted crimson azaleas and white rhododendrons were banked behind the altar, while small trees and branches of magnolias, forsythia, and apple blossoms were arranged on the sides. There were no other flowers in the church.

The bridesmaids, in creamy ivory dresses, carried loosely arranged sheaves of flowers which were a cheerful medley of jonquils, tulips, lilacs, carnations, daisies, and others, and wore floral circlets on their heads. The bride, in pearl-encrusted lace, had a tulle headdress that foamed back from her face like that of a Spanish infanta and made her look even smaller and daintier than she is. Her bouquet—a mixture of sentiment and political savvy—combined white rhododendrons for West Virginia, white violets for Illinois, and white roses for New York.

After the couple had been pronounced man and wife, the full Rockefeller Chapel choir and most of the Chicago Symphony's first-chair men let loose a rendition of Vaughan Williams' *O Clap Your Hands* that was so jubilant it made one shiver.

In short: the setting and the service were so beautiful that all of us ladies who had badgered our husbands into getting us to the church forty minutes early so we could get aisle seats felt wholly justified in having done so.

By the time we came out of the Chapel—with the Laura Spelman Rockefeller carillon spilling music overhead—the rain had stopped and the crowd had grown. Ten deep, they lined the path the wedding guests were following to the hall across the street, stood on the lawns, sat in the trees. It was a cheerful crowd whose main interest was in spotting celebrities. They saw the George Romneys, the Thomas Deweys, the John Lindsays, the Art Buchwalds, Maurice Chevalier, *and* Lynda Bird Johnson with George Hamilton.

From the rear ranks of onlookers I heard some female (surely teenage) voices plaintively query, "Where's George Hamilton? Did anybody see George Hamilton?" In counterpoint, a group of male students mimicked in falsetto tones, "Where's George Hamilton? We want George Hamilton!"

Everyone smiled and jostled each other good-naturedly, and I hope that some of them actually did see George Hamilton. He had a lovely tan.

It is to the credit of the newlyweds that they stood in a receiving line for over two hours and shook over fifteen hundred hands. George and I spent some time chatting with other wedding guests—especially those conservatives from the North Shore suburbs who hadn't been out to the University since the Red witch-hunts of the 1930's—and admiring the giant mixed-flower bouquets that adorned the rooms. But long before the receiving line had shortened sufficiently for us to join it, I found myself desperately in need of space and quiet. *This has been happening rather too much lately*, I thought, with a twinge of real apprehension; but to get away from that seething crowd of people was suddenly imperative. So we went home. Perhaps sparing the newlyweds yet another pair of hands to shake was the best wedding gift we could have given.

Speaking of which: young Mrs. Rockefeller, with hundreds of gifts to acknowledge, later wrote me a two-page letter that could have been a model for the many brides of my acquaintance who have never (and with far less excuse) acknowledged wedding gifts at all. And young Mr. Rockefeller wrote George a letter thanking the University for the time and effort that had been expended on their behalf, asking particularly that the letter be circulated among all those, including the Buildings and Grounds people and the campus cops, who had helped. Given the instincts of a politician and the training of a gentleman, how can he fail?

A month and a half later, the Chapel was the scene of another "spectacular," only this time it was a bigger and better version of Dan Robins' 1965 stroke of genius, a Carillon Gala.

That musician of uncompromising standards, who ordinarily gave short shrift to composers other than Bach, Handel, and Scarlatti, had in 1965 programmed a concert that included *Wir Werden Uberkommen*, a title with a good classical ring to it but a piece with a most contemporary sound; Hewitt's *Battle of Trenton*, a very noisy sonata composed in 1797 and dedicated to General George Washington; Saint-Saëns' *The Swan*, featuring a tuba solo: and Sousa's *Stars and Stripes Forever*.

This latter work had required, in addition to the carillon, a mass of bass drums, cymbals, tubas, bell lyres, and piccolos—which were played from the Chapel roof. It had taken forty people to pull it off; forty *fit* people, for the roof is a hundred feet above the ground, and these instrumentalists had been positioned just behind a low stone parapet with little protection from a tearing wind. *Or* from the surprise finale: the unfurling of a forty-foot-long American flag from moorings just in front of them. The wind had caught it handsomely; had blown it back over the drums and piccolos ("It was like being caught in an undertow," one said); and had then flung it up and outward in a burst of red, white, 'n' blue glory.

The 1966 version included some eye-level treats. One of them was a twenty-piece orchestra whose members performed on tambourines, triangles, finger cymbals, and a Turkish instrument called a schellenbaum, which one plays by whanging it up and down like a pogo stick. Dan Robins had also found both a calliope and an antique portable carillon (the kind in which the bells and keyboard are mounted on a truck bed), and parked these on the Chapel lawn. He ran down from the tower in order to play a Soler concerto in duet with the owner of the calliope, a frail-looking lady with a lot of muscle power. For her Chicago concert debut, she chose a red chiffon evening gown and a white mink jacket. Dan was resplendent in white tie and tails.

Overhead, sixteen tubas brayed *Isolde's Liebestod* into the night, and Mozart's *Toy Symphony* emerged as a cacophony of amplified sound: tower carillon plus harmonicas, whistles, kazoos, and a striking cuckoo clock. A huge fan had been installed up there somewhere; under a blaze of colored floodlights, it kept in constant motion a rainbow burst of long crepe paper streamers. And, as before, Sousa's *Stars and Stripes Forever* was the finale —only this time, George and I were halfway up the tower, on small porches, banging away on snare drums; and the calliope and orchestra on the lawn were chiming in, too.

The crowd (so large it blocked the street) stamped its feet

and clapped and chanted, "More! MORE!"; and everyone went home in great good spirits.

That was on a Friday. The following Sunday was Pentecost, and I had a feeling that the sermon might have been amended on Saturday. One of the most inspired parts of Friday's foolishness had been the installation on the Chapel tower and along the roof of brilliant red and blue pennants on high staffs, where they had snapped and crackled in the wind, lending a romantic day-of-the-tourney look to the Gothic building they surmounted.

Not that everyone agreed. George had immediately received complaints, as had Dean Parsons. So to decorate the Chapel, the callers said, was sacrilegious. Others objected to the presence on the Chapel lawn of a calliope or to crepe paper streamers being fan-driven from the Chapel tower.

Perhaps it was in response to these critics that the Dean reminded his congregation that Pentecost is "the happy holiday when we celebrate the birth of the church," and suggested that although University people "have rightly honored the disciplines of the mind, we may have done it at the expense of other aspects of our humanness. Holiness and hilarity may stand closer together than we sometimes suspect."

Edward Mondello, the University organist, is so good that Chapel congregations had spontaneously adopted the custom of sitting through the Postlude as if it were part of the service. But on that particular Sunday, I didn't listen very attentively to the music. My thoughts were still on the theme of the sermon: that it is not enough to describe and dissect; people *feel*, too, so let us not be insensitive to the emotions; let us accord to the needs of the spirit as much respect as we give to the needs of the body. *This is also what the dissident young are trying to tell us, isn't it?*, I thought.

The Chapel always invited reflection. Sometimes there was nothing else to do there. I went to the Convocations when students were graduated, more out of a sense of duty than because I had a special interest in seeing someone get a diploma. But after I had entertained myself by leafing through the program and reading the titles of dissertations which had earned Ph.D.'s for their authors ("Solvolytic Studies of 1-Phenyl-1-chlorocyclopropanes"; "Twana Phonology"; "Response Stability as Related to Implicit Role Demands and Subject-Item Distance," etc.), there was usually an hour or more when my thoughts could turn elsewhere.

During a special Convocation in the spring of 1967, "elsewhere"—in time if not in space—was implicit in the program itself. The occasion was the official celebration of the University's Seventy-fifth Anniversary, an event which was being commemorated by the conferring of honorary degrees upon twenty-six distinguished scholars. As a souvenir, a booklet listing all the honorary degrees that the University had ever awarded had been distributed—and it transported me right out of the present. Specifically, forty-nine years back.

How astounding! In 1911, an honorary degree had been given to Count Johann-Heinrich von Bernstorff, German Ambassador to the United States and "servant of enduring peace between two related nations." But the University had *rescinded* the degree in 1918, and in 1919 had given one to Cardinal Mercier, Archbishop of Malines, for "nobly strengthening the hearts of a suffering people."

I wish I had known the period of World War I, which seems to have excited the passions of the civilian populace to a much greater degree than World War II. I remembered a conversation with Mary Wirth, who had started off with reminiscences about compulsory chapel attendance when she had been a Chicago undergraduate, then had recalled the 1917 day when the University Chaplain had prayed, "We thank God that we have learned to hate." A number of students had walked out of the service in protest, and had later appealed to the Dean of Students to excuse them from further chapel attendance "on religious grounds." (He did, too.)

The untenured professors in the German Department had been asked to leave; the French Department had been asked to teach "military language"; and the University's three students who had been drafted but refused to go to war because they were conscientious objectors had been roundly condemned by all save that handful of fellow students who had corresponded with them while they were in Leavenworth Penitentiary.

Now, that's what can happen, I thought, *when a university lets itself become politicized.* This, of course, was the direction that the militant young of the 1960's were trying to push the universities. They wanted the nation's institutions of higher learning to advance particular social and political goals, whereas the traditionalists were doing their best to preserve the universities as neutral places where no one cause or course of action was advocated but where all could get a hearing.

A particularly shaggy young man was sitting just across the aisle from me. *You!* I thought. *The universities have always had to withstand pressure from the outside, pressure to teach only what is orthodox and to satisfy only tastes that are popular. Now you guys are making things twice as difficult by attacking from the inside. Quit it!*

In the course of these indignant ruminations, I had actually turned toward him, and now he became aware of the glower I was directing his way. He stirred uneasily, glanced to his left to see if someone else was misbehaving, then furtively slid his glance back to me.

Good heavens, I don't mean you personally. For all I know, you're a member of "Up with People." So I gave him a big smile and a nod, which confused him even more. What kind of nut *was* that woman across the aisle? When the Convocation ended, he scooted out of his place as if the Furies were after him. Maybe he thought I'd been trying to engineer a pick-up.

So I shook myself back into 1967; went home; and made up for my inattention during the ceremonies by gushing inordinately over the honorary degree recipients when they came next door for the post-Convocation cocktail party.

Redmond came home for one day that spring, on the saddest of errands. His college roommate had been killed in Vietnam, and Red served as pallbearer. Joe had been an interesting boy, one whose progress through life would have been worth watching. I hadn't known him well, and grieved for him as another kind of symbol of his generation: the young men who went to war without a sense of mission but because they thought it was their duty, then did what was expected of them for the same joyless reason. To perform valiantly under such circumstances was no small virtue. Their travail was genuine, and commanded respect. In contrast, there was something synthetic and shabby about turning an argument over college grading practices into a righteous cause; it demeaned righteousness.

Yes, the campus was again bubbling and boiling with a continuation of the 1966 rank-in-class controversy—an issue that hadn't seemed, to me, worthy of all the passion it had generated the first time around, and that in its 1967 version had become a mean little exercise in disputation for the sake of disputation alone. The background was this:

The "fuller discussion" that everyone had seemed to want in '66 had occurred, and in February of '67 the faculty Council had acceded to the demand of Students Against the Rank that the comparative grade records of male students should not be calculated separately. However, the Council said, class rankings using the records of both men and women would still be compiled, because such records are required by many graduate schools and prospective employers. They could also be presented to a draft board if a young man wanted to make such use of them.

The Council didn't believe that many men would, however. College women tend to get better grades than men, and the inclusion of their grade records depresses the men's ratings. Any male student seeking deferment would at that time have been wise to take the national Selective Service test and send that (presumably higher) score to his draft board. Therefore, the Council announced, in fairness to male students who had been counting on a male class rank for deferment purposes, such ratings would continue to be compiled until the first date at which students could register for the Selective Service test.

This decision had been hailed by some students as "a victory for student power" and by others as "an empty gesture." Students Against the Rank immediately decided that what they had actually been against from the beginning was *all* ranking. ("To compare one student with another is undemocratic.") They also complained that the Council's decision had been made without enough student participation, and for good measure added the issue of retention on the faculty of a young historian who had not been re-hired for the following year. He was popular with the students not only because he spent a lot of time with them but also because he espoused radical causes. They couldn't believe that his colleagues in the history department preferred not to re-hire him for professional reasons, and interpreted his termination as a dark plot hatched by University administrators to oust him for political reasons.

These various disaffections had simmered along throughout the late winter and early spring months. George had lost track of them altogether, for he had been ill. This time a series of severe dizzy spells had actually put him in the hospital.* In the offices of other administrators, I would guess, problems of greater urgency had swamped out any concern for ranking as it affected those eligible for the draft; if they thought about it at all, it was as a dead issue. A new draft law had been passed which (after June 30) would make irrelevant a student's academic standing relative to other students.

In any case, and for whatever reason, it never occurred to anybody in University officialdom to announce at regular intervals through the spring that, because no national Selective Service test had yet been scheduled, male-only class ranks were still available to those who wanted them.

* Because people in academic circles are great gossips, especially where the president of a university is concerned, every effort was made to keep George's illness a secret. He was smuggled into Billings Hospital via a steam tunnel; his room was unlabeled and plastered with NO VISITORS signs; and his name appeared nowhere on the lists of patients which are routinely circulated to various offices in the University. But when he was discharged and walked home from the hospital, the first person he met— the foreman on a campus construction job—said, "Hello, Mr. Beadle. I hear you've been in the hospital since last Thursday. Feeling better now?"

The students, however, interpreted this omission as evidence of administrative duplicity. They also bore down harder on the issue of ranking in general. In early May, they circulated a petition asking that all ranking be abolished; collected a thousand signatures; and two weeks later accused the faculty Council of "stalling" because it did not regard the petition as a mandate for compliance. By the end of the month, then, the place was in an uproar; and Students Against the Rank announced that they would take over the Administration Building for a "nondisruptive study-in" until such time as their demands were met.

Regardless of what you call it, the University's officers decided, a sit-in is a sit-in, and University policy forbade them. Up went the notice, therefore, that "any action in furtherance of the stated intention of occupying the Administration Building . . . will subject the participants to disciplinary measures."

Ninety-some students moved into the building anyway. They were then verbally warned; given time to vote on whether to stay or go; and about a third of them left. The rest, certain that the talk of disciplinary measures "up to and including expulsion" was a lot of bluster, remained. That same evening, they all received summonses to appear before a Disciplinary Committee within the week.

In due course, and after a tremendous lot of quibbling over hearing procedures, fifty-eight of them were suspended for at least one quarter.

And then the agony began.

Nobody can argue fine points better than academic people, and dozens of arguments (among students, faculty, and administrators) went on simultaneously. Since the "study-in" had begun after the Administration Building had closed for the day, and the building had actually been vacated that same night, what was so "disruptive" about the demonstration? Besides, look at who was calling it disruptive: the University Administration, following a policy laid down by the faculty. Inasmuch as students had had no part in making that policy, it had no legitimacy. Further, who was meting out discipline? That same

University apparatus. Judgment was being rendered by the adversary in the dispute, and that was *wrong!*

Or, abandoning legalistic argument, what about provocation? The study-in was justified. For a whole year, students had patiently been "going through channels" in order to get class ranks abolished, and the University had disregarded their appeal. Shouldn't the authorities at least be willing to discuss definitive expressions of student opinion? Instead, they suppress such opinion!

Or, from the human standpoint, consider what might happen to those who had been suspended. Some would lose fellowships or grants-in-aid. Others might be drafted. Wasn't this too harsh a penalty for individuals to pay whose only crime was a principled and peaceful protest against the repressive and reactionary University Establishment?*

Thanks to all this tumult, the end-of-the-academic-year activities took place in a tense and joyless atmosphere. With misgivings, I scheduled our usual series of Open Houses for graduates. Out of fifteen hundred to whom invitations were sent, a hundred and twenty came. Convocation was a dismal affair, with a quarter of the students wearing white armbands to protest the suspension of the sit-inners. A dozen students refused to shake George's hand after he presented their diplomas. Another dozen ostentatiously walked out of the ceremony in order to further emphasize their opposition to the University's "re-

---

* In the heat of the post-mortem protest, it tended to be forgotten that the Disciplinary Committee, at the same time that it had announced the suspensions, had *lifted* them for twenty first-year students because they hadn't been on campus in 1966 and might not have fully understood the reason for the University's ban on sit-ins. (Nor was *that* a popular decision with everyone. One of our less permissive faculty members snorted in disgust and exclaimed, "Some precedent! They're saying in effect that everyone is entitled to one sit-in as part of his liberal education!")

And many people also forgot that the Dean of Students, who is permitted by the University statutes to ameliorate penalties imposed by the Disciplinary Committee, did so in the case of several graduate students. Insofar as I know, no suspended student was drafted during the period when he was not enrolled at the University.

pressive policies." At the following reception for graduates and their families, a new B.A. and her parents—all three wearing white armbands—came through the receiving line just so they could castigate George for "the awful thing the University has done" and to demand redress.

When we finally got home that night, I said to George, "Well, thank God, there's only one more year of this."

(He would be sixty-five in 1968, and the announcement of his forthcoming retirement was soon to be made.)

Seeking to cheer me—after all, we *did* have to put in that additional year—he said, "Things will be better by fall, honey. You'll see."

But he looked as dispirited as I felt.

Thirty-one

George was wrong; things weren't any better in the fall. However, our batteries had been recharged during the summer, and both of us went into the new term with more composure and more humor than we had possessed at the end of the last.

George himself had a fine summer holiday, loosely disguised as work. In July, he went on a long tour of the Far North, sponsored by the Arctic Institute of North America; and returned in great spirits, tanned and fit, with tales of musk ox and mining towns and salmon as big as *this*.

His love affair with the arctic dated from the 1950's, when he had climbed mountains in Alaska's Brooks Range, and thereafter he had returned at regular intervals to that austere but (to him) exhilarating country. So I was not too surprised when he announced that he had found some land that would be just right for our retirement home.

"Near Anchorage?" I asked. "Or Fairbanks?" (That's where the University of Alaska is.)

"No," he said. "In Yellow Knife, Yukon Territory."

"I can hardly wait," I said. "Does it have a zip code?"

And then I noticed that he was serious.

He was so serious that he wrote the town clerk to find out how much the land he liked would cost us. The town clerk replied that because that particular plot of ground had good topsoil (in those parts, a greater rarity than gold), its price was $100,000.

WHERE HAS ALL THE IVY GONE?

I breathed easier. I really did not want to spend my sunset years chasing moose out of the garden.

My own "summer holiday" had been postponed into the fall, when I was to visit Guatemala with a group from Chicago's Field Museum; but I didn't mind staying in the city, anyway. The weather tended to be better than at most of the nearby resort areas, and there were all kinds of pleasures to engage in in Chicago if one had the time.

A special delight of that summer was the dedication of a fifty-foot-high steel sculpture designed by Pablo Picasso for the city's new Civic Center Plaza, an acquisition that belongs with those other out-of-character civic activities that make Chicago an interesting place in which to live. From time to time, its burghers forget that they are hog butchers to the world and undertake such audacities as the reversing of a river, the establishment of a university like Chicago—or the construction of a sculpture that not one citizen in a thousand can understand or appreciate.

The architects of the new Civic Center building, led by William Hartmann of Skidmore, Owings, and Merrill, got this particular bright idea. They left the job of negotiation to Bill. He stalked Picasso for months, purse in hand, and finally snared him—not with money but, I think, with the basically incongruous idea of a Picasso sculpture becoming the symbol of Chicago. Instead of money, Picasso accepted a complete library of Chicago Symphony Orchestra recordings, a White Sox uniform, and an autographed photograph of Mayor Daley. He then did a sketch (there are those who use the word "doodle"), and the American Bridge Division of U. S. Steel cast it in the kind of steel that is supposed to rust.

It has no title other than "the Chicago Picasso." Some say it represents a human head, others say it's a bird. An alderman with no taste for abstract art has called it "a vulture." Another (one of the mayor's minuscule opposition in the City Council) believes that it represents "a taxpayer picked clean." The mayor himself, pestered by reporters who wanted him to characterize it

and comment on its significance to the city, said that *he* didn't
know what it represented but that it was a great addition to the
whole metropolitan area.

"Chicago has always been charitable about sharing our culture
with the suburbs," he blandly remarked.

I don't like the sculpture. It is flat, hard, unpattable, and un-
lovable. But whether you like it is actually immaterial. It is big
and bold and dramatic, in proper scale for its site, and its air of
authority suits its surroundings.

Everyone was on hand for the unveiling: hippies wearing
crowns of daisies; trustees of the Art Institute in custom-made
suits and Dior ties; Women March for Peace, the Picasso doves
on their picket signs displayed against a tasteful shade of blue;
stock boys, salesgirls, and secretaries; women in housedresses
with their hair in rollers and their babies in strollers; Black-Is-
Beautiful types (the aggressive vanguard of those who would
shortly be sporting Afros and wearing dashikis); shoppers from
the suburbs in expensive little seersucker suits with pearl circlets
on the lapels; seedy hangers-on at City Hall. Smack in the middle
of the mob was the whole Chicago Symphony Orchestra—nervous but valiant, as strayed children leaned on the music racks
or stood spellbound at the musicians' elbows. There were too
many speakers and the oratory was fulsome, but one didn't have
to listen. Just letting the scene soak in was a joy.

It wasn't a wholly carefree summer, of course. We always
cleaned house thoroughly during July and August, and in 1967
(since the University was further stepping up its pursuit of that
$160,000,000) I had to co-ordinate the arrival and departure dates
of wall washers and rug shampooers with the luncheons scheduled before presentations to possible donors. There was a party
or two for summer-session students, the reception for distinguished guests after the August Convocation, and a tea for the
wives of delegates to a medical conference. Our total tally of
guests now stood at just over thirteen thousand.

Once or twice a week I put on my white gloves and went off
to be a Sidewalker. This activity was part of an anti-litter cam-

paign which could have been a success, but wasn't. Launched the previous year, it had never progressed beyond its "demonstration area," Fifty-third Street. There, a small band of ladies put in an hour a day, ostentatiously picking up other people's nasty droppings—beer bottles, waxed paper smeared with catsup, candy wrappers, greasy bones, and so on—and dropping them in the litter baskets. We wore white gloves in order to emphasize the dirtiness of the job.

Those who did it were good and loyal and I herewith salute them—Elsie Krueger, Florence Stout, Inge Maser, Jean Anderson, Sylvia Mann, Jean Coulter, and a dozen more—with gratitude and affection. However, in addition, we needed troops of men to fix the observed litterer with a steely eye and say, "Put it in the basket, Bud!" They did not materialize.

Said troops might even have been the police, enforcing the ordinances forbidding littering. But the district commander patiently explained to me that if his men were out of their squad cars writing tickets for people who threw pop bottles into the streets they wouldn't be able to respond to emergency calls as quickly as if they remained on patrol.

We ladies of the white gloves would also have welcomed a band of high school students who had been brainwashed into believing that "It's real neat!" could be applied to one's environs as well as to the latest album by the Beatles. They did not materialize, either. Or the Boy Scouts. Or college-age militants; but then, it wasn't yet fashionable for them to be concerned about ecology.

The streets could have used some beautification, too, but those few optimists who annually filled the concrete or redwood planters outside their stores with petunias soon lost their plants to petunia thieves or had them smothered in litter. About the only really luxuriant floral offering in Hyde Park that summer was the newsstand at Fifty-seventh and Kenwood. In the dark of one night, some anonymous artist had painted great splashy blooms all over it.

To that cheerful sight, another was shortly added—on a vacant lot a block west; a tiny one, no more than thirty feet wide. There, a professionally lettered sign (it must have cost a mint) appeared one day, announcing that

On This Lot Will Be Erected the
FRANK LLOYD WRIGHT
MILE-HIGH BUILDING COMPLEX
Containing
10,000 Apartments . . . Parking for 8,000 Cars . . .
Golf Course . . . Marina . . . Polo and Football
Field . . . Swimming Pool . . . Bowling Alley . . .
Restaurants . . .   Plus Private Tunnel Direct
to the Loop and O'Hare Airport
*
FOR INFORMATION CALL 943-0622

The telephone number given connected the caller with Dial-a-Prayer.

Members of the Harper Court Board, that summer, needed whatever encouragement a call to 943-0622 might have provided. Two of our artisans had gone bankrupt; the gallery run as an artists' co-operative had closed its doors; and we kept getting promises or bad checks from several specialty shop owners who were skating on very thin ice. We took one tenant to court in order to recover back rent, and got a judgment which we were never able to collect. We also lost some potential income. A cabinetmaker with more ingenuity than conscience dickered for shop space, obtained a key he shouldn't have had, and used the space for three months (working only at night) before Charlie Fox found him out. Then he refused to pay for it, because he hadn't signed a lease.

The skylights leaked, and some brick retaining walls began to lean toward the Equator. Vandals discovered how much fun it was to write obscenities on our light-colored buildings. There were alleged sightings of prostitutes in the environs, and the center continued to be plagued at night by loiterers who looked as if they'd as soon as not plunge a knife into your ribs. We asked the police for as much and as frequent surveillance of the Court as they could give. They were most co-operative, and it helped. In fact, they were almost too co-operative. . . .

Ernie Leonard* is one of those people you describe as "a nice little man"—not because he is small in stature but because he is quiet, clean, and rather diffident. A man of advancing years, he clerks in a store on Fifty-third Street, lives in South Shore, and is unmarried. People tell me that he likes an occasional glass of beer and bowls a bit, but "nothing to excess" seems to be his motto.

The Fifty-third Street stores stay open late on Thursdays, and one warm September night Ernie decided to stop off at a tavern near Harper Court for a quick one after work. He couldn't find a place to park, so he tucked his car into a lot behind one of the Harper Court buildings (a lot that is normally reserved for the use of its merchants); and went off to the tavern.

When he exited, three hours later, he had a female companion, a woman in her thirties or forties. Both of them were drunk. They staggered in a northerly direction, past a dozen teenagers who were lounging on the grassy banks of Harper Court's courtyard and serenading the moon on their bongo drums.

A few minutes later, high-pitched screams issued from the merchants' parking lot.

A nearby apartment hotel has a doorman who doubles as a security guard. When he heard the screams he called the police. Then he raced outdoors to see what was going on.

The woman was lying on the pavement beside Ernie's car. "He's raping me! He's raping me!" she was screeching.

Ernie was leaning over her. He was hanging onto a door handle with one hand and waving the other, palm down, as one does when trying to shush a child who is having a temper tantrum. At the same time, however, he was yelling at the top of his lungs, "I'm not! I'm not!"

It didn't appear that a rape was in progress, but the hotel door-

---

* That is not his name; and if there actually is an Ernie Leonard who works on Fifty-third Street and lives in South Shore, I don't mean him.

man was taking no chances. He grabbed Ernie's free arm in an attempt to pull him away from his alleged victim.

Ernie apparently became a tiger when in his cups. He spun around in place and not only aimed but landed a punch on the doorman's nose.

"Take your hands offa me!" he bellowed.

At the same time, the doorman yelled, "What the hell do you think you're doing?"

Lights were going on in adjacent buildings and a few windows were flung wide open. Residents began to stick their heads out and give voice.

"Pipe down, whoever's making all that racket!"

"Mabel? Mabel! Can you see anything down there?"

"Someone ought to call the cops!"

There was now enough commotion to be heard above the bongo drums, so the teenagers came charging over to see the action.

Concurrently, two squad cars arrived from the north. All that yelling and screaming could mean only one thing: a riot. And who starts riots? Teenagers, of course. So the cops ordered the teenagers to line up against the wall and started to search them.

Now the kids were yelling, too.

A third police detail arrived, this time from the south. Hearing the din but not yet seeing its source, the policemen leaped out of their car with guns drawn, and one of them fired his pistol into the air.

That brought open *all* the windows in the surrounding buildings, and about thirty people in pajamas and robes—all crying, "What's happening?" or "I heard a shot; did *you* hear a shot?"— surged into the street.

A couple of squadrols were on the scene by now. The alleged rape victim was yelling, the alleged raper was yelling, the doorman was yelling, the teenagers were yelling, and the onlookers were getting in everybody's way. So the cops decided it would be easier to sort things out at the precinct station.

They didn't have much trouble loading the teenagers into a

squadrol, but Ernie was stubborn. He was still spinning and flailing, and in fact managed to belt the doorman once more. It took three policemen to get the handcuffs on him.

In the precinct house, at 2:30 A.M., a hastily summoned lawyer friend of Ernie's found the battle still in progress. Ernie would not, positively would not, have his fingerprints taken.

"What's the charge?" the lawyer asked.

"Battery; and attempted rape."

Ernie was outraged. "You idiots," he howled. "I *couldn't* have raped her. My God, I'm sixty-two years old!"

Then he passed out.

Meanwhile, the teenagers—unbooked—were sitting morosely on benches waiting to be sent home.

And the lady who had precipitated the melee was being examined in the Emergency Room at Mercy Hospital. She had not been raped.

The next day, when everyone concerned felt better, it turned out that neither of the principals had the slightest recollection of the night's events. The doorman decided to be generous and not press the charge of battery. The teenagers even got their abandoned bongo drums back.

On Sunday, when I was updating the previous year's speech for the Newcomers' Reception, I came to this sentence: "Hyde Park is a very lively community, one in which something interesting is always going on." I giggled, and said to George, "Shall I document it?"

Thirty-two

George's forthcoming retirement had been officially announced at the end of June, and a search committee for the University's new President had been formally appointed. I don't know how hard or how far they looked, inasmuch as Edward Levi was the obvious choice. Nevertheless, the forms had to be observed.

One of the inviolate rules in this situation is that an outgoing president does not name his successor. Even a hint of his trying to use influence on behalf of a particular candidate is the kiss of death. All through that summer, therefore, I sat on the sidelines and observed the development of an administrative deadlock that was both entertaining and exasperating.

It began when the Dean of the Division of the Biological Sciences offered George a post-retirement appointment as a faculty member in that division—subject, as in the case of all appointments, to the approval of the President and the Provost of the University.

But the President thought that whatever role he might play in the future life of the University was dependent upon the identity of his successor, so he asked that the recommendation be put on ice for the present.

That suited the Provost fine, because he was reluctant to make any new faculty appointments for 1968–69. The new President, Edward said, should be stuck with as few of someone else's decisions as possible.

George, of course, not only hoped but expected that Edward would be the University's next President. Edward was a fine Provost and had been a fine Dean of the Law School, and his talk of a return to full-time teaching was unrealistic. Everyone knew that he kept getting offers to head other institutions, and it seemed likely to George that if the search committee didn't offer him the University of Chicago presidency pretty promptly, he'd be tempted to go elsewhere.

So, while the waiting was going on, George tried to keep Edward's mind off of "elsewhere." The best way to do this was to keep him involved in planning for the future of Chicago. Which Edward didn't want to do because of uncertainty about the identity of the new President. And so on full circle.

Edward, similarly, knew that George was getting offers of post-retirement jobs at other institutions. He also knew that if he were to be the next President of the University, he'd want to keep George at Chicago. But he couldn't say so, and therefore he spent the waiting period keeping *George's* mind off of "elsewhere."

"Don't commit yourself to anything just yet," he kept saying.

"But you're both so silly!" I exclaimed to George one evening. "It's like that old Alphonse and Gaston joke, the one about the men who couldn't get through the door because they were too considerate of each other. Why can't you come right out and admit to each other that Edward is likely to be the next President?"

"Why, honey!" George said, in pretended reproof. "That'd be against the rules." And then, dead serious: "Damn! I wish they'd decide."

They did—in September; and Edward accepted the job.

He certainly had no illusions about it. There had been riots at Cornell that year. Wisconsin was in turmoil. San Francisco State was beginning to disintegrate. Berkeley had never settled down since the first explosion of the Free Speech Movement, and the conservatives among the University of California's regents had finally decided that it was all Clark Kerr's fault—so off with his head.* In short, the public backlash was beginning. Pacing it, the militant mood of students was turning nastier.

Yet the universities still had the familiar old problems of needing more money than they possessed and of attempting to provide more services than they could—or of withstanding social pressures to do so. There was no reason to assume that the University of Chicago would be free of these problems, and every reason to assume that the presidency would be more of a man-killer in the seventies than it had been in the sixties.

Even so, Edward was willing to give it a try. By then, I think, he had such a deep emotional investment in the University of Chicago that he *had* to go the whole route. Anyway—and thinking only of short-range benefits—it was going to be good for the University to have a President-elect a year before he would take office. It would assure continuity between administrations and would preserve the forward momentum of such major enterprises as the fund drive and the reorganization of the College.

Like Edward, Kate Levi had grown up in Hyde Park, in a family with close ties to the University (her father had long been a trustee, for example), and she too knew what she was in for when she became the institution's First Lady. She would be good for *it*, as well. Just as it may have been an advantage to the University to bring a complete outsider to the presidency in 1961, it would now be an advantage to have born-and-bred Chicagoans in the President's House.

Kate knew everybody; had social instincts that I couldn't begin to match; and would engage in civic and philanthropic activities quite different from those that had been associated with my tenure. Whether the wife of a university president likes it or not, the causes she espouses acquire some of the

---

* When Kerr was dismissed, the University of Chicago had immediately offered him a professorship in its School of Business. His academic specialty is labor relations; but because some of his prospective colleagues doubted that he had been able to "keep up" in that field during his years as an administrator, one of them said, "If we're hiring him as a scholar, I'm against it. But if we're hiring him as a hero, I'm for it." As it turned out, Kerr declined the offer.

prestige associated with her husband's office or of the university itself; and now certain groups or activities to which I had given little time or interest would have their fair share of attention. Perhaps most important of all, the prospect of living in the Manse didn't seem to give Kate the cold shivers. I had wasted a lot of emotion on fighting the place.

The University's future leadership, in short, would be in good hands. But those hands wouldn't be at the helm for another year—and therefore George's and my activities went on as before.

The class of 1971 arrived, met in assembly in the time-honored manner, and were assured in the time-honored manner that they were the brightest group ever to be admitted to the University. But they didn't respond to this sally with the usual self-conscious little stir, triggered partly by pride and partly by fear (because of the competition they posed for each other). They just sat. All through Orientation Week, in fact, they played everything so cool that I began to wonder if they were alive.

They were sufficiently curious about "the Administration" to come to the President's Reception, but at the same time they were ashamed of themselves for attending something as conventional as they rightly guessed it would be. Receiving-line repartee is not very enthralling at best, but this year many of the students wouldn't even go halfway and merely grunted in acknowledgment of our greetings.

There is a question on the College's application form that asks prospective students to list their "special achievements" or "distinctions," and a couple of years earlier a girl had ignored her status as a National Merit Scholar in order to reply, "I have a remarkable ability to hold my breath under water for exceptionally long periods of time." That kind of impishness, of being able to mock without malice, was missing in this year's class. There was no *zest* in them.

And they were already grubby. In former years, our new undergraduates had been clean and tidy, and had looked like individuals for two or three weeks after the start of classes. In 1967, however, they arrived on campus in tattered jeans and bare feet, and could see no reason to dress differently for the President's Reception. Those of us in the receiving line no longer wore evening dresses or dinner jackets (we had abandoned that custom two years before), but we had continued to observe the formal etiquette of the receiving line itself. This was now a complete anachronism, and I resolved on the spot that the next year's reception—if there was one—would be a picnic.

Afterwards, I said to George, "Talk about a visual demonstration of the generation gap! That was it. This year, I wasn't even certain as to which ones are GRITS Kids."

By which I meant that the hippie-oriented youth culture had penetrated to the backwoods. GRITS stands for Grass Roots Talent Search, which is the University's colloquial designation of a program officially called the Small School Talent Search. The program had been inaugurated just before we came to Chicago, and its aim was to recruit students from small-town or rural high schools. The College's administrators thought that young people with that kind of background would add a leavening touch to a student population that is predominantly urban or big-city suburban. In addition, they wanted to find out whether a small school background really did disqualify a student for a college experience like the one offered at Chicago, as was then widely assumed.

Much has been written in recent years about equalizing educational opportunity for underprivileged youths (usually black) from the city ghettoes, but not much attention has been paid to youngsters (usually white) who attend country schools that cannot offer as rich an educational program as larger and more populated districts do. If you only graduate ten students a year, you're going to hire *one* science teacher and expect him to substitute ingenuity for fancy lab equipment. The city and suburban schools, on the other hand, can hire specialists and give them fine teaching tools. Big systems have more complete libraries than small-town and rural schools, and also possess the supplementary services of municipal libraries and art or natural history museums. For all these reasons, students in small-

town and rural districts tend to get somewhat lower scores
on college board exams than those with urban backgrounds, and
this puts them at a disadvantage when applying to selective private colleges or universities.

Not that many of them do. That's the other disadvantage
of their environment. Small-town and rural communities are
more enthusiastic about basketball teams and marching bands
than about intellectual achievements, which means that high-IQ
students are not pushed very hard in school. In addition, those
who are motivated to go to college aren't often encouraged to
think bigger than the nearest state college. Estimable though
these institutions often are, they tend not to produce members
of the learned professions—and it's wasteful of the nation's intellectual resources to let a really bright youngster become a
home economist or a high school football coach when he or she
is capable of becoming a statistician or a physician.

The University of Chicago initially recruited its GRITS Kids
from small towns and rural school districts in the Midwest. Their
college board scores were given less weight than usual, and their
principals' recommendations were given more weight. Most came
into the College with full-tuition scholarships. The first year was
usually hard for them academically (because they had never
had to read as much, or as critically, as the typical first-year
student in Chicago's College is expected to). But in the later
college years they did as well as students from urban and suburban backgrounds, and their dropout rate for social or emotional
reasons was no greater.

Therefore the program was extended to the entire United States
and Canada, and by 1967 almost four hundred GRITS Kids had
gone through the College or were then enrolled. About a quarter
of them had progressed to graduate school, many with Wood-
row Wilson fellowships or similarly coveted awards. One had
been a Rhodes Scholar.

Scarsdale children are in and out of the Metropolitan Museum
of Art from the time they are big enough to climb into a school
bus without a boost. Lacking such experience, young people from

America's small towns and wide open spaces can still be excited at age eighteen by a first look at an Old Master; and the priceless gift they had brought to the University of Chicago was enthusiasm. They were not only willing but eager to participate in organized activities, and had correspondingly enriched the extracurricular life of the College.

At the President's Reception in '67, I thought, sadly, *If even the GRITS Kids are now suspicious of anyone over thirty, some bad times are ahead.* And then a second thought: *I wonder if there are drug pushers, now, in places like Broken Bow, Nebraska?*

The reception for graduate students went better. In general, graduate students have a particular, and scholarly, reason for being at a university—although this was less true in the sixties than it had been a decade earlier. They therefore get along better with the faculty (and vice versa) than undergraduates, who are still trying to find out who they are and what they want to do with their lives.

The reception for new faculty members was a pleasure. We had an interesting "catch" that year, and as I went over the lists and brief biographies before we left the house I said to George, "You know, I complain a lot about all those departmental cocktail parties we have to go to, but I *am* going to miss the association with such a varied lot of people."

"Such as?"

I read from the sheets in my hand:

"Ronald Emmerich, old Iranian languages. David Bevington, sixteenth-century drama. They're both visiting professors.

"Henry Kingdon, allosteric activity of proteins.

"Leonard Linsky, 'expert on the theory of denoting and the theory of reference.' What do you suppose that means?

"Jack Stevens, surgical management of rheumatoid arthritis. He's from Glasgow.

"Mariano Yogore, parasitology. Specialty, schistosomiasis. That's the snail disease, isn't it?

"Oh, here's another visitor: John Wolf, 'author of a diplomatic history of Baghdad railroads, also has a new biography of Louis XIV in press.' Isn't that a great combination, all in one brain?"

George did an extra amount of traveling that fall: Pittsburgh, Tulsa, New York, Los Angeles, Dallas, Washington, anywhere the money was. But he was home for the October ground-breaking of the new Regenstein Library, a building that was going to outmode every other university library in the country. (Capacity: three million books.) We had a special soft spot in our hearts for that library, because the Joseph and Helen Regenstein Foundation had happened to pick George's birthday in 1965 to give the ten million dollars that was making possible its construction.

From the sketches it appeared that Walter Netsch's massive and marvelously proportioned limestone building would be as distinguished an architectural addition to the campus as the Saarinen-designed Law School. But the site had presented a problem. The logical place, central to everything, was Stagg Field; and the old alums didn't like that prospect at all. To eliminate the turf and grandstands where so much history of collegiate athletics had been written seemed disrespectful to the memory of Chicago's great coach.

"They're pretty upset about it," the Alumni Director had reported to George.

"Even though the new athletic facilities"—a few blocks west and north—"will be bigger and better, and will still be called Stagg Field?"

" 'Fraid so. It's just not the same *place*."

Then George had had an inspiration. When work began in earnest on the library, alumni who had been especially active in athletics had gathered on the site. Led by Jay Berwanger, the famed "one-man team" of the 1930's, they had then formed a procession and had carted some symbolic wheelbarrow loads of Stagg Field topsoil over to the new location. So at least a part of the loved place had survived.

That same month was marked by another event that gave George special pleasure, not in his academic role as President of the University but in his community role as president of the South East Chicago Commission (which, together with the Hyde Park-Kenwood Community Conference, continued to keep tabs on the progress of urban renewal in the neighborhood). This event was the dedication of the Lutheran School of Theology at Chicago, a new amalgam of three small seminaries, located in a handsome new building at the corner of Fifty-fifth Street and University Avenue.

It is not generally appreciated how important the "anchor institutions" are to the stability of a city community like ours. It's true that a good many people live in Hyde Park or Kenwood because they like the diversity of its population and the liberalism of its political outlook. But other people live here because they have jobs here, and they sufficiently prize the convenience of living within walking distance of those jobs to put up with such discomforts as polluted air, dirty streets, insufficient elbow room, and the presence of people whom they might not normally choose for neighbors. This applies especially to middle-class whites who are engaged in managerial, clerical, or service jobs. They are not necessarily free of racial bias, but those of this type who stayed in Hyde Park through the 1950's and continue to settle here today do so because it's a joy to be spared a commute to work.

And where do they work?

At the University, of course, as members of the faculty, as research assistants, as librarians, in office jobs, as nurses and medical technicians in the University hospitals, and so on. The University of Chicago, with some ten thousand workers on its Midway campus, is among the twenty largest employers in the city.

But there are similar jobs too at the Chicago College of Osteopathy, the Illinois Central Hospital and Woodlawn Hospital, the American Bar Center, the Center for Research Libraries, the Museum of Science and Industry, the Child Care Society, the U. S. Weather Bureau Regional Forecast Center, the Pritzker Center of the Jewish Children's Bureau, the Public Administration Center, in the several big hotels located in East Hyde Park, and in the neighborhood's numerous elementary and secondary schools.

There also used to be jobs for local residents at George Williams College, which (among other objectives) seeks to train inner-city social workers. Indeed, Hyde Park-Kenwood and its neighboring communities provide a perfect laboratory for such training. George Williams College had been most supportive of the urban renewal effort in the 1950's, during the presidency of John McCurdy, but under a new administration in the 1960's it had a change of heart and moved to one of Chicago's all-white suburbs.

George was disgusted. "How the hell can they justify training inner-city workers in a synthetic community like that?" he said.

Furthermore, he was furious because the University had felt constrained to buy the George Williams physical plant in order to control its usage.

While this defection was still smarting, the vanguard of the Lutherans had arrived. They *wanted* to be in an inner-city community; their students, they said, preferred to be where the action was. Their faculty thought it would be stimulating to be close to the other theological seminaries that for years had clustered around the University of Chicago, and to be associated with the University itself. The land they picked was being cleared by the city's Department of Urban Renewal, but it wasn't quite enough—so the University of Chicago had sold them some adjacent property upon which were apartment houses occupied both by students and by permanent residents of the community.

A great tempest had immediately brewed. The heartless University of Chicago was again displacing the poor, the downtrodden, the powerless. And for what? Still another institution! As the anti-Lutheran pickets had tramped back and forth outside our house, George had snapped, "My God, look at them! And where were they when George Williams moved out?"

My husband seldom shows anger, but throughout that particular controversy he did. Even now, he slaps down with uncharacteristic passion the assertions of the new college generation that the Hyde Park-Kenwood urban renewal project was a malevolent scheme forced by the University and other community institutions upon a helpless citizenry. Without the University and those other institutions, he says—and I agree—Hyde Park and Kenwood would today almost surely be as blighted and as segregated as the communities directly north and south of us, communities which lack the institutional "anchors" for an economically, socially, and racially diverse population.

The dedication of the Lutheran School of Theology occurred on a fine Sunday afternoon in October, and was preceded by a religious service in Rockefeller Chapel. At its conclusion, all two thousand people in attendance marched in procession along University Avenue for the six blocks that separate the two buildings. To representatives of many academic institutions, in brilliantly colored ceremonial garb, and to the Lutheran clergy of several different synods there were added devout laymen carrying flags and banners representing the different ethnic traditions that had merged in the creation of the new school. No marshals kept stragglers in line; the people chatted to each other as they went along; and the pace varied from brisk to leisurely. It was not in any sense a march. It was a pilgrimage. It was also a very moving sight.

Thirty-three

It is impossible to name one person, or even ten, who should be credited with the discovery of atomic energy. True, its first controlled release occurred in the United States, at the University of Chicago, under the leadership of Enrico Fermi. But he, and all other nuclear physicists of his generation, were heir to four decades of research that dated from William Roentgen's discovery of X-rays just before the turn of the century. From then until the 1930's, the point of such research was simply to find out how atoms are structured and how they behave. The pioneers did not contemplate, and perhaps did not even imagine, an application of their findings (whether for bombs or for industrial power plants).

By the mid-thirties, it was possible to study atomic structure by bombarding substances with subatomic particles until the atoms had been knocked apart, and Fermi was one of the leaders in this field. He had even used uranium as the element under bombardment. But he didn't know enough chemistry to realize the significance of what happened to the various products of its disintegration.

The people who found *that* out, in 1939, were the Germans Otto Hahn and Fritz Strassmann. In their case, though, the chemistry of the reaction interested them so much that their report skipped lightly over the physics. It was left to Hahn's long-time associate Lise Meitner—already in exile in Copenhagen

—to realize the true import of their discovery, and to make clear to physicists the staggering implications of the process which she christened "fission."

As is usual when some great scientific "breakthrough" occurs, the professional journals couldn't keep abreast of developments. News of what's new was therefore transmitted informally by the people who were in the forefront of discovery—at scientific congresses, during visits to research centers in other countries, by writing colleagues in distant places, and so on.

Niels Bohr, for example, came straight from Lise Meitner to Columbia University, and there had long conferences with Enrico Fermi and Leo Szilard, a Hungarian-born physicist in the same lab. From there he went to two conferences and on to other universities. At these, as everywhere else in the specialized world of the physical sciences, atomic energy had suddenly become Topic A.

That much excited talk about the incredible power locked in atoms could not escape the attention of non-scientists—among them, ministries of war. Hitler's armies were already on the march in early 1939, and by the middle of the year the German Ministry of Munitions had organized a research group to explore the uses of nuclear fission. This scared the émigré scientists in America half to death.

People like Fermi and Szilard knew firsthand what to expect if Fascism were to dominate the world, and they spent futile months trying to get someone in the United States Government to take their warnings seriously. Finally, using the entrée to the White House of a Russian-born economist, Alexander Sachs (who was an industrial consultant to President Roosevelt), and the prestige of Albert Einstein (to be sure that a letter to the President would actually be read by the President), they managed to get a federal Advisory Committee on Uranium appointed. This committee was a mix of alarmed scientists and complacent military men. Its eventual appropriation of a puny six thousand dollars for research was recommended as much to keep the scientists out of the military men's hair as for any other reason.

That was in early 1940. By then, the nuclear physicists of the non-Fascist countries had voluntarily agreed not to publish any more scientific papers. The lid of censorship had already clamped down in Germany. Not only had the supranational brotherhood of science been ruptured by the oncoming war, but in addition the scientists of both sides were from this point onward to work in ignorance of what those on the other side were learning, and how their knowledge was being applied.

I knew the story, but in the fall of 1967 it came alive and developed new dimensions because of two twenty-fifth anniversary celebrations in which many of the participants in the American effort to unlock the secrets of the atom were present. The atmosphere suggested a reunion among survivors of a catastrophe, or a battle group, or veterans of any other experience that had been marked by high drama, high uncertainty, and mutual support among daring young men. The young men were graying now, but they still remembered how it had been in the early 1940's when they had been recruited for jobs so secret that they didn't know what they had agreed to do until after they had agreed to do it.

When you tear atoms apart, you can get isotopes of the same element, which are chemically almost alike but differ in physical properties; or you can get products that are chemically quite different. Uranium 235 is the isotope of uranium that is fissionable. Uranium also yields a product called plutonium, an element which was not (in the 1940's) known in nature but which was created in the holocaust of a cyclotron. Its discoverers were a team of Berkeley physicists. Once created, plutonium is very stable, and like U-235 it is fissionable. Since it can be separated from uranium more easily than U-235, American scientists were quick to realize that plutonium might be a better nuclear fuel than U-235. At least, it should be available as an alternative.

The only problem was that there was so little plutonium in existence in 1940 that you couldn't see it with the naked eye. The first order of business, therefore, was to produce more; and two of the country's cyclotrons ran night and day in an effort to make enough so that its properties could be further studied. It was already known, however, that even this crash program would yield an extremely small amount of plutonium, too little even to be weighed by the instruments and techniques then available. What good would it be to any experimenter to have some plutonium, if he couldn't tell how much he was using?

To create a usable oxide of the stuff and to work out ways to weigh it fell to Glenn Seaborg, one of the discoverers of plutonium. A group under his direction therefore moved to the University of Chicago in mid-1942. In August of that year, they isolated a pure compound of it—thanks to skills both scientific and domestic. Once, a centrifuge came apart and if someone hadn't sopped up the escaping liquid with a sponge, the experimenters would have had to start all over again. Then a beaker broke. That time they recovered their plutonium by evaporating it from the copy of the Chicago *Tribune* into which it had soaked.

On September 10, 1942, they managed to weigh it. One of the by-products of this effort was the development of that branch of science called ultramicrochemistry. Using its techniques, one can weigh micrograms of substances. (A microgram is one millionth of a gram.) It turned out that they had 2.77 micrograms of plutonium; if you want a comparison, a dime is 900,-000 times heavier.

In bulk, there was such a small amount of plutonium that the fewer people who had access to it the better. So its keepers showed their VIP visitors a small vial of green ink. Since nobody knew what plutonium ought to look like, this "sample" was very impressive.

There can't be many college classrooms in the United States which have been officially designated as National Historic Landmarks, but Room 405 of the George Herbert Jones Laboratory at the University of Chicago is one of them. That's where the weighing of plutonium took place, and it was to celebrate the installation of the plaque marking the site that the first of our 1967 memorials to the birth of the atomic age took place.

While Seaborg and his group had been concentrating on plutonium, Fermi and his associates in the Metallurgical Lab had been constructing their pile of uranium and graphite. December 2, 1947 was the date on which they had achieved the first controlled nuclear chain reaction. But the twenty-fifth anniversary celebration of the event began on December 1, with a formal symposium on the uses of atomic energy. There were also informal sessions for alumni of the Met Lab and its successor, the Manhattan Project.

The story of what they had done between 1942 and 1945, and how they did it, is too well known for me to repeat in detail here, but as they retold it on that reunion occasion it was fascinating to hear the small additions or amplifications that reflected the particular experience of the tale's teller. These reminiscences also dramatically documented the makeshift and sometimes casual character of the enterprise, the participants' fearful sense of groping their way in the dark, and the emotional stress they endured because they didn't know at any point whether their efforts would be successful.

The pile, for example: why was it placed in the squash rackets court under the Stagg Field grandstands? Answer: chance chose the site. The intended research spot was in a forest near the present location of the Argonne National Laboratory, a rural hideaway in the best tradition of mystery-suspense fiction. But the building there wasn't finished on schedule, so any other available high-ceilinged place would have to do.

It didn't occur to anybody to check the heating in the squash court, and there wasn't any. During the winter the only way to keep warm was to do manual labor; for this reason, even Fermi took a turn machining graphite. The security guards were less fortunate, because they had to stand at the doors. They almost froze—until somebody found a cache of old raccoon coats, and dressed them in Joe College style.

Not that "security" meant what it does today. Possible radiation damage was measured by the condition of a few cages of mice and rats that were kept near the pile. If they seemed healthy, the assumption was that the people were. As for restricting the workers to those who had "clearance": Fermi himself was classified as an enemy alien; and, at the other end of the scale, odd jobs around the place were done by high school students who had been hired simply because they were strong, willing, and available.

What seems to have kept the project secret was self-censorship. A psychiatrist then on the staff of Billings Hospital said, "Hundreds of people knew that something was going on that they *mustn't* know about, and so they just pulled down the shades of knowledge." (Although he didn't say so, this may have been the same psychic phenomenon that affected non-Jewish Germans who lived near enough the concentration camps to be fully aware of what was going on there but didn't dare to "know.")

On the twenty-fifth anniversary of the first controlled release of atomic power, all but a few of the Met Lab people had managed to reassemble. They paid tribute, of course, to those who had died; among them, Fermi (in 1954) and Samuel K. Allison (in 1965). Sam Allison had headed the Met Lab's chemistry division, and had been present when the first chain reaction was recorded. (He always insisted, though, that "the people who were immortalized as being present on the afternoon of December 2, 1942, were only the ones who had nothing to do and could hang around to see if Fermi would produce.")

I had special reason to recall him with appreciation. In 1964, when the University was trying to persuade the Italian Government to contribute a memorial to Fermi and a banquet was held in honor of the great Italian architect Pier Luigi Nervi, Sam Allison had made an after-dinner speech. His remarks were so simple and unvarnished that he turned the evening into one of those memorable public occasions when the private man comes forth. The science writer Ruth Moore was in the audience, took notes, later gave me a copy, and has now said that

I may reproduce them. Here then is part of what Professor Allison had to say that night:

> What were the consequences of the event?
>
> Scientists deal with numbers and I cannot forbear using numbers to illustrate. For most of civilized history we have depended for heat and light on one chemical reaction—the burning of coal into carbon dioxide. Without this reaction we would be as Australian aborigines.
>
> Physicists like to think in terms of atoms.
>
> One atom of coal turned into CO_2 yields two or three electron volts. One atom of Uranium-235 in fission yields 200,000,000 electron volts.
>
> These are the basic figures: two and 200,000,000. An entirely transcendental source of energy had been tapped.
>
> We all felt the importance of the event. Everyone understood about the 200,000,000 electron volts.

For the next three years, the problem was development. Plants for the manufacture of U-235 and plutonium were built at Hanford, Washington, and at Oak Ridge, Tennessee. Huge cities, unmarked on maps, grew up around them. The atom bomb itself was built in yet another secret city, Los Alamos, high on a mesa near Santa Fe, New Mexico. There, for several unreal years, the best scientific, engineering, and industrial talent in America was pooled in an activity that the workers thought of as the key to the life or death the nation. Among them was Samuel Allison, head of the laboratory's technical and scheduling group. Listen to him once more:

> The pressure was intense. I personally was in the hospital two or three times. If we did not succeed, we would not catch the Germans. They were the leaders in physics. We could not imagine that they were not ahead of us in atomic development.
>
> One incident illustrates the feeling of time:
>
> After the Army took over and set up the Manhattan

Project, all those working there were required to have their fingerprints taken. Everyone did, with the exception of Eugene Wigner [a Hungarian-born physicist, who had emigrated to the United States in 1935]. He refused.

"The Germans will develop an atom bomb before we do," he said. "They will win the war. When they come to Washington, they will get a list of those who collaborated on our bomb and will identify them by their fingerprints. They will shoot every one, and I don't intend to be shot."

The generals were dumfounded by this, but Wigner's fingerprints were never taken.

Not until well after the war did the Allies learn that the Germans had given little attention to the development of atomic power. They thought it would take twenty years to develop an A-bomb; and, besides, they expected a quick victory without it. In the early 1940's, however, their activities were as shrouded in secrecy as ours. Presumably, they got hints of our work on atomic power, just as we got hints of their work on rocketry; but nobody really *knew*. Crawford Greenewalt, DuPont's man in the Manhattan Project, has said that he didn't dare read the newspapers on D-Day because he was so fearful they would report German use of an atomic bomb on the Allied armada.

And so, in the United States, work proceeded all through '43, '44, and '45 under the relentless pressure of an unknown deadline. Risk taking was inevitable. The military boss of the Manhattan Project later said that he had been prepared to declare martial law throughout the whole Southwest in the event that the first A-bomb test blew up half of New Mexico.

It was Sam Allison's voice that had echoed across the desert during the countdown before that blast. And here, many years later, is his voice again:

There was a discontinuity in military science from the moment of Hiroshima—a pre- and post-bomb period. Remember that 200,000,000. A new order of magnitude of destruction was in our hands.

I am mostly pessimistic. No sane government or individual would engage in activity which might precipitate war with atomic weapons. But we may end with the weapon in the hands of some irresponsible individual, inflamed with a desire for revenge on an enemy. The instinct for destruction of enemies is strong in the human race.

I see just a crack of light. We may squeak through, if we get it in our minds that this is something new, and that war is insane and impossible. We may then realize the peaceful benefits of this great discovery.

On the site of the squash court where the atomic age was born, there now stands a massive twelve-foot-high sculpture by Henry Moore. Its dedication was the second major event of Chicago's 1967 salute to the birth of atomic energy; and that occasion was thoroughly contemporary.

December 2 was a dismal day, gray and windy and with an intermittent near-freezing mist. The shivering students holding the flags on either side of the open-air podium nearly had their arms jerked out of the sockets. The student-hung banners across the street—PEACE, on a white ground, and HIROSHIMA, on blood red—flapped as if alive. There were appropriate remarks, mercifully short, by appropriate dignitaries; and then, precisely at 3:36—twenty-five years to the minute after Fermi's instruments had confirmed that controlled fission was occurring inside his graphite pile—Laura Fermi pulled the rope that unveiled the six-thousand-pound bronze called *Nuclear Energy*.

At a dinner the night before, Henry Moore had been the guest of honor. (A small round man with a cheery cherub face, he doesn't at all match his sculpture.) I had always thought that bronze was bronze and that was that, but I learned from him that bronze can come in a variety of colors and textures. He said that he had made the top of this sculpture a bright gold color and had given it a shiny finish because the piece would be visible for almost a block on either side, and he thought that "it should beckon."

It does. Its polished dome rises above a rough-textured, three-pronged base, inside which there is space enough for a person to sit; and students sometimes do. The view into it, the view above your head, the hint of what's around the next curve: every step, as one circles it, changes its aspect. Like the Pevsner in the Law School's reflecting pool, it is sculpture that incorporates the onlooker into its own dynamics.

And what does *Nuclear Energy* represent? The sculptor allows the viewer to decide. The dome could be a mushroom cloud, Henry Moore has said: a tribute to man's instinct for the destruction of his enemies. Or it could be a skull, a brain case sheltering something wonderful and vital: a tribute to man's ability to solve problems by the use of his intellect. One can extrapolate to broader generalities: man the destroyer or man the creator; id or superego; historic man or future man. People will probably be arguing the point a hundred years from now—if there are any people.

Thirty-four

A lot of people expected us to return to Southern California
when George retired, but we'd gotten it out of our system. Nor,
with one exception, were the offers from institutions east of
the Rockies especially tempting. The one exception would have
taken us to a state university set in beautiful countryside—
but also miles and miles from anything bigger than a hamlet.

One Sunday afternoon in December, we were discussing the
offer. I looked out the window at Chicago's begrimed winter
landscape and said, "It'd be nice to look at white snow, wouldn't
it?"

"And fall color in the trees," George responded. "The whole
area is forested, you know. Full of rabbits and foxes and
raccoons. I'll bet you've never seen a raccoon out of a zoo, have
you? Nice animals. Everything's clean and green and quiet
there."

Just then an ambulance went tearing west along the Midway,
its siren ripping the air.

"Speaking of quiet," I said, "do you realize that's the first
siren we've heard today? What do you suppose all the wife
beaters and fire bugs and dope addicts have been doing instead?"

Almost together, we smiled at each other. We *had* become
urbanized. George shrugged his shoulders and said, "Well, honey,
I guess we're hooked."

Some faculty friends have a weekend place in the nearby

countryside and the wife once said to me, "Every time we drive back to the city and begin to smell it, I say to myself, 'Why do we do this?' Then we hit the South Side. Just seeing it makes me sick, and I think, 'How crazy can you get?' Finally, we reach Hyde Park, where we paid twice as much for half as good a house as we could have found anywhere else, and where the air isn't fit to breathe, and I get that great lift that means I'm *home*."

It is commonly said that the community derives its unique atmosphere from its village-in-the-city character. It *does* give one the sense of "place" that comes from repeatedly seeing the same people, of knowing about their affairs, of being able to count on neighbors to be neighborly when you need them; yet at the same time the urban attitude of not trying to run other people's lives is pervasive.

From the beginning, Hyde Park had entranced me for two main reasons: its citizens' independence of mind, and their activism.

Even the children. A fifth grade of legend had been split by its teacher into Republicans and Democrats, for an exercise in practical politics—only none of the kids wanted to be Republicans. So they caucused; reorganized as the Independent Voters of Illinois; lured half the Democrats into their camp; and annihilated the remnants.

Hyde Parkers are not competitive about possessions or status. They don't talk about who did or didn't get invited to a party. It doesn't matter whether you have a color TV, and in fact a few people don't have *any* TV. (As Ned Rosenheim says, it's a community that practices conspicuous abstention.) The one thing that people are snobbish about is art, and Hyde Park housewives will forego the acquisition of a new coat in order to buy a porcelain bowl from Ruth Duckworth at the Fifty-seventh Street Art Fair.

The community is overorganized. I'd sometimes get fed to the teeth with the frequency of meetings, the inevitability of someone's disputing almost any proposed course of action, the perennial sprouting of new committees in behalf of this or that cause. And yet . . . how splendid it is to feel the juices rise, not with the foreknowledge of success but because it seems right to *try*.

George always became angry when students, often from homes in all-white suburbia, dismissed the Hyde Park-Kenwood urban renewal effort as just a great big exercise in "Negro removal."

"Certainly, some Negroes were displaced," he'd say. "So were some whites. And some businessmen. And some buildings. The point is not the removals but the reason for them, and what happened afterward.

"Hyde Park-Kenwood is now about thirty-five per cent non-white, the same proportion of Negroes that it had before urban renewal began, and this is a larger non-white population than the sociologists say a community can accommodate without 'tipping.' Yet we're stable, and have been for at least five years. Do you know of any other community that used to be practically all white which can make that claim?

"We've proved that property values don't have to drop because black people move in; in fact, they've risen here by as much as fifty per cent. The vacancy rate in rental housing is two per cent, compared to a rate of seven or eight per cent for the city as a whole.

"And our black residents aren't all rich psychiatrists, either. We've got middle- and low-income Negroes, too. We have public housing that didn't have to be forced on us. Can you name any other basically middle-class community of which that can be said? What about *your* hometown? Are you taking your fair share of the poor, especially the blacks?

"You ought to be *proud* of the University and *proud* of Hyde Park-Kenwood for demonstrating that it's possible to stabilize a changing community and make it a decent place for all its residents to live in!"

The students were never convinced. All that urban renewal stuff, and the reason for it, was before their time. What mattered to them was their inability to find a cheap apartment in Hyde

Park, their romantic belief that society would function well if no constraints were placed on anyone, and the need to find a villain to blame for the inequities they could still see all around them.

One day I had ridden home from downtown Chicago in a taxi whose driver was very black, very literate, and very bitter. "Live in Hyde Park because whites have a duty to stay in the city, hey? Earning points with Jesus, hey? I reckon it makes you feel good all over when you mingle with us colored folks," he had said.

And more of the same: fifteen minutes of it. I had felt at the time that he should have paid me for providing therapy instead of asking me to pay him for transportation. And of course he had made me angry. I do believe that whites have a duty to stay in the cities, but I had never thought—consciously, anyway—that I was doing anyone an especially big favor by living in Hyde Park.

Besides, it isn't the community's inter-racial character alone that makes it interesting. It has the social diversity of a European city neighborhood. According to the census figures, the biggest single occupational group are the "professionals"—but they account for less than 30 per cent of the total. There are almost as many "clericals," and a smattering of every other category right down to "laborers." Educational background? The biggest single group has had four years or more of college, but they represent only a quarter of the total. Almost as many quit at the end of high school, and a sizable percentage didn't make it past eighth grade. Income? More people belong in the $10,000 to $15,000 bracket than any other, but they are less than a quarter of the total; the rest of the population distributes itself fairly evenly across ten different income ranges. Age? Same story: the largest group accounts for only 10 per cent of the population, and all ages are represented—from babes in arms to people over eighty-five. Marital status? Better than half are married, but almost 30 per cent are single and 15 per cent are widowed or divorced.

And perhaps the greatest of the community's assets is "the Hyde Park mystique." People have been telling each other for at least three generations that this is a great place to live; that it is "different"; that it is "better." You come to feel that if you disagree, there's something wrong with *you*.

There was nothing wrong with George and me: we set out to look for a retirement house in Hyde Park-Kenwood. It had to be a house, so that George could have a garden. Maybe somewhere in Kenwood, where frontages can run to two hundred feet. And it had to be a *new* house, because I was sick of ministering to the needs of a structure built in 1895. When we found just the right place, it was a Hyde Park row house on a twenty-seven-foot-wide lot, a house that had been built in 1893 and was still piped for gas lights.

We bought it in January of 1968, the idea being that we'd move in by March and thus make possible whatever redecoration or renovation of the President's House that the Levis wanted to do before his inauguration in November.

Our thinking was fuzzy. We were so fully occupied with University activities that we had neither time nor energy to dismantle one household and set up another one. It would be more sensible, maybe, to turn the President's House over to the Levis in July—a schedule that would give both Kate and me four months to get our respective new habitations ready for occupancy.

We were to discover that such dovetailing worked better on paper than in practice, but at least we made a good beginning. All through the late winter and early spring, Kate's architect and interior decorator prowled through the President's House, making cost estimates of proposed changes; and their equivalents prowled through my new house for the same purpose.

For me, it was a strange period, emotionally. My thoughts and many of my activities were directed toward a future that was still many months distant, yet the present in which I was living seemed (in terms of both place and behavior) like the past. This sense of disorientation in time was not ameliorated by an article in the Chicago *Daily News* which praised George for his accomplishments at the University but read like an obituary because he as well as his administration were referred to in the past tense.

What *had* he done (and, to be exact, was still doing)?

In his gloomy periods, George would sometimes say, "About the only thing I've accomplished around here is to get some good lawns started. And that was mostly because nobody was really against grass and I'm so much for it. That's a hell of a note, isn't it? To be remembered as the President who was psychopathic about grass."

"Well, you had a baby named after you.* And by the time you quit you'll have raised a hundred and sixty million dollars. How about *that?*"

"I mean, something I accomplished by myself. Think of it: I couldn't even make a dent in the Biology Division. They're still fiddling around trying to get that building designed, and the course work isn't anywhere near as good as it could be."

"There's precedent. Bob Hutchins' great interest was in the humanities, and the University was strongest in the physical sciences during his regime. You're a scientist, and look at all the good things that are going on here in the humanities."

"Thanks to Edward."

George was right in saying that he would leave behind no specific program or institutional structure which would forever be linked with his name and personality. University presidents rarely do, these days. They often get public credit for the successful fund drives, the new buildings, or the curricular innovations that occur during their administrations, but these are never their personal achievements. The time when a William Rainey Harper or a Charles W. Eliot could literally force his wishes on an always-obstructionist faculty has long since passed. Any important measure now has to pass multiple checkpoints

* George Wells Suhm, born in 1967, when his father was a graduate student in the School of Business.

before it is accepted, which means that the autocrat of yesterday has become the diplomat of today.

But that is not to say that a university president cannot make a great impact on his institution. I could not appraise George's administrative skills, because I had never seen him in action in the office; but I could and did sense the behavioral climate that he had created. His regime was marked by an internal atmosphere of goodwill which had made possible many of the institutional achievements that were externally visible.

One of George's most conspicuous traits is honesty. In fact, he is a man of such probity that he almost radiates it. People find it exceptionally difficult to be deceitful in dealing with someone who treats them as if they are honorable, and even the students had responded to this quality. (They had not, in all the turmoil they had engendered, attacked George as an individual—only as a symbol of "the Administration.") He was a visible presence on the campus—one professor described him as "indefatigably mobile"—and he obviously cared about what was going on there. It is also very difficult for people to goof off on the job when the executive head of the organization is working so hard at *his* job.

As for the "Mr. Outside" aspect of his presidency, George had healed some Town vs. Gown wounds. People in the immediate community had found it a little more difficult to think of the University as completely cold-blooded and self-centered when its President did a stint on Fifty-third Street as a collector of litter, clearly enjoyed the company at the annual Kenwood Ball, and was on a first-name basis with the proprietor of the local hardware store.

Downtown, the captains of Chicago's commercial and industrial Establishment—many of whom distrust "intellectuals," especially the kind who believe that the First Amendment means what it says—had found George an agreeable companion. They knew he was a Nobel laureate and could see for themselves that he had a penetrating mind, but there was no arrogance in him;

and by extension the University came to seem less remote, more likable, and more worthy of respect.

There were times when it might have served the University well if his rhetoric, that of a cool and rational man, could have been more responsive to that of students and young faculty who had rejected reason. There were times when it might have been good for everybody if he could have unleashed his emotions in public. And there were times when the University could have used a President who naturally wore a cloak of majesty. But on balance, and in a period when many institutions of higher learning were held suspect by the public and were being torn apart by internal dissension, it had been no small contribution to the University of Chicago to have kept the peace, mended the fences, and grown some grass.

Thirty-five

In January of 1968, Harper Court got a new management, and things began to look up. The Board of Directors had reasoned that we needed a manager who was based close enough to the center to get there quickly when the ejector pump broke down . . . someone with no other job to distract attention from Harper Court . . . someone with unusual empathy for businessmen who didn't think of themselves as businessmen.

We considered management by a real estate firm located in Hyde Park but came in the end to accept Bruce Sagan's suggestion that in this case we avoid the professionals and seek a gifted amateur. "Find a Hyde Park housewife who knows how to keep books and has run some local project," he said. "She can learn on the job how ejector pumps work."

So we hired Jeanne Orlikoff and Nancy Shlaes, each on a half-time basis (to backstop each other, in case the children got sick). What they subsequently learned about ejector pumps was an infinitesimal part of their education; in fact, it was a good thing they were already seasoned Hyde Parkers, or they might have quit before they got started.

On their first day on the job, I forwarded a letter from a shop owner who was going into bankruptcy; our lawyer told them that a shopper had fallen down some stairs in the courtyard and was filing suit for damages; and a tenant in one of the lower-level stores called to complain because a sexual exhibitionist had unzipped in front of her show windows and was performing for her. (By the time our new managers and the police got there the man had vanished, but while the cops were writing up their report he most obligingly returned and repeated the show—so all they had to do was step outside and scoop him up.) This was not a typical day in our managers' experience only because they were never to experience a typical day.

Some of the shakiest enterprises folded up that spring. Some of the more successful merchants asked for additional space. We got a number of promising new tenants. Those of the older tenants who had the most business savvy began to make their influence felt. We noted with pleasure that owners of property in the immediate vicinity of Harper Court had begun a clean-up, paint-up campaign. Of course, the City Parking Lot wasn't finished yet, and the Small Business Administration still hadn't paid us the full amount of the mortgage—but by and large the project was beginning to shake down. Those of us who for five years now had been concerned in the affairs of Harper Court began to feel a bit less like nervous mother hens.

At the University, the administrators who dealt most directly with students didn't know whether to be nervous or not. There were no overt signs of another big convulsion in the making, and perhaps this spring the militant few wouldn't find an issue to inflame the moderate many. . . .

It was easy to be myopic about "the college student" during the 1960's. Those of us at institutions which had become embattled early in the decade tended to forget that many campuses *weren't* embattled, and so did the mass media, which by their fulsome reportage of campus disorders helped to create more.

That spring, for example, we attended a dinner party at which another guest was an administrator at a state college on the southwest side of Chicago. He said that the college had to hire Chicago's Civic Opera House for its graduation ceremonies

WHERE HAS ALL THE IVY GONE?

because such a high percentage of its graduates were the first in their families to receive a college diploma and huge assemblages of relatives had to be accommodated. All the grandparents, aunts, uncles, and cousins wanted to share the great moment when Tony or Stefan got his B.A. For young people of this sort, there was still something marvelous and mystical about "a college education," and they didn't want anything to interrupt their achievement of it.

Then, too, there were thousands of young people at sectarian colleges. These, by their very nature, attract students who do not challenge authority. I rode back to Chicago one day on a train from the suburb of Wheaton, site of such a college, and was fascinated by the conversation of two attractive youths sitting just ahead of me. They began by reviewing the interpretation that one of their professors had given some part of the Gospels, but spent most of the time describing the sense of spiritual uplift that each had experienced upon "fully and finally accepting Christ."

I don't know what percentage of all college students in the United States in 1968 were non-militant for the reasons just suggested, but I do know that the militants tended to cluster in the non-sectarian and elitist colleges and universities. Those are the ones that demand the high level of intellectual achievement which is commonly the product of being reared in a home where at least the parents (and often several generations) have been college-educated. One of the ironies of the period was that Michigan State had gone out and actively recruited Merit Scholars, in order to upgrade itself intellectually, and then found that its Merit Scholars were the ones who led most of the campus protest activity.

It was commonplace to hear outside observers of the campus scene say that "all this trouble" was being caused by "an irresponsible minority" but that the majority of the students were "good, decent kids." The implication of such remarks was that there was a sharp line of demarcation between the irresponsible minority and the good, decent kids—and there wasn't. The young people of the sixties, as a group, had a culture that differed from that of older people; and all the young shared it to greater or less degree. Even those Wheaton College students I listened to on the train had longish hair, and although I'm sure they didn't use drugs themselves I'll bet they knew people who did.

Chicago's student body was probably pretty typical of those then at the country's non-sectarian and elitist institutions. Here is how our Dean of Students, Charles O'Connell, described them (at a meeting of faculty wives) in the spring of that year:

> Despite the headlines, a substantial majority of our students are primarily interested in personal concerns. What shall my philosophy of life be? What style of life shall I follow? What should my vocation be? (They use "vocation" in the sense of "To what activity am I called?"—not in the sense of "What shall I do to make money?" And they want their vocation to be relevant to their philosophy of life.)
>
> They are more interested in social and political problems than immediately preceding generations of students, but this interest is still not central to the life of the majority of students here.
>
> They are still willing to use established channels and recognize established forms of social behavior, but they do so with a certain degree of unease. They have been much affected by the studies of men in gray flannel suits, by the Vance Packard exposés, by articles charging that the mass media propagandize and corrupt.
>
> They are very questioning, and are unwilling to wait for answers.
>
> It is an experimental generation. Its members are skeptical about the motives or actions of other people or institutions, but they have a naïve trust that their own experiments won't go wrong—whether it's LSD or university reform they're trying.
>
> "Relevance," "involvement," and "concern" are the im-

portant words. There is little regard for what one is involved in or concerned about. To *be* concerned is all-important, and will excuse excesses.

Both the hippies and the radical activists differ from the majority of students in that they carry to extremes certain of the traits common to the majority.

For hippies, sincerity is the cardinal virtue and hypocrisy is the cardinal vice. *Feeling* is what matters, and their problem is: How can you get at the truth without going through a lot of intellectual processes? They draw many of their ideas from primitive cultures, or from the mystic philosophies of the Orient.

The radical activists have transmuted their personal preoccupations into preoccupation with some social or political cause.

Despite their rhetoric, their ideas are not very closely linked with Marxist or Maoist ideology; rather, they draw upon the philosophy of anarchism and upon the tradition of native American localism and individualism. Among the works most frequently quoted by members of our campus SDS chapter are Thoreau's *Walden* and *On Civil Disobedience*.

They are missionaries. How can we determine what is the true philosophy of life, and adapt the world to it? How can we suppress bad vocations? ("Bad" usually means business or industry.) How can we, and everyone, be truly free? (To eliminate all social controls is the usual answer to this.)

Out of over eight thousand students on this campus, only thirty to fifty are consistently active in SDS. This group endlessly searches for issues that will appeal to less radical students, hoping that they can tap the wellsprings of concern and augment their numbers greatly in terms of pressure for change. When they think they have an issue, they send up a trial balloon. If a hundred or so come to the meeting, that's the issue they choose. If no one comes, they drop it and try for another issue.

It is sometimes difficult to deal with the SDS because its members do not always report accurately to the students as a whole what goes on at meetings with University administrators. One answer to the problem is to reply in writing to the questions they have raised and distribute both questions and replies to the entire campus.

And so far we have been able to convince the majority of students—although *not* the members of SDS—that we are not "entirely corrupt," and that we have more than a measure of good intentions, good faith, and even good sense.

As I look back now, I think the University of Chicago came closer than many other colleges or universities to preventing the kind of campus polarization that saw all administrators and faculty as bad guys and all students as good guys. But the cards were stacked against the country's institutions of higher learning. National events that spring and summer conspired to polarize the entire population of the United States, and it was inevitable that rising emotions everywhere would exacerbate the tensions on the campuses.

On April 4, Martin Luther King was killed. Militant young blacks had already deserted the ranks of his followers, but they still respected him for what he had meant to the civil rights movement. Older Negroes—those who had not yet lost their faith in the American Dream, those who still believed with King that there was a basic morality in the nation—saw his death as the dissolution of their hopes.

Or so I surmise. I know what *happened* after his assassination, but I am no longer confident of my ability to explain *why*. The events of that April taught me that no white person of my background can appreciate the black experience.

I had long thought, for example, that my Negro friends were as comfortable in mixed society as I was. We were of the same social and educational background, had the same cultural tastes, had many common interests, so surely such details as skin pigmentation or cast of features didn't matter? Ah, but they did! I had once heard Whitney Young say, "The psychological lynching of a man's soul can be more damaging than the physical lash of the bull whip"; and the death of Martin Luther King revealed psychological scars on the souls of people I had naïvely assumed bore none.

At a meeting, a gentle-mannered woman whom I thought I knew well suddenly flared into harsh condemnation of "you whites."

A community organizer, speaking of businesses based in the ghettoes, said, "We black cats are going to kick you white folks out. Maybe later you can come back. On *our* terms."

A group of social workers announced that they no longer felt any responsibility to their agencies but only to the people they served. "We're through talking to whites," their spokesman said. "There's nothing more to talk about. You know what we want. You just don't give a damn. Now we're going to take it."

This was big talk, harsh talk, unrealistic talk. The social workers knew perfectly well that they, like employees everywhere, would have to take orders from supervisors or governing boards, at least some of whose members were white; and the community organizer knew perfectly well that if white capital and business experience should be lost to the ghettoes there would be nothing to take their place. Yet, during that brief period of shock, educated and theoretically "assimilated" black Americans indulged in unrestrained talk of this nature, and nothing could have more sharply dramatized for me the depth of the psychic wounds which they must have at some time in their lives experienced.

The less educated and less controlled simply went berserk. The high school kids began it with public marches that soon disintegrated into riots and arson and death. Block after block on Chicago's West Side went up in flames. The firemen worked under a hail of rocks, and in fear of bullets from the guns of snipers on adjacent buildings. The National Guard was mobilized, and Mayor Daley issued his famous "shoot to kill" order. (This remark was made in the heat of passion, and reflected his agony at the wanton destruction of his beloved city—but once said, it could not be unsaid, and would haunt him forevermore.) In the course of that hellish three days, who could identify those who were "guilty" and those who were "innocent"? It was a time of madness.

Mrs. Carter had once lived on the West Side and still had friends there. She told me that one of them, a woman long active in an organization for community improvement, had telephoned her, weeping, and had said, "The best workers in my block group! They're out there too, smashin' windows and takin' things!"

What happened on the South Side was thoroughly bizarre.

The National Guard troops lined up along Sixty-third Street, in Woodlawn, in anticipation of violence there; and nothing happened. Meanwhile, twenty-some blocks farther south, hardly a store window along Eighty-seventh Street remained unbroken. What made the difference was the cooling action of the Blackstone Rangers and the East Side Disciples.

Some insiders corroborated the street gangs' assertion that they had preserved order for reasons of civic virtue. Others said that the gangs had used the occasion to extort protection money from Sixty-third Street businessmen (mostly white). But if the latter is true, at least they honored the commitment: the peace *was* kept.

That weekend even produced a truce between the gangs.

I was upstairs in my study on Sunday afternoon, and thus had a good view of the Midway as a long line of black youths came marching along from the southeast, chanting, "Two, four, six, eight, we're the Rangers and we're great!" At the same time, from the southwest, came another column of marchers; these were the East Side Disciples. There must have been several thousand of them, all told, and they filled a block-long stretch of the Midway just east of Woodlawn Avenue—one gang along the grassy banks at the northern side of the mall, the other gang on the southern side.

Curious onlookers and nervous police cars gathered 'round (but kept their distance) as the leaders of the two gangs carried kitchen chairs into the open space between their lined-up supporters. There they sat, in splendid isolation, and talked for ten minutes. There was something medieval about the confrontation. Where or when in modern times has anyone seen rival barons and all their vassals engaged in a peace parley?

The outcome of that meeting was a solemn pledge by both gangs to keep things cool from then on "in memory of Dr. Martin Luther King." The truce lasted, as I recall, about ten days. By the end of the month, Billings Hospital was again full of wounded warriors.

The separatist trend had already begun to destroy the alliance of young black and white militants that had been forged initially in the civil rights movement when it had been centered in the South. Separatism was greatly accelerated after the death of Martin Luther King; and from the spring of '68 onward, college and university administrators had to worry about attacks from two groups.

Black students began to demand that more blacks be admitted; that more black professors be hired; that "black studies" be added to the curricula; that dormitories or social facilities restricted to blacks be provided. White students concentrated on anti-war protests; on achieving more student participation in policy making; on "restructuring" universities to make them more "relevant." Thank goodness, Women's Lib was yet to be born.*

* Speaking both of Women's Lib and the rapidity of change in student attitudes that made the sixties so difficult a period for adults who had to deal with the young:

In 1966, the Women's Board of the University (a group of some three hundred Chicagoans who perform a variety of supportive services for the institution) had sponsored a series of afternoon teas for undergraduate girls. These were planned in co-operation with a student advisory group and featured panel discussions on post-college choices, all the speakers being young women no more than a few years out of college. They were chosen to exemplify the multitude of choices that are actually available to girls in their twenties, and to demonstrate that women do not have to choose between "getting a man" and "contributing something worthwhile to society" but can in fact have their cake and eat it too.

Only a handful of girls came. The student advisory group then did a

But even without the girls in a separate camp, there was a general heightening of tension between the races, between young and old, between the Establishment and the Rebels. And contact or confrontation, when they came, were marked by greater irrationality than before. For example:

In mid-April, a University of Chicago undergraduate was shot and killed while walking home from the campus through one of the "best" and "safest" sections of Hyde Park, and for no apparent reason except that he and the gunman happened to be in the same place at the same time. Shortly after his body was found, a girl student reported that she had been nearby soon after the murder, and had observed a man cleaning a gun.

But she flatly refused to look at photographs in Police Department files to see if she could identify him. Her reason. The police had handled the riots after Martin Luther King's death "in an unfeeling way and with unnecessary force," and therefore she wouldn't co-operate with them.

---

little retrospective polling and reported to the Women's Board that University of Chicago coeds refused to admit publicly (as they would have, by appearing at the teas and participating in discussion) that the accident of their sex posed special problems for them. They were determined to think of themselves as "people," not as "women."

But only three years later, college girls were among the most active members of the new feminist movements that are today lumped together as "Women's Lib." Their common assumption is that people do have different problems because of their sex.

Thirty-six

One of the ironies of the anti-militarism movement of the 1960's was that students picked both the Reserve Officers Training Corps and the Institute for Defense Analyses as targets. The ROTC feeds men with a civilian outlook into the armed forces, and thus helps prevent the growth in this country of a military establishment which is so inbred that it develops a junta mentality. IDA, a non-governmental agency whose job is to analyze and evaluate research supported largely by the Department of Defense, provides a civilian check on the research and development activities of the military—unless one happens to believe, as many student activists did, that IDA's board members had "sold out" to the military and that the universities with which they were affiliated were, through them, helping the United States engage in "imperialist aggression" in Vietnam.

IDA had been organized in 1956 by a group of American universities, each of which sent a representative to its board of directors. As members of that board, however, the university representatives functioned as individuals, if only because much of IDA's research was "classified" and board members couldn't share it with people at their home institutions. At least, that was the case at Chicago. For years, we had had a representative to IDA, but it was essentially a meaningless relationship because he didn't report to anybody on campus about the agency's activities.

As the anti-war war on the campuses heated up, members of SDS at Chicago had been unable to make the ROTC a target, because Chicago had no ROTC unit. But they *could* aim at IDA, and in the fall of 1967 they had begun a campaign against the University's affiliation with it. George had therefore appointed a faculty committee to review the relationship; in February of 1968, the committee had recommended that the association with IDA be terminated; and in March, the faculty Council had voted to do so.

The study committee had said that it considered IDA's military stance—"be it that of dove, hawk, or dodo"—irrelevant, and based its recommendation for withdrawal on the fact that there was no real interaction between IDA and the University. However active a role the sponsoring universities might have played in IDA in its beginnings, by 1968 they were doing no more than providing the organization with board members who might as well be serving on their own time. So why not drop the corporate affiliation and let IDA recruit its own board members?

The students who had protested our institutional association with IDA would have been much more pleased by the University's withdrawal if the faculty committee had sat in moral judgment on IDA, so they didn't savor their victory. Some SDS members were even disappointed by the University's action, because it robbed them of a good issue for rallying the troops. In May of that same year, a professor heard one of our militants say to another, "Damn the Administration! I wish we had IDA back!"

As with the University of Chicago's decision in the 1930's to stop playing big-time football (which didn't sit well with some of the Big Ten universities), this decision was not hailed with joy by all of the eleven other universities which sponsored IDA. Perhaps they derived benefits from it that the University of Chicago didn't. Perhaps they made more institutional use of their representative on IDA's board than Chicago did. For whatever reason, some did not like the idea of a Chicago pull-out;

and George consequently spent hours on the phone conferring with the presidents of other member institutions—trying to work out procedures and a timetable of withdrawal that (in accordance with our faculty committee's directive to him) "would take full account of the University of Chicago's current responsibility to IDA as well as to the other member universities."

One of these universities was Columbia, and Columbia was not anxious to sever its corporate ties with IDA; or at least not soon. Its militant students, encouraged by Chicago's action, correctly recognized this reluctance as immediately exploitable. And Columbia, unfortunately, was extremely vulnerable to attack. It had no body like our faculty Council which could express itself on policy matters affecting the whole university; in fact, it had been years since Columbia's entire faculty had met in a joint session. Its administrators temporized when (hindsight showed) they probably should have taken repressive action. When they did take repressive action, it radicalized the uncommitted moderates. In short, the student assault on Columbia was a repeat of Berkeley's experience four years earlier, except that it was more violent and destructive and the wounds to the institution went correspondingly deeper.

Our most militant students were envious. They looked at the famous photograph of a Columbia student sitting at the president's desk and reading his private papers while smoking one of his cigars, and realized that their own aspirations had not been high enough.

IDA had been denied to Chicago's SDS chapter but had served well at Columbia. Would Columbia's other "issue" serve Chicago equally well? That issue was racial. Columbia was building a gym which was intended to serve the adjacent Harlem community (because it used two acres of a city park) as well as the university's students. The gym had two entrances—one on Morningside Heights, for the students, and one at the park level down below, for community residents. A majority of community groups in Harlem had approved the erection of the gym, and understood that the two entrances were not dictated by a policy of racial discrimination but by topography. Nevertheless, Columbia's militant students had managed to tar the university with a charge of "Gym Crow"; and people who had been apathetic about the university's relationship to IDA had gotten excited about this alleged proof of Columbia's alleged "institutional racism." What equivalent situation, Chicago students asked themselves, do *we* have?

It was an easy question to answer, because just south of the Midway, a University expansion program was in progress, paired with some urban renewal in Woodlawn.

Now I have to digress for a bit of Woodlawn history.

That community, comparable in size to Hyde Park and Kenwood, had a split personality. On its west side, it was not too blighted physically and its inhabitants were hard-working, respectable, middle- and lower-middle-class families. Its east side was a different story: there, its taverns, its prostitutes, its drifters and drunks and unemployables were clustered. The crime rate was high; and anyone who thinks that black people are less fearful than white people about crime in the neighborhood is greatly mistaken. Black people also dislike overflowing garbage cans and rat-infested alleys as much as white people do. Unfortunately, most cities—and Chicago is no exception—have a double standard of municipal services. Black neighborhoods frequently need more service because their people are jammed so tightly together, live under greater stress, and can't get away from it; but they usually get less service than the city's white neighborhoods.

Woodlawn's more solid citizens had therefore decided, in 1960, to "organize" the community. Perhaps, united under one banner, they could exert some pressure on the city authorities. They had hired Saul Alinsky to help them organize, and that tough-minded gentleman had guided them during their first few years. Saul Alinsky is a highly controversial figure, but I think the main reason is that people who dislike his techniques misunderstand his purposes. He is not interested in what comes *after* a community organization is built—in other words, in the objectives of the organization; he is interested only in building the organization.

The history of The Woodlawn Organization (TWO) is a case in point. It is easier to get people to co-operate in some common cause if they have a visible enemy to fight, so Alinsky picked the University of Chicago as that enemy. Inasmuch as he is a very intelligent man, he must have been well aware that this ploy would delay the solution of many problems that TWO sought to solve.

It was as important to the University as to Woodlawn to reduce the crime rate there, to rehabilitate blighted buildings, upgrade community health, and so on. Woodlawn would be the site of University expansion, groups of students were already living there, and the community might in time provide housing for the University's faculty (as it once had). So it was ridiculous to say that the University was Woodlawn's "enemy."

From the time he took office, George had waved the olive branch at TWO; and University people were active in individual Woodlawn organizations all through the period when the University was being used as a symbol of oppression—but none of these efforts had wrought much significant change. That had to wait until TWO had become a strong community organization. By 1964, it had; and Saul Alinksy went on to another job. It was then possible to get down to the ways and means of solving Woodlawn's problems.

The leaders of TWO realized as well as anybody that the only way to get rid of slum buildings is to tear them down; that the only way to reduce the excessive population density which creates slums is to displace people; and that the kind of people who must be displaced are the transients, the dope pushers, the prostitutes—all the people whose presence in a community encourages crime and civil disorder. In other words, TWO's goal in the urban renewal of Woodlawn was just about what Hyde Park-Kenwood's had been. An essential difference, however, was that Woodlawn had a great middle group of "shiftless poor" who weren't really vicious but simply couldn't cope with urban life and inadvertently made all kinds of trouble for themselves and their neighbors. Some of these people, unfortunately, would have to go, too.

And how did the University of Chicago fit into this enterprise? As an institution, it had influence and expertise, and these were both offered and accepted. In some cases, the University's help was channeled through the South East Chicago Commission, in other cases through the academic divisions.

Money expended on urban renewal by universities and similar institutions can generate federal "credits" (that is, tax dollars to be spent on urban renewal elsewhere in a city), and the University of Chicago's "credits" had been earmarked for Woodlawn. This money, plus foundation grants, had by 1967 made possible a highly innovative scheme: the start of a housing development for middle- and low-income families and a shopping center, both of which would be operated by TWO. A complete urban renewal plan had also been approved; spot clearance was proceeding; and some rebuilding had occurred.

Legal research by the University plus TWO's skill in rounding up voters had made possible a ban on the sale of alcoholic beverages in one precinct of Woodlawn. This largely unpublicized and truly remarkable action by the citizens of that community had closed down the tavern row on Sixty-third Street where so much crime had originated.

The University had opened a children's health clinic, staffed by medical personnel from our hospitals but governed by a community board chosen by TWO. A similarly organized mental health clinic had also been established, and the University was in process of acquiring funds for the operation of a social services center. It would gather into one spot the offices of many agencies that serve the city's poor, and would be allied with our School of Social Service Administration.

The University was also working with TWO and the Chicago Board of Education to set up a community school board that would give the citizens of Woodlawn closer contact with and more control over their public schools.

These were all formal alliances. As before, individual members of the faculty, faculty wives, and students continued to work as volunteers in programs whose goal was to improve the quality of life in Woodlawn. University of Chicago faculty wives, for one example, played a significant part in raising funds for a new YWCA building.

Some University administrators and faculty took a dim view of these co-operative programs, not because they had anything against helping Woodlawn get on its feet but because they believed that the University should be spending its energies and its money on teaching and research. In view of the institution's primary mission, they considered its social welfare activities in Woodlawn to be excessive—and nobody could have been more taken aback than they were when our militant students in May of 1968 launched an attack on the University because it wasn't doing *enough* for Woodlawn, for the poor in general, for black people in general, and for poor blacks in particular.

The attack came in two waves.

Two groups of black students demanded an 11 per cent quota of black undergraduates; special programs of compensatory education for those who weren't qualified to do the academic work required by University of Chicago standards; an all-black dormitory; and more "black studies" in the curriculum. They engaged in a brief sit-in at the Administration Building, but left after only four hours because of the threat of disciplinary action by the authorities.

Their demands were then incorporated into the manifesto of a white students' group. Its backbone was, as usual, formed of SDS members, but this time they called themselves the Committee for a Responsible University. They upped the demanded quota of black students to 20 per cent, wallowed in penitence for their own racist sins, and pointed accusatory fingers at everyone else. They ignored the existence at the University of a compensatory program for black high school students, a tutoring program for black undergraduates who were in academic trouble, a special program to recruit more black students, the availability of adequate scholarship funds for them, a special program in the School of Business to prepare more blacks for executive jobs in industry, more courses in African and Afro-American studies than the students were registering for, and an adult education program among the employees which was intended to qualify poorly educated blacks (and whites, for that matter) for better jobs within the University.

The CRU also demanded that the University "cease all destruction of housing in Hyde Park and Woodlawn until it has provided adequate substitute housing in the immediate vicinity at the same or *lower* prices." (My italics. The students' reasoning was that the University had a lot of money, so why not subsidize housing for people who couldn't pay the going rates set by the market? The economists in the Business School had a fit.)

Further, the University "should abandon all secrecy in its arrangement of redevelopment plans for Woodlawn. All future plans must be made in co-operation with and ultimately under the control of the people of Woodlawn. This means abandoning the pretense that deals with TWO represent real community participation." This section of the manifesto really sizzled TWO. If it didn't represent "the people" of Woodlawn, who did? At a public meeting on the University's campus, the president of TWO told the white students that Woodlawn could get along very nicely without their help, thank you, and in fact, STAY OUT UNTIL WE ASK YOU IN.

The part of the manifesto that made Goerge so angry I thought he might have a stroke was the militants' proposed alteration in plans for "the student village," an especially cherished project of his. Responding to demands for more student participation in policy making and student complaints about housing, he had two years previously appointed a committee to draw up a set of specifications for a residential community within the borders of the campus. Over three hundred students had expressed their ideas; the architect had spent months on it; and the final plan was a beauty.

It was a complex of apartments and town houses that would have accommodated nine hundred students and some faculty members, and also had such amenities as restaurants and an auditorium. The students now viewed the complex as a "dormitoried fortress," and demanded that it be redesigned as an extremely low-cost housing development which would be open to the public, especially "victims of urban renewal." The student village as planned would have cost $25,000,000; and I am using the past conditional tense because the militant students of 1968 lost George the one donor who had shown interest in it. It still remains unbuilt.

No sit-in was planned by the Committee for a Responsible University; this time, it was to be a strike. Its organizers made a fundamental mistake, however: they called an open-air meeting, which attracted a lot of students who were curious rather than committed, and when the strike vote was called the group voted it down 150 to 110. One of the committed, in accepting temporary defeat, promised that in time the New Left would "get this campus out of its mood of sick acquiescence."

Actually, what had happened was that the issues were phony, or fabricated, and the administration had managed to disseminate the facts widely enough so that even the student newspaper had editorialized against the strike. But the cost had again been great. Hours and hours had again been spent on meetings, reports, attacks, rebuttals.

When a group of moderates had brought a petition to the Dean of Students deploring "the irresponsibility of a few of our fellow students" and requesting the University "to continue to keep in mind the interests of the serious student," they had complained because the SDS seemed to take up so much of the administrators' time. The Dean couldn't say so, but the reason was that the administrators never knew—given the volatile atmosphere on campus—whether a given probe by the SDS (and there were so many!) was going to be successful. It was like sitting on top of a volcano that might or might not erupt, and being unable to predict where the first fissure would open in case one did.

As is obvious, I had complete contempt for the SDS. They were liars and cheats; and means *are* as important as ends. In addition, and on the personal level, I seemed powerless to control sour attitudes toward other students, attitudes arising from reaction to the behavior of student radicals. It made me feel ashamed of myself as well as angry at them because I had become so untrusting of the young. I knew how many blows to the spirit young people had taken that year. The death of Martin Luther King. The riots afterward. The shock of seeing Chicago's April 27 Peace Parade turned into a bloodbath by the calculated repressiveness and harshly punitive actions of the city authorities. The death of Robert Kennedy, the only major political figure left on the national scene in whom young people put any trust. Why would any sensitive and intelligent kid want to be a part of a society that so violated its own basic principles? It was a miracle that so many of the young had hung on, *wanting* to believe, and had kept the faith. I told myself this over and over, but nevertheless found myself wary and suspicious in my dealings with students. Always in the back of my mind was an expectation of a double cross, a fear that the volcano might blow while I was with them.

One day a student twice stopped by the house in an effort to see me, and Mrs. Galloway refused to let him in.

"He's one of those dirty ones," she said.

Then he telephoned. He wanted my help in getting an appointment to see George, and was turning to me because he hadn't been able even to get past the receptionist in the office at the Administration Building.

"What do you want to talk to Mr. Beadle about?" I asked.

"It's a private matter," he replied. "Honestly. Not University business. *Please*. It'll only take five minutes."

He sounded like a nice boy.

But one never knew, these days.

Should I, or shouldn't I?

Finally, I told him that if he could get up early enough to catch George in the garden the following morning, there would be an opportunity for a private chat. Then I spent the rest of the evening fretting about my decision. What if this were to be another of those painful confrontations that made George so sick at heart that it poisoned the whole day?

The next morning, the student came. He *was* one of the dirty ones. He was also a nice boy. He was about to be initiated into a campus club, and had been set the task of "doing a favor for the President, and getting a signature to prove it."

George had him pull two weeds; signed the document; and they parted cheerily.

I went upstairs and had a good cry because I had become a person who was afraid to admit a boy who had only wanted to do a favor for the President.

Thirty-seven

It was a schizophrenic spring because, in the midst of all the New Left protests, certain innocent pleasures from the era of Joe College experienced a revival. Some students celebrated May Day by dancing 'round a maypole that they had set up in the main Quadrangle; another lot repaired a disused telescope on the roof of Ryerson Hall, invited us to have a look at Mars, and served champagne in Dixie cups; and a third group let themselves be talked into participating on the TV program "College Bowl."

This latter was not at all a University of Chicago kind of thing, and the student body felt most ambivalent about it. Naturally, our team would win, and perhaps it was good to demonstrate to the whole country how brainy we were. But at what a cost! The master of ceremonies insisted on identifying our contestants as "juniors" or "seniors" (when they were, of course, "third year" or "fourth year" students); and they had to sit there with straight faces when he introduced them as "the Varsity Scholars from the University of Chicago." That, in fact, became one of the campus' favorite derisive terms that spring: anyone beating the books in the library in preparation for finals became known as a "varsity scholar."

But perhaps nothing was so astounding to the administrators as the Student Government's action in approving the official return of intercollegiate football to the campus. Here is the editorial that appeared in the student newspaper:

> We had to do some pretty careful listening after the SG meeting Wednesday night to hear any cries of righteous indignation at that august body's proposal to reinstate varsity football at Chicago next fall. So far as we could tell, there were no placards in sight. No one threatened a sit-in, there was no fiery rhetoric about the decline of the Aristotelian ethos, and hardly a soul exhumed the spirit of our beloved leader, Robert M. Hutchins.
>
> When the University announced its decision to abolish football in 1939, it took courageous action to halt an insidious trend away from academic concerns in American universities. But that was over a quarter century ago, and now that the point has been emphatically and successfully made, there is no longer a valid reason for sacrificing football to Chicago's unique form of ancestor worship.
>
> As a number of others schools have demonstrated, varsity football when kept in proper perspective need not be incompatible with the academy. So long as it is not allowed to infringe on more important matters, it remains nothing more than an outlet for people to do their thing. . . .*

Our thing was fundamentally unchanged, although I was entertaining guests much less frequently, now that I was coming into the home stretch. We had the Phi Beta Kappa tea as usual, as well as the annual dinner for the Aides, the reception for high school seniors who would be coming to the College in the fall, and the party for members of the executive committee of the faculty Council. There was the usual seasonal upsurge of concerts and dinner dances sponsored by various women's groups as benefits for worthy causes; the testimonial dinners for civic

---

* And when intercollegiate football *did* return, in the shape of games with small liberal arts colleges, Chicago students regarded attendance as a sort of "high camp" activity. It was an early example of the nostalgia that would become a nationwide phenomenon in the 1970's. Large crowds attended the games. There were cheerleaders and a marching band—whose members played only kazoos—and everybody had fun.

leaders or faculty members on the brink of retirement; the conferences and congresses whose delegates had to be welcomed to the University of Chicago. I was going to miss these: they had so often opened windows for me into unknown areas of scholarship.

King Olav V of Norway paid a visit to the city in May. He looked tired; visiting royalty *always* looks tired. That day, the King had ridden in a parade on State Street, then had gone to a civic luncheon, next to a reception before the evening banquet which we attended, and would end his day with an after-dinner reception. What kept him going (and other traveling Heads of State) was self-discipline, devotion to the national interest, and the outpoured love of expatriate countrymen. All through the evening banquet in King Olav's honor, little old ladies in homemade dresses and freshly set hair kept coming to the head table in order to shake his hand, their faces alight with pleasure to be briefly linked with the home country.

In June, the Shah of Iran was our guest. (He looked tired, too.) Security was so tight that all those invited to the dinner in his honor were sworn to secrecy ahead of time, and a four-block-square area around the Oriental Institute was cordoned off. It was a fine party, the ladies in their best ball gowns and jewels, the gentlemen in ruffled Edwardian shirts and brocade cummerbunds—except for one aggressive nonconformist in a tweed jacket and canvas sneakers, and the wife of the President of the University of Chicago, who kept her feet well tucked under her chiffon evening dress because she had a sprained ankle and was wearing bedroom slippers.

My conversation with His Imperial Majesty was "social." He had just been in St. Louis buying airplanes. He would go on to New York to see his favorite dentist. He would refuse painkillers; to do so was, with him, a matter of principle. His children would be educated in their own country. He felt it had been a mistake for himself to have been sent away from home to a boarding school when he was very young.

The only time the table talk got really animated was when

the conversation turned to horticulture and then to seedless watermelons (which George was currently trying to raise). The Shah was fascinated by diploids and triploids, and took notes. I think he even forgave George for almost forgetting to ask him to make some after-dinner remarks. This is something that one just doesn't *do*—either to a Shahinshah or to someone who has come to your institution for the express purpose of giving you three million dollars.

The next day the site of the Pahlavi Building was dedicated. Two of the three million dollars were earmarked for its construction,* and the other million was to support a program of Middle Eastern studies. The crowd in attendance at the dedication consisted largely of security people, the press, and picketing students who carried placards alleging that the Shah was a CIA agent and urging him to STOP KILLING IRANIAN STUDENTS. His Imperial Majesty was not amused.

Throughout the brief ceremony of dedication, a young Iranian woman stood at the barricades and wailed. An aide told me that she was praying to Allah in hope that the Shah would take notice of her, and just before he left the site he went over to her. With tears streaming down her face, she held out her baby for him to—well, *bless*. If ropes and policemen hadn't impeded her, she would have prostrated herself at his royal feet. This abject adoration made a strange and moving contrast to the line of picketing students just behind her.

A few weeks later, I participated in another kind of dedication.

On the morning of the ceremony, I said to George, "Honest to goodness, I feel as if I've been in this thing from the beginning of time."

And no wonder: it had been four years since Miriam Elson and I, at some point of low resistance, had agreed to raise funds for the acquisition of sculpture for the community's new neighborhood parks—and we were only at the midpoint of the effort.

* Construction costs were subsequently to skyrocket to such an extent that the building couldn't be built for two million dollars, and the University would return to the Shah the money he had paid.

It was an interesting problem, given the astronomical cost of sculpture when purchased from recognized artists and, at the same time, the high incidence of urban vandalism. The solution that our committee had hit on was to sponsor a contest for students of sculpture at the Art Institute of Chicago, and then to commission three of the prize works. (The money had come partly from residents of Hyde Park-Kenwood and partly from a foundation.) The students' creations were as handsome as many a professional's. They pleased the educated eye, yet at the same time used forms and materials which children could touch, climb on, or tug at without damaging either themselves or the sculptures—or at least not much.

The first piece, a white organic shape of fiberglas, had been installed in 1967. (Letting the sculptor, Jerome Skuba, do it in *white* had been a mistake.) The piece we were now dedicating was a fountain by Gary Wojcik, a dynamic swirl of bronze pipes whose jets shot a pinwheel of droplets into a shallow pool. The third piece would be installed the following year (or so we then thought). We had also experienced somewhat fewer difficulties than usual in dealing with the Chicago Park District during 1968, and were feeling optimistic about the future of the project. Therefore we gave the fountain a good send-off.

The loyal supporters of worthy causes who always come to this sort of thing were there, and the alderman, and the superintendent of the local public school district, and some beaded and bearded hippies in Nehru jackets, and a delegation of religious from St. Thomas's school across the street. Their pupils had raised almost two hundred dollars for the sculpture by selling cupcakes and popsicles. A squad of Little Leaguers was on hand to backstop the one of their number who had been chosen to turn on the fountain's jets, and the Unitarian Church's Children's Choir turned out in force to sing some English *Glees* (in Italian). A loose child entertained herself during the ceremonies by stalking around and around the pool on stilts, a stray dog took a splash bath in it, and assorted toddlers had to be restrained from following suit. Throughout, reporters from the city dailies—none of whom, as usual, had been given (or had read) our news release explaining the project—kept tapping people on the shoulder to ask, what's this all about? It was a typical Hyde Park civic event, and I treasure the recollection.

Similarly, a civic banquet which we attended on July 9 lives in memory as one of the good ones. It should: the Citizens Board and the Women's Board of the University hosted it, and George and I were the guests of honor. I don't know how many hundreds of people attended, but none of them came because they had to, and it was a grand and touching occasion. The speeches were short, and the speakers avoided either a tone of sticky sweetness or that eulogy-at-the-casket manner that so often characterizes these occasions. We were grateful.

The July date, early for someone who was retiring in November, was set at my insistence. The point of it was to clear the decks for the Levis. I thought that the academic year of '68–'69 should be wholly *their* year, and I wanted us to be as inconspicuous as two grains of sand on the beach by the time September came around. This was a foolish dream. After all the years of experience I had had with university people, I should have known how unwise it is to set one's heart on any given outcome when Ruling Bodies are involved. All through the coming fall, therefore, the Levis and the Beadles were to be bracketed at welcome-and-farewell events.

Nor were the Beadles as helpful to the Levis in regard to giving possession of their future domicile as I had hoped to be. We were still living in the President's House in July . . . and in August . . . and for most of September. George was determined not to go out of office until the $160,000,000 was in hand. (Thank goodness, he got it by November 1, or Edward might still be waiting to be inaugurated.) Consequently, he was at home hardly at all that summer, and I closed up the house myself.

With hugs and tears, Mrs. Galloway and I parted company. She went to a job which would not require her to feed fifteen thousand guests over a seven-year span—but, on the other hand, a job that wouldn't provide her with occasional princes and millionaires to cook for. Mrs. Carter and Mr. Coleman stayed on for a while to help with the clean-up, and Red came home to dispose of his own things and to pack up all the books.

I was so pushed and pressed that I forgot he was my son, not a hired workman, and I never got around to asking him if he had found a nice girl yet. If I had, I might have found out months earlier than I actually did about the existence of my daughter-in-law-elect: dear Suzie. Red had met her at Harvard but was courting her by mail, her specialty being East Asian studies and her address at that moment being somewhere in Taiwan. He still wasn't sure of her, however; so he probably wouldn't have bared his heart to Mom that August even if Mom had been other than a boss foreman.

There were still two months of University activity to get through, for George would be President until the day that Edward was inaugurated (November 14). But I had always equated my job with the President's House and not with the President's Office, so I date *my* retirement from the September day when we moved to our own house.

I was glad to get out of the Manse, but at the same time I was aware that our departure marked a milestone in my life. The years in that house had been exciting ones, personally more broadening than anything I could have anticipated when we moved in, productive of friendships that I would continue to cherish, useful to the University and to the community. On balance, they'd not been bad years, not bad at all. It was like childbirth; already the memory of pain was dimming.

We made the move on a day when the rains were so torrential that the movers couldn't fully unpack the van when they got it over to our own house.

The place was bare and cold and smelled funny.

The cats slunk around the edges of rooms, bellies down and ears back, as if they expected some huge bird of prey to swoop down on them.

There were TV dinners in the oven; the first in seven years.

George lit a tiny fire—just for cheer—and clouds of smoke immediately billowed into the room.

I was sitting on the floor, where the sofa would have been if the sofa hadn't been spending the night in the moving van, and George caught me wiping my eyes.

"It's just the smoke," I said. "Irritating."

"Yes," he said. "Mine smart, too."

EPILOGUE

The fireplace draws well, now. It was just a small matter of adding a twelve-foot extension to the chimney, reaming out the rubble inside the flue, doing some tuck-pointing and flashing, and recementing the firepit. This cost us less than a thousand dollars, and I wish I could say the same of other small matters that have required attention during the three years we have lived in this house.

But we still like it. In a place of this vintage, you don't have to spread the floor wax: you just dump some on the northwest side of the kitchen floor and it rolls south by southeast all by itself. In a neighborhood like ours, you don't have to turn on the FM station: when you want grand opera, you just listen to the voice teacher across the street. (In fact, you listen even when you don't want grand opera.) In a retirement like ours, you don't have to take up needlepoint or stamp collecting: you just go back to doing the kind of things you did before a university presidency intervened. George is again involved in genetic research, and I mix housewifery with writing and civic dogoodery.

Harper Court is still managed by one of the women we hired in 1968. Jeanne Orlikoff has guided the center through two good years; the shops are all rented; and we have a waiting list. We're hurting a bit again because insurance rates, taxes, and costs of maintenance have risen sharply and we can't raise the rents as much as we ought to, because half the tenants have twenty-five-year leases. Yet that in itself is a measure of the success of the project: the twenty-five-year leases were required by the Small Business Administration for our original tenants, and for half of them to have survived this long beats the average for small business men of their type by an imperial mile.

Mrs. Galloway, Mrs. Carter, and I keep in touch, and a couple of the graduate students who used to work for us send Christmas snapshots of their wives and children. Mr. Coleman's back gave out on him a year ago, but he now runs a newsstand just a block from our house and we see him regularly. We don't see the caterer or our favorite waitresses any more; in fact, we haven't entertained more than four guests at any one time since we moved in here, and the three-year total is well under fifty. We still attend University events, but we go rarely enough so that these occasions are always a pleasure and never a duty.

Red and Suzie have been married for over two years, so *that's* off my mind.

In short, it's a nice life we're leading. I'm no longer such a slave to the calendar and the clock. And I've had time to reflect.

People around here still say to George, "You got out at just the right time, didn't you?"

Some of them are referring specifically to the events of 1969, when the University experienced its worst sit-in. It was sixteen days in length, terrifically costly in terms of damaged property and hours lost from productive work, more bitter than any of the others in terms of rhetoric, more polarizing in its effect upon the University community, harsher in the punishments meted out to the militant students. The officers of the University once again dealt with the disruption by using what had become known as "the Chicago style" (abandoning the Administration Building, refusing to negotiate with the militants, refusing to call the police)—but the psychic cost was heavy.

Or perhaps those who congratulate George on the timing of his retirement are referring more generally to the extremely violent phase of student militancy that characterized the whole nation during 1969 and 1970 and that escalated through massive

destruction of buildings by fire and bombings to loss of lives by
gunfire.

I agree that George was lucky to "get out," but not just for
those reasons. To be a university president is an impossible job
these days, even when the campus is outwardly at peace.

Edward Everett, who was the president of Harvard between
1846 and 1849, once wrote to his friend Daniel Webster:

> Owing to the complicated machinery of the College gov-
> ernment & the habit formed by my predecessor . . . of
> leaving every thing to the Faculty on the one hand & the
> Corporation on the other, I found there was nothing left
> me but to act as a kind of clerk to the two bodies without
> power of discretion to do any thing of importance myself.
> The first official duty I was called to perform as head of
> the University which considers itself first among American
> Seminaries, was to administer a private admonition to a
> Sophomore for pinning the coat-tail of the boy who sat
> before him to the settee. I saw in that one instance that I
> had made a woful mistake; but I determined to give the
> office a fair and manful trial . . .
> I found that I was living at the rate of five years in one;
> and felt that I had a right to resign.*

University presidents still live at the rate of five years in one,
still act as "a kind of clerk" to the faculty on the one hand and
the trustees on the other, and no longer have the authority to
administer private admonitions to anyone. But at the same time,
they are held as responsible for what happens on campus as if
they *did* have the power to govern it.

In terms of service, Notre Dame's Father Theodore Hesburgh
is one of the most senior of American university presidents. He's
been on the job for almost twenty years, and says that he now
has only one tenth as much control over university affairs as he

* This excerpt from Everett's unpublished papers is included here with
thanks to Redmond, who found it while working on a research project
of his own; and through the courtesy of the Massachusetts Historical
Society, which has kindly granted me permission to quote it.

had when he was appointed in 1952. He, and all other university presidents today, spend their time trying to reconcile the often opposing interests of trustees, faculty, students, alumni, and public groups of varying opinions—all of whom love to veto proposals made by the others and so hate to yield an inch that it can take months of talk to resolve even the simplest of issues. Father Ted believes that this "balancing act" is what drives presidents out of office.

Between 1967 and 1970, thirty of the country's most prestigious institutions lost (before normal retirement age) presidents who were capable, seasoned men. In 1970, something like three hundred colleges and universities were looking for presidents. On the average, the ones who are inaugurated this year will be finished within six years—fired, tired out, or dead.

Possible solutions are obvious. Give the presidents more authority or less responsibility. Create a campus policy-making group within which all holders of veto power must reconcile their differing opinions before the president is asked to take any action. The difficulty is that those proposals, which sound lovely on paper, would require such a massive shake-up in the structure of the colleges and universities that they wouldn't be good for much of anything for a long time, and they might well emerge from the experience unable to function as well as they do now.

My own proposal is more modest. It asks only that everyone concerned with the country's colleges and universities—a group that includes the general public—should begin now to find answers to two questions:

1) How can the faculties do a better job of governing the internal affairs of the colleges and universities?

2) What is the purpose of these institutions of higher learning?

It is a truism among administrators that "when things are going well, the faculty runs the university but when there's trouble it's up to the administration to solve it." Chicago has been lucky; overall, its faculty *does* guide and support its administrators. But many college and university faculties put self-interest or self-indulgence above the welfare of the institution whose internal affairs they are so insistent upon "governing."

The self-interested ones won't serve on university committees or inform themselves sufficiently about the institution's problems to be of use in solving them. They won't yield a fraction of their control over curriculum and staff, despite widespread—and legitimate—student dissatisfaction with courses of study and quality of teaching. This dissatisfaction was one of the root causes of the campus disturbances of the 1960's.

The other major cause of the turmoil was dissatisfaction with national policy, notably the Vietnam war, and here it was the self-indulgent faculty members who performed a notable disservice to their institutions. I can understand why many faculty members shared the students' concern over national policy. In fact, the majority of people, young or old, on university campuses were anti-war. But I can't understand why faculty members actively supported students' attempts to use the universities as tools to change national policy. Realistic adults should have known that the fire-bombing of an ROTC armory on a college campus was not going to change the course of the Vietnam war.

It has been suggested by some psychologists that faculty members who "overidentify" with students do so because they have been denied, or haven't earned, the admiration or respect of their older colleagues. They turn therefore to the young and immature, who are less critical and easier to manipulate.

But this also is essentially a faculty problem. Many of the older men are "too busy" to teach, leaving the younger ones with instructional loads so large they don't have time for research; or attend few departmental meetings because they are so often in Washington and elsewhere, serving as consultants to some agency or industry; or so resent the challenge to their own scholarly opinions of the young fellows' new ideas that they close their hearts as well as their minds to the oncoming generation.

Much of this non-constructive activity derives from the

faculties' uncertainty as to the purpose of colleges and universities in general, and of their own institution in particular.

Should it pass on "the high culture" of society, or train professionals, or be responsible for the moral improvement of citizens?

Should it isolate itself from mundane affairs, criticizing and analyzing instead of participating? Or should it be a staging ground for social and political action?

Should it be a service station for the public: testing products; giving advice to farmers, businessmen, and housewives; providing managers and consultants for enterprises not related to its educational mission?

Is it up to the colleges and universities to equalize educational opportunities for discriminated-against minorities? To finance community rehabilitation? To become patrons of the arts by supporting repertory theaters and maintaining artists-in-residence?

I don't believe that it is the faculties' job to answer these questions. It is the trustees' responsibility to make policy; and the only way any governing board can decide which of a multitude of demands to accept is to know what its objectives are. No university can do *all* the things that are implicit or explicit in the list above, yet all are currently under pressure to do most of them. It's high time for trustees to make some choices. Out of such choices would come a whole range of basically single-function institutions that could do well whatever they have chosen to do.

If I were a university trustee, I would judge every proposal by the degree to which it would enhance or diminish my institution as an independent, critical body. I would fend off the people who want it to provide social services or manage projects, insisting that my university discusses and analyzes the problems of society but does not try to solve them.

The main reason I would make that choice is that this is what colleges and universities are already geared to do. Society needs "neutral" places where all ideas can be aired and evaluated, and if our academic institutions were to cease performing this function, someone would have to re-invent them. To search for truth, wherever it may lead: if the faculties do not do this as well as they should, let them concentrate on doing it better. *Demand* that they do so; and see to it that they are not diverted by extraneous activity.

Other agencies will take on the jobs that academic institutions are now performing poorly, or shouldn't be performing at all—if the colleges and universities refuse to do them. And once everybody connected with our institutions of higher learning has a clear idea of their basic reason for existence, they will be more manageable.

There was a time when a man accepted the presidency of a university for the pay, the prestige, the perquisites of office, and the chance to put his personal mark on the institution. Today, some vestiges of the prestige and the perquisites remain, but a university president can make more money for less work in almost any other kind of job, and he knows that he is unlikely to be an Eliot, an Angell, or a Harper. So why do people continue to accept the job?

It may not be wise to generalize. After all, I know only a few university presidents (or ex-presidents) well enough to guess at their motives; and I have to guess, because they grow evasive or seek refuge in clichés when one puts the question. But I can't believe that the motives I impute to those I know are foreign to the others. I believe that the majority of university presidents so venerate the idea of the university, its ethos, the animating principle behind all those libraries and laboratories, that they cannot refuse a call to serve it.

George will not like the ecclesiastical tone of that last sentence. Edward might be more willing to accept such language. The militant students of the 1960's would vigorously dispute its implications. Idealists? Men with a *mission?* Those gray-flannel-suited, buttoned-down bureaucrats? Those cold fish, always talking about money? Those dehumanized advocates of "reason"? Yes. Because those same men believe that nothing but reason can save us; that only the colleges and universities can preserve such shreds of it as the world has left; and that the

bureaucracy and bickering and even the blundering down irrelevant bypaths can be endured if at the same time one can
increase the probability that men will learn to think before they
act.